EARTH'S THREATENED RESOURCES

Timely Reports to Keep
Journalists, Scholars and the Public
Abreast of Developing Issues, Events and Trends

Editorial Research Reports
Published by Congressional Quarterly Inc.
1414 22nd Street, N.W.
Washington, D.C. 20037

About the Cover

The cover was designed by Kathleen Ossenfort

Copyright 1986 by Congressional Quarterly Inc.
publisher of Editorial Research Reports

PRINTED IN THE UNITED STATES OF AMERICA

Editor, Hoyt Gimlin
Assistants: Leah Klumph, Elizabeth Furbush, D. Park Teter
Production Manager, I. D. Fuller
Assistant Production Manager, Maceo Mayo

Library of Congress Cataloging-in-Publication Data

Earth's threatened resources.

Bibliography: p.
Includes index.
1. Man—Influence on nature. 2. Conservation of natural resources. 3. Environmental protection.
I. Editorial research reports.
GF75.E17   1986   333.7   86-4204
ISBN 0-87187-391-5

Contents

Foreword

Modern technology is transforming mankind's relationship with nature at an accelerating pace that often threatens plant, animal and even human life. The well-being of many species, including our own, is at stake in the race between technology and understanding. Each report in this collection seeks such understanding. Taken together, they offer the reader a troubling picture of what lies ahead — and sometimes a tribute to human resourcefulness in meeting challenges.

Although there is currently a surplus of food in the world, a drought in Africa can kill hundreds of thousands, and even in "good" years millions of the world's poor suffer crippling malnutrition. Soil erosion, especially in developing countries, gravely threatens future food supplies, and food production by the world's fisheries is no longer keeping up with population growth.

The human race has made progress in protecting a species it has threatened with extinction — the whales — and is striving to protect other wildlife and wilderness areas threatened by "advancing" civilization. But the water under our ground is being contaminated by hazardous wastes, and the rain from heaven, showering acid from industry and auto exhaust, is killing fish in our lakes and may be killing trees in our forests. Even the water lapping our coasts is nibbling at the continent as we reconsider using the ocean as a dump. Overseas, 28 million acres of rain forest are destroyed annually by clearing for agriculture and commercial logging.

This book describes these conditions, gives the various viewpoints, examines the origins of the problems, and looks toward future dangers and opportunities. The opportunity to understand ourselves and our environment better is what we hope this book extends to its readers.

Hoyt Gimlin
Editor

April 1986
Washington, D.C.

ACID RAIN:

Canada's Push
For U.S. Action

by

Roger Thompson

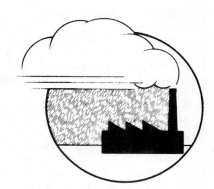

Mar. 7
1 9 8 6

Editor's Update: After meeting with Canadian Prime Minister Brian Mulroney, President Reagan March 19, 1986, fully endorsed a special envoys' joint U.S.-Canadian report on acid rain. Mulroney, under pressure at home to show progress on the issue, hailed Reagan's endorsement as "new and very significant." The National Coal Association and the Edison Electric Institute also welcomed the report, but the National Clean Air Coalition, which favors stronger emission controls, called it "a step backward."

Sen. Robert T. Stafford (R-Vt.), chairman of the Senate Environment and Public Works Committee, March 18, 1986, introduced a bill to reduce both sulfur pollution from power plants and nitrogen oxides emitted by motor vehicles.

A report sponsored by the National Academy of Sciences, released March 14, 1986, found that emissions of both sulfur dioxide and nitrogen oxides contribute to reduced atmospheric visibility, increased acidity in lakes and declining fish populations. The report also said that acid rain is a leading suspect in the decline of some Appalachain forests.

ACID RAIN

For years the Canadian government has accused the United States of dumping its air pollution garbage, particularly acid rain, in Canada's front yard. Canadian officials say half of the sulfur dioxide, the primary ingredient in acid rain, that falls on Canada's eastern provinces drifts across the border from the United States. The cumulative effect has been devastating. By Canada's count, 13 salmon-bearing rivers in Nova Scotia and at least 1,600 of Ontario's lakes are "acid dead," incapable of supporting fish life, and almost one million lakes in Ontario and Quebec provinces are listed as vulnerable to acid rain damage.

Similar complaints have come from various places in the Eastern United States, especially New England and upper New York state *(see box, p. 9)*. But their appeals for help from Washington, endorsed by environmentalists nationwide, have been nullified by opposition from the upper Midwest and Ohio River Valley, regions whose industries are great users of coal high in sulfur content and are identified as prime sources of the acid rain troubling eastern Canada and the Northeastern United States.

After a decade of complaining about this unwanted U.S. export, Canada last year embarked on an ambitious program to cut its own industrial sulfur emissions in half by 1994.[1] Having moved to put his own house in order, Prime Minister Brian Mulroney now is in a better position to push forward his country's campaign to persuade the United States to take similar steps. The Reagan administration, however, has doggedly insisted that not enough is known about acid rain to mandate a multibillion-dollar national control program. President Reagan has called instead for more research.[2] The gap between the two countries' positions has made acid rain an increasingly contentious issue, elevating it to the chief topic of discussion when Mulroney meets with Reagan in Washington on March 18.

A recent report issued by special envoys of the two leaders

---

[1] The Canadian program calls for cuts in sulfur dioxide emissions to 2.6 million tons a year, one-half of the 1980 level, and tighter controls on vehicle emissions. Total costs are estimated at more than $1.5 billion, mostly borne by industry. The government's expenditures are estimated at $150 million.

[2] According to press reports, Reagan has privately questioned whether acid rain is a man-made problem. In an unguarded moment during the 1980 campaign, Reagan suggested that trees and other vegetation, not unregulated industry, caused most air pollution.

made clear that acid rain is a man-made problem in need of prompt U.S. attention.[3] Reagan suggested the report when he and Mulroney met last year in Quebec City on Saint Patrick's Day, the so-called Shamrock Summit. The report includes joint recommendations from Drew L. Lewis, Reagan's former transportation secretary, and William G. Davis, the former premier of Ontario. They seek a middle ground that satisfies the need to make progress without causing either side to renounce previous positions.

Rather than recommend costly pollution controls to curb emissions from U.S. coal-burning utilities, the chief producers of sulfur dioxide, the report called for a $5 billion, five-year program to develop ways to burn coal cleanly. This reflects a concession from Davis, since Canada has long sought immediate cuts in U.S. sulfur emissions. For its part, the United States officially acknowledged for the first time that industrial emissions are the primary cause of acid rain. The report also calls for the establishment of a bilateral advisory group to provide a forum for continuing consultations on air quality. In his letter transmitting the report to the president, Lewis wrote: "[T]here should be no doubt that acidic air emissions are being transported through the atmosphere and over the U.S./Canadian border. That transboundary air pollution is causing serious environmental concern in both countries because of the ecological, economic, and cultural value of the resources at risk."

The report culminates nearly a decade of joint discussions on acid raid but without concrete action. In 1978 the two governments agreed to set up the Bilateral Research Consultation Group to study the problem. A year later, the governments issued a Joint Statement on Transboundary Air Quality, pledging to work toward an agreement to control air pollution, including acid rain. In 1980, Canada and the United States signed a Memorandum of Intent to develop a bilateral air quality agreement "as soon as possible." Five working groups were established to provide scientific advice, but no agreement resulted from their efforts. That is where things stood when Reagan met Mulroney last year.

Reactions to Envoys' $5 Billion Proposal

"We can't keep studying this thing to death. We've got to do something about it,'" Lewis told news reporters after delivering the report to the White House on Jan. 9. Davis, in his letter of transmittal to Mulroney, advised the prime minister that his ultimate goal "should be to negotiate with the United States a

---

[3] Drew Lewis and William Davis, "Joint Report of the Special Envoys on Acid Rain,"January 1986, p. 8. For background on U.S.-Canadian acid rain problems, see "Acid Rain," *E.R.R.*, 1980 Vol. I, pp. 445-464.

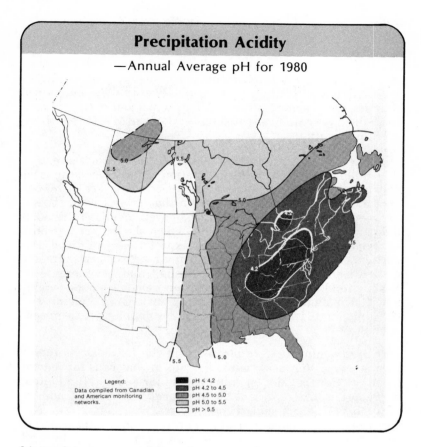

Precipitation Acidity

—Annual Average pH for 1980

Legend:

Data compiled from Canadian and American monitoring networks.

- pH ≤ 4.2
- pH 4.2 to 4.5
- pH 4.5 to 5.0
- pH 5.0 to 5.5
- pH > 5.5

biateral agreement [treaty] on transboundary air pollution, including an emission reduction program with a reasonable timetable for implementation."

Reagan called the report "an important step forward," but he has not said whether he will endorse its recommendations. Senior advisers, including State Department officials, are reported to have urged him to do so during Mulroney's visit. Tom McMillan, Canada's environment minister, underscored the political significance of the issue during a speech Jan. 22 before the New York Board of Trade. He called the acid rain issue "a litmus test" for U.S.-Canadian cooperation. "If we can't make progress on acid rain, with its terrible consequences for all of us, how can we hope to work on other issues where self-interest is less clear-cut?"

Utility and coal industry groups, which have bitterly opposed new sulfur emissions controls, applauded the Lewis-Davis report's call for accelerated development of clean coal technologies. The National Coal Association reiterated its position, however, that "there is no scientific consensus that coal

5

combustion is the cause of acidity in the environment." The $5 billion cost of the proposed program would be divided equally between the federal government and industry, primarily from coal-fired power plants in the Ohio River Valley and upper Midwest, the heaviest emitters. About 80 percent of the nation's sulfur dioxide comes from 31 states east of the Mississippi River or bordering it.

The Lewis-Davis proposal is similar in intent, if not size, to a $400 million, three-year demonstration project on clean coal technology approved by Congress last December *(see p. 18)*. At the time, Reagan threatened to veto that project even though that would have meant rejecting the government's entire $368 billion fiscal 1986 appropriations in which the project was buried. Some industry leaders do not expect Reagan to back the more expensive new proposal. Ben Yamagata, executive director of the Clean Coal Technology Coalition,[4] told a conference in Washington Feb. 19: "Given the current debate over the federal deficit, it is highly unlikely that the president will commit the $2.5 billion in federal cost-sharing for development of clean coal technologies. . . ."

Environmentalists were pleased that the Lewis-Davis report acknowledged that acid rain is a problem that calls for federal attention, but they do not think it goes far enough. If adopted, the report would represent "a major advance in past administration positions," said Richard Ayres, chairman of the National Clean Air Coalition. But it "shrinks from making concrete recommendations to remedy the severe threat posed by acid rain." he continued. "It is a way for utilities to get five more years without having to clean up." Said Debbie Sheiman of the Natural Resources Defense Council: "We don't need new technologies, what we need is to garner the political will to use present technology to reduce emissions." [5]

In Canada, the report received a lukewarm to poor reception. Environmental Minister McMillan described it as "not an ideal report" because it did not call for specific emission reductions. Canada's efforts alone to curb sulfur dioxide emissions will not eliminate acid rain damage from sensitive eastern provinces, said Bruce Jutzi, an environmental specialist at the Canadian Embassy in Washington. Mulroney's political opposition has made an issue of the report. Adele Hurley of the Canadian Coalition on Acid Rain said "disgust is the right word" to describe her reaction. "It's like having somebody dump garbage

---

[4] The coalition is an ad hoc group of more than 40 organizations, including electric utilities, coal companies, equipment suppliers, construction firms, state and local governments, the National Coal Association and the Edison Electric Institute.
[5] Persons quoted in this report were interviewed by the author unless otherwise indicated.

on your front lawn, and the ultimate insult is they tell you they don't see what you are talking about." In a letter delivered Feb. 12, the coalition urged Mulroney to make a personal appeal to Congress for laws to cut emissions leading to acid rain. The letter stated that it was "clearly time to tell the Americans what they must do to protect the North American environment from acid rain." Mulroney offered no response.

Scientific Consensus on Causes, Sources

For all the debate over acid rain policy, there is at least a scientific consensus on its causes and sources. Acid rain is the popular term that describes a phenomenon more appropriately called acid deposition. It occurs when sulfur dioxide (SO_2) and nitrogen oxides (NOx) emitted from coal-fired power plants, smelters, vehicles and other sources are transported through the atmosphere, sometimes hundreds of miles, and return to earth as acid compounds.[6] SO_2 is roughly twice as acidic as NOx, making it the chief target of proposed emission controls.

Electric utilities accounted for two-thirds of the 20.8 tons of sulfur oxides emitted nationwide in 1983, the latest year for which figures have been made available by the Environmental Protection Agency (EPA). Industrial boilers and processes ranked second, sending 4.1 million tons into the air, and smelters (chiefly copper) produced 1.1 million tons. All other sources made up the rest. These emissions are concentrated in the Ohio River Valley in six states: Illinois, Indiana, Ohio, Kentucky, West Virginia and Pennsylvania. They and two other high-emitting states, Missouri and Tennessee, produce 46 percent of the U.S. total.

The amount of nitrogen oxide was almost as great in 1983, some 19.4 million tons. But since the main source is motor vehicle exhaust, these emissions were more evenly distributed across the country. However, three of the highest-producing states — Illinois, Ohio and Pennsylvania — are also in the Ohio River Valley. After auto exhaust, the next biggest source of NOx emissions is the burning of industrial fuels. NOx is released into the air when any kind of fuel is burned, because nitrogen and oxygen in the air combine at high temperatures.

Once in the atmosphere, SO_2 and NOx may fall back to the earth within a few miles, or within several hundred miles of their source. Research suggests that about one-third of the sulfur compounds deposited over the Eastern states originated from sources over 300 miles away, one-third from sources between 120 and 300 miles away and the remaining third from

---

[6] According to the Lewis-Davis report (p. 8), natural sources contribute only about 3 percent of the sulfur and nitrogen compounds that cause acid deposition in the Eastern United States and somewhat more in the West.

sources within 120 miles.[7] "It is very clear that there is a solid link between acidic emissions and acid depositions in the United States," stated the Lewis-Davis report. "The areas of highest acid deposition coincide with or are downwind and to the northeast of the areas of highest emissions."[8] Prevailing winds on the North American continent are from west to east. While the industrial East Coast creates much air pollution, it either falls locally or tends to be blown out to sea.

Pollutants responsible for acid rain return to earth as rain, snow, sleet, fog or dew — collectively known as acid precipitation — or as dry particles or gases. The relative amounts of wet and dry acid deposition varies with location and weather conditions. It is estimated that roughly equal amounts of wet and dry deposition fall over the Eastern states. In areas distant from pollution sources, such as New York's Adirondack Mountains, wet deposition may account for 80 percent of the sulfur deposited, while in cities dry deposition predominates.

Dry deposition is difficult to measure; the 170 measuring sites maintained by the National Atmospheric Deposition Program measure only acid precipitation. A recent World Resources Institute study of dry deposition in the western states found, however, that it probably is a bigger problem there, particularly as a threat to visibility in national parks. In addition, dry deposition was found to be 15 times greater than wet deposition in the Los Angeles Basin.[9]

Excess acidity in precipitation arises primarily from the reaction of sulfur and nitrogen oxides with water. Acidity is measured on what chemists call a pH scale. Measurements range from 0, most acidic, to 14, which is alkaline and thus shows no acidity. A reading of 7 is neutral. The scale is logarithmic, meaning that a change of one point represents a tenfold change in acidity. For instance, pH 5 is 10 times more acidic than pH 6; pH 4.2 is twice as acidic as pH 4.5. Unpolluted rainfall generally is considered 5.6, although there are naturally occurring regional and seasonal variations.

Harmful effects have been most clearly shown on streams and lakes. When waters become more acidic than about pH 5, some species stop reproducing and die, and the aquatic ecosystem changes drastically. Numbers of water plants, snail and insect species begin to disappear when pH drops below 7. Substantial evidence indicates that acid deposition is most harmful in areas where the soil cannot adequately neutralize the acid before it

[7] Office of Technology Assessment, "Acid Rain and Transported Air Pollutants," U.S. Government Printing Office, July 1984, p. 5.
[8] Lewis-Davis, *op. cit.*, p. 11.
[9] Philip Roth, et al., "The American West's Acid Rain Test," World Resources Institute, March 1985.

State Acid Rain Action

Several states, primarily in the Northeast, have enacted laws or signed agreements with Canadian provinces to control acid rain. "This is a good example of a regional approach in the absence of federal action," said Larry Morandi, of the National Conference of State Legislatures.

Massachusetts recently passed a law requiring industry to cut sulfur dioxide emissions by 30 percent over five years. New Hampshire requires a 25 percent reduction by 1990, and New York a 17 percent reduction by 1988. A bill to cut sulfur emissions in Maine appeared headed for defeat in the current legislative session.

New England governors and the premiers of three eastern Canadian provinces signed a regional agreement last June 17 on acid rain control. The agreement calls for an overall 32 percent reduction in sulfur dioxide by the mid-1990s, although percentages may vary from one jurisdiction to another. Those participating are Connecticut, Maine, Massachusetts, New Hampshire, Rhode Island and Vermont, and the provinces of New Brunswick, Nova Scotia and Quebec. At least three other states — California, Minnesota and Wisconsin — also have enacted acid rain controls.

Seven states and four environmental groups filed suit in federal court last December charging that the EPA violated the Clean Air Act by not tightening its standards for sulfur dioxide emissions. According to the 1977 act, the agency was supposed to revise the standards in 1980 and every five years thereafter, based on the latest scientific data on pollution's effects.

The suit, filed in federal district court in New York, was joined by Connecticut, Massachusetts, Minnesota, New Hampshire, New York, Rhode Island, Vermont, the Environmental Defense Fund, the Natural Resources Defense Council, the Sierra Club and the National Parks and Conservation Association.

---

enters the water. Soil that is sandy or underlain by granite rock is especially ineffective.[10]

In the 31 easternmost states, the Office of Technology Assessment estimates that 3,000 lakes and 23,000 miles of streams are extremely vulnerable to further acid deposition or have already become acidic.[11] Those in New England and New York's Adirondack Mountains have been greatly affected. About 180 lakes in the Adirondacks no longer support brook trout and some have lost six or more species of fish.[12] An EPA report

[10] General Accounting Office, "An Analysis of Issues Concerning Acid Rain" U.S. Government Printing Office, December 1984, p. 10.
[11] OTA, op. cit., p. 11.
[12] GAO, *op. cit.*, p. 13.

9

released last August estimated that 60 percent of the lakes in New England are highly sensitive to acid rain — more than in such other areas of sensitivity as Florida (54 percent), the upper Midwest (41) and Appalachia (36). The agency estimated that 1,000 lakes in the East already have succumbed to acid rain. The survey used pH 5 as the cutoff for ecological damage. But a study reported in *Science* magazine last June indicated that damage may begin at the 5.59 level or even higher.[13]

Acid deposition also is diminishing the acid-neutralizing capacity of sensitive soils in the West, including areas of the Cascade Mountains in Washington and the Rockies in Colorado. Although lakes and streams in many Western mountainous areas receive an annual jolt of acid deposition from melting snow, "no aquatic ecosystems in the West have acidified completely," said the World Resources Institute study.[14]

Uncertain Effects on Forests and Health

Acid rain once was thought to be the prime cause of a decline in forest growth in the United States and Europe, but current research has not established a cause-and-effect relationship. Damage figures, however, continue to mount, according to the World Resources Institute study. It reported that the extent of damage to West German forests rose from 34 percent in 1983 to 55 percent last year, while 10 percent of the trees in southern Scandinavia and Czechoslovakia have been damaged. In the United States, stands of red spruce in high elevations in Vermont have declined by about half. Similar declines have been reported in the Adirondacks and the southern Appalachians.

Though the cause of this damage has not been clearly established, acid rain remains a prime suspect. It may harm trees by removing nutrients from the leaves or by altering the soils in which the trees grow. However, observed growth declines also may result from drought, temperature extremes, insects, heavy metals (such as aluminum), ozone or other pollutants. Writing in *The Environmental Forum* magazine, two forest industry researchers summed up the current state of scientific knowledge: "[O]ver the past years, forest products industry scientists have studied all major forest locations having undiagnosed damage symptoms. Not only were we unable to conclude that this forest damage is definitely linked to acid rain, but industry scientists also could not positively conclude that other specific air pollutants — acting singly or together — were the culprit." [15]

---

[13] D. W. Schindler, et al., "Long-Term Ecosystem Stress: The Effects of Years of Experimental Acidification on a Small Lake," *Science,* June 21, 1985. Schindler was chairman of a landmark 1981 National Academy of Sciences' study on acid rain.
[14] Philip Roth, et al., *op. cit.,* p. 19.
[15] L. Wayne Haines and James N. Woodman, "Air Quality and Forest Health: The Forest Industry View," *The Environmental Forum,* November 1985, p. 29.

Likewise, damage to crops from acid deposition under natural conditions has not been documented. Years of research in this area "suggests that acid deposition's impact on agriculture is not a cause for concern," said a 1984 General Accounting Office (GAO) report.[16]

Acid deposition does have a well-recognized potential to damage building materials, such as stone, paint, steel and zinc. Dry deposited SO_2 and sulfate, a secondary product of SO_2, combine on moist surfaces to form sulfuric acid, which is more corrosive than acid rain. It is difficult to determine, however, which portion of damage is done by pollutants swept in from long distances as opposed to those emitted locally. It is equally difficult to apportion damage between acid deposition and other factors, such as weathering. Nonetheless, a 1985 draft study by EPA, Brookhaven National Laboratory and the Army Corps of Engineers set a preliminary midpoint estimate of $3.5 billion for annual building materials damage caused by acid deposition.

Direct effects of acid deposition on human health so far have not been proven. There is some fear of indirect effects, such as contamination of fish or drinking water supplies. It is thought that acidified water can contribute to elevated levels of dissolved mercury, which in turn can produce toxic concentrations of mercury in fish. However, no human health problems have been associated with mercury dissolved by acid rain.

Some researchers see a larger threat from breathing extremely small particles of sulfur dioxide. Sulfates contribute to poor visibility across much of the United States, including national parks in the West where copper smelters are the primary source. Sulfates mixed with other particulates "could be responsible for about 50,000 premature deaths a year, particularly among people with preexisting respiratory or cardiac problems," concluded the Office of Technology Assessment (OTA).[17] It is not known, however, whether harmful effects are caused by sulfates or other particulates with which they are associated.

While the OTA study is widely cited by environmental groups, William H. Megonnell, an environmental specialist at the Edison Electric Institute, an industry research and information organization, says it has no validity. "The study concluded that deaths attributable to sulfates ranged from 0 to 150,000, so they came up with 50,000 as a midpoint," he said. "It has absolutely no scientific credibility."

---

[16] GAO, *op. cit.*, p. 19.
[17] OTA, *op. cit.*, p. 47.

U.S. Policy Dilemma

A cid raid has emerged as a major political issue because current laws do not adequately address the problem of pollutants being carried long distances by the winds. The Clean Air Act, the nation's primary law for controlling and preventing air pollution, sets standards for *local* air quality. Enacted in 1970 and amended in 1977, the law establishes emissions limits for the seven most common toxic pollutants: sulfur dioxide, nitrogen oxides, particulates (soot and dust), carbon monoxide, hydrocarbons, ozone, and lead. The law permits EPA to set industrywide performance standards that are enforced by the states.

Under the law, much stricter requirements apply to new sources of pollution than old ones. Existing industries were required to achieve a moderate degree of emission control. The 1977 amendments required all new stationary sources to install the best available technology to reduce pollution. For coal-burning electric power plants, this has meant installing scrubbers — equipment using wet lime or limestone — to remove 70 to 90 percent of the SO_2 emissions from the flue gas.

Compliance with the Clean Air Act now costs an estimated $25 billion annually, according to the Council on Environmental Quality. And results have been encouraging. About 98 percent of the nation's counties are in compliance with national standards on sulfur dioxide and nitrogen oxide emissions. Between 1940 and 1970, SO_2 emissions increased 56 percent and NOx emissions 200 percent. Since then, NOx emissions have remained fairly constant. After reaching a peak in 1973, SO_2 emissions dropped 28 percent over the next decade. For electric utilities, these emissions dropped 19 percent while coal consumption increased roughly 60 percent during this period. The chief reason for this reduction has been the installation of scrubbers to remove most of the pollutants before they come out of the smokestacks. There are 119 scrubbers in use at utility plants and 100 more are planned or being installed, according to the Edison Electric Institute.

Ten-Year Legal Battle over Tall Stacks

Local air quality standards, however, have not controlled the long-distance spread of sulfur dioxide. In fact, under current federal regulations, the Office of Technology Assessment projects that these emissions will grow 7 to 11 percent by the year 2000.[18] The National Coal Association challenges these

---
[18] OTA, *op. cit.*, p. 61.

figures, saying that its own recent survey of coal-fired utilities indicates that SO_2 emissions will continue to drop. Whatever the case, it is clear that current regulations permit utilities to meet local air quality regulations while emitting large quantities of SO_2. They do so by using tall smokestacks. Tall stacks, those over 200 feet, disperse pollution by propelling it up to a mile high, casting pollution problems to the winds.

The Natural Resources Defense Council (NRDC) has led a decade-long battle to require EPA to outlaw tall stacks. The council maintains that the Clean Air Act allows tall stacks only in rare instances when available pollution controls are not sufficient to protect local health. Yet, since 1970, utilities have built 102 tall stacks in violation of the Clean Air Act, said Richard Ayres of the National Clean Air Coalition. There are 23 stacks taller than 1,000 feet, the tallest rivaling the Empire State Building at 1,203 feet. NRDC estimates that forcing utilities to install scrubbers on these "illegal" tall stacks could reduce sulfur dioxide pollution by up to 7.6 million tons a year.[19]

EPA has lost two lawsuits and several appeals over tall stacks during the past decade. Just last June the agency acted under court order to issue the latest regulations governing tall stacks at utilities and smelters. Within weeks, the NRDC filed suit in the U.S. Circuit Court of Appeals for the District of Columbia seeking modification of the new regulations. "The agency's new policy might yield no reductions at all, and in some cases pollution would even be allowed to increase," said Ayres. Dwain Winters, chief of EPA's acid rain program, said the agency objected to using tall stack regulations "as a backdoor way to control acid rain." It's up to Congress to pass laws to control acid rain, he added. "It would be presumptuous for us to push the law for acid rain control when Congress is still debating the issue."

New England vs. Midwest and Ohio Valley

The Clean Air Act's failure to address the problems of pollution carried by the winds across state and national boundaries has prompted members of Congress to introduce corrective legislation in recent years. The acid rain issue has proven so divisive that no laws have been enacted. It is largely responsible for blocking a renewal of the Clean Air Act. Funding authorization for the act expired in 1981 and has been continued year to year since then.[20] Proposed acid rain controls pit one region against another, threatening the livelihood of coal miners in

---

[19] Natural Resources Defense Council, "Tall Stacks, A Decade of Illegal Use; A Decade of Damage Downwind," March 1985, p. 2. Fifty other tall stacks built after 1970 are considered legal because they were "grandfathered" by EPA in 1976.

[20] For background, see "Environmental Conflicts in the 1980s," *E.R.R.*, 1985 Vol. I, pp. 121-144.

Appalachia and raising the possibility of substantial higher-priced electricity in the Midwest in return for lifting the threat to lakes and streams in New England.

The Senate Environment and Public Works Committee in 1984 approved 16-2 an acid rain control bill that would have required the 31 states bordering and east of the Mississippi River to cut sulfur dioxide emissions by 10 million tons by 1994. The cost of the program would be borne by ratepayers in the affected areas. The committee was controlled by New Englanders whose states stood to gain environmentally and Westerners whose states stood to gain financially. The bill, authored by committee Chairman Robert T. Stafford, R-Vt., would have encouraged utilities to meet clean air standards by using low-sulfur Western coal. Under current law, utilities have little incentive to burn low-sulfur coal because all new plants are required by 1977 Clean Air Act amendments to install scrubbers no matter what the coal's sulfur content. The bill would not have required scrubbers at plants meeting air quality standards.

The measure never made it to the Senate floor for debate largely because it was bitterly opposed by senators from Ohio River Valley and Appalachian states. Electricity users in those areas would have shouldered much of the $10 billion annual cost, calculated to cause 5 to 10 percent rate hikes in Indiana, Ohio and West Virginia.[21] There was also fear that many West Virginia and Kentucky coal communities would turn to ghost towns if utilities switched to low-sulfur Western coal.

Also killed in 1984 was a House bill that would have required scrubbers on the 50 dirtiest utility plants to reduce sulfur dioxide emissions by 70 to 90 percent. The bill would have imposed a nationwide tax on non-nuclear electric power to pay 90 percent of the capital costs. As with the Senate bill, annual costs were projected at $10 billion. The measure, sponsored by Reps. Henry A. Waxman, D-Calif., and Gerry Sikorski, D-Minn., died in subcommittee on a 9-10 vote. Most Western members argued that it was unfair to charge their constituents for cleaning up pollution they neither created nor suffered from. Those from the Midwest, such as Rep. John D. Dingell, D-Mich., chairman of the powerful Energy and Commerce Committee, generally oppose any acid rain controls for fear of imposing higher utility rates on consumers.

Waxman and Stafford plan to introduce new acid rain legislation this year. An aide to Waxman said the congressman is still trying to resolve the issue of "who pays" for acid rain controls. A spokesman for Stafford said the senator's bill would include

[21] OTA, *op. cit*, p. 15.

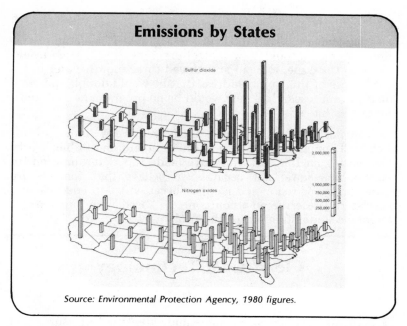

Emissions by States

Sulfur dioxide

Nitrogen oxides

2,000,000

1,000,000
750,000
500,000
250,000

Emissions (tons/year)

Source: Environmental Protection Agency, 1980 figures.

new controls on motor vehicles in an attempt to broaden its appeal. Sen. Daniel Patrick Moynihan, D-N.Y., already has introduced a bill that would incorporate the recommendations of the Lewis-Davis report. But Moynihan went a step further, saying that "improving technology is only part of the answer to acid rain." His measure also incorporates the major provisions of Stafford's previous bill, including the 10-million-ton reduction in sulfur dioxide emissions by 1994. Moynihan is the author of the only acid rain legislation passed to date: the National Acid Precipitation Act (NAPA) of 1980. The act established a 10-year research program into the causes and effects of acid deposition.

Research has been the most visible element of the Reagan administration's approach to the acid rain issue. During fiscal year 1982, NAPA's first budget year, the program received $17.4 million and has grown to $85 million this year. The administration has committed increasing amounts to research to underscore its belief that not enough is known about acid rain to mandate new controls.

Former EPA Administrator William D. Ruckleshaus reportedly was prepared to announce a comprehensive policy on acid rain control in late 1983 until he visited the White House, where he encountered opposition from David A. Stockman, then director of the Office of Management and Budget, and other Reagan advisers. Stockman had calculated that Ruckleshaus' plan would have cost $6,000 for every pound of New England fish saved from acid rain. Reagan's advisers also were worried about election-year political fallout in the Midwest if the administration endorsed a tough new control program. Not to seem insensitive to the issue, Reagan announced three months later in his 1984 State of the Union address that he would double spending on acid rain research. There would be no program, he said, until more was known.

That position has remained unchanged. EPA Administrator Lee M. Thomas told the Senate Environment and Public Works Committee on Dec. 11: "We have made this determination [to oppose new laws] not because we believe that controls are unnecessary or too expensive, but because it is premature and unwise to prescribe emission controls based upon our current scientific understanding of the problem."

Clean Coal Technology

P olitical polarization at home and intensified pressure from north of the border spurred special envoys Lewis and Davis to seek a middle ground where the United States and Canada could claim some progress toward resolving the acid rain issue. "Our recommendations must be realistic," they wrote. "They must not ask either country to make a sudden, revolutionary change in its position." In this context, clean coal technology emerged as a possible solution to an intractable problem.

Coal burning techniques have remained largely unchanged for most of this century. Coal is crushed, fed into a boiler and ignited. The heat boils water that turns to steam, which in turn drives a turbine that generates electricity. Efforts to develop ways to burn coal without fouling the air have been under way for several years. Most projects to date have been small-scale research efforts, but their results have been very promising. Some of the new technologies meet or exceed the most stringent clean air requirements. In addition, facilities using the new technology may be cheaper to build and operate than conventional plants outfitted with flue-gas scrubbers.

"Scrubbers have proven to be among the most costly and least reliable pieces of equipment in the utility industry," said Richard E. Balzhiser, senior vice president of research and development at the Electric Power Research Institute.[22] A single scrubber can cost $100 million, accounting for up to 40 percent of a new plant's total cost. A typical scrubber uses up to 1,000

---

[22] Leslie Braunstein, "Clean Coal Technology: Just in Time," *Electric Perspectives*, fall 1985, p. 9.

gallons of water per minute, consumes 3 to 8 percent of the power plant's total energy and produces a mountain of sludge waste that is difficult to remove.

Promising Ways for Burning Coal Cleanly

The leading new technology is called fluidized bed combustion (FBC). It involves injecting a mixture of powdered coal and limestone into a furnace where jets of air suspend the particles as the coal burns. The air jets cause the mixture to act like a liquid. Calcium in the limestone combines with the sulfur in the coal to form a harmless dry waste product, calcium sulfate. This technique removes upwards of 90 percent of the coal's sulfur and eliminates the need for flue-gas scrubbers. The process greatly reduces NOx emissions because the coal burns at about 1,600 degrees Fahrenheit — 500 to 1,000 degrees lower than in a conventional boiler. Another important feature is that FBC works equally well with high- and low-sulfur coal. Conventional fluidized bed boilers operate at atmospheric air pressure. A more advanced version operates at the pressure of 15 atmospheres, about 225 pounds per square inch. A major advantage of pressurized fluidized bed combustion is that the boiler is more compact and therefore less costly to build.

More than 40 industrial fluidized bed combustion boilers now are in operation or under construction in the United States. The utility industry is attempting to adapt the technology for large-scale electrical generation. The Tennessee Valley Authority currently operates a 20 megawatt (MW) atmospheric fluidized bed combustion boiler at Paducah, Ky., and is building a 160 MW commercial demonstration plant at the same site. The operational date is set for 1988. The Northern States Power Co. is building a 125 MW plant at Burnsville, Minn., to start up in August. Colorado Ute Electric Association is building a 110 MW plant at Nucla, Colo., to begin operating in 1987. The American Electric Power Service Corp. is planning a 70 MW demonstration pressurized fluidized bed facility at the company's deactivated Tidd Plant near Brilliant, Ohio. Wisconsin Electric Power Co. also is making similar plans.

The most advanced clean coal technology involves the conversion of coal to clean-burning gas. The process is called gasification combined cycle (GCC) because the power plant uses both a gas and a steam turbine to produce electricity. The synthetic fuel runs the gas turbine while excess heat generated throughout the plant is recovered and used to power the steam turbine — hence a combined cycle facility. A 100 MW demonstration plant began operation in California's Mojave Desert in the summer of 1984. The Cool Water Generating Station is operated by California Edison near Barstow. The plant removes

95-99 percent of the coal sulfur and has met "the toughest environmental regulations of any plant in the world," said Dwain Spencer, vice president of the Advanced Power Systems Division of the Electric Power Research Institute. The plant's success has prompted other utilities to explore adopting the coal gasification process.

Economic Advantages of Innovative Designs

The new technology is being touted as the best means for the nation to meet future demand for electricity and to replace deteriorating power plants. Utility executives believe growth is expected to average between 2 and 4 percent annually through the year 2000. Approximately 1,300 coal-fired boilers currently produce about 55 percent of the electricity in the United States. That figure may increase to 70 percent by the end of the century. Declining oil prices probably will have little effect on the push to perfect the new technologies, said Thomas R. Kuhn, executive vice president of the Edison Electric Institute. Problems that have arisen with nuclear power plants make it doubtful they will add significantly to future power supplies. No new nuclear plants have been ordered since 1978.[23]

New coal technologies also will help utilities better manage the financial burdens of new plant construction. Fluidized bed and coal gasification plants can be built in modular fashion, enabling utilities to match unit size with incremental growth in the output of electricity. Many components can be made off-site and transported to the plant for installation, lowering construction costs and shortening the time needed to add new capacity. Fluidized bed technology also seems well suited for adaptation to old power plants, eliminating the delays and expense of obtaining approval of new plant sites.

Although utility and coal companies seem convinced that clean coal technologies offer economic and environmental incentives for widespread adoption in the 1990s, they have turned to Congress to help underwrite development costs. The utility industry, the chief beneficiary of the new technology, argues that demonstration projects are so expensive and the rewards so problematic that it cannot conduct the projects alone.

Industry's appeal for assistance has gotten a sympathetic hearing on Capitol Hill. In 1984 Congress authorized $750 million for clean coal demonstration projects, but it did not act on a bill to implement a clean coal program.[24] Last year the $750 million, which had not been appropriated, came under intense pressure from the Gramm-Rudman-Hollings budget-cutting

---

[23] For background, see "Nuclear Power's Future," *E.R.R.*, 1983 Vol. II, pp. 553-572.
[24] The money came from $7.35 billion rescinded from previous appropriations to the Synthetic Fuels Corporation. Congress last December voted to dismantle the corporation.

law.[25] The Office of Management and Budget wanted to use the money to reduce the federal deficit. Reagan vehemently opposed creating a federal clean coal program on philosophical grounds, arguing that industry should shoulder the expense. Despite Reagan's veto threat, Congress in December agreed to a three-year, $400 million clean coal program, leaving $350 million of the original $750 million set aside for future use. Reagan reluctantly signed the bill incorporating the program.

Less than a month later Lewis and Davis issued their joint report recommending that the United States embark on a five-year, $5 billion clean coal technology program. Given the budget pinch created by Gramm-Rudman-Hollings, industry leaders are not optimistic that Reagan will endorse the Lewis-Davis proposal. Speaking to a clean coal conference in Washington in mid-February, Carl E. Bagge, president of the National Coal Association, said the $400 million program already approved by Congress "should serve as the foundation for the American response" to the Lewis-Davis report.[26]

Legal Incentive for Utilities Not to Change

Despite industry's embrace of clean coal technology, some observers contend that utilities lack incentives to adopt the new technologies once they are proven. The issue centers on regulations covering the overhaul of old coal-fired boilers. The Clean Air Act requires all new boilers to meet strict emissions standards. The same standards do not apply to overhauled boilers unless the work exceeds 50 percent of the unit's replacement cost, which rarely happens. Thus, there is no requirement that an overhauled boiler burn any cleaner than it did before.

This poses a big problem for the future of acid rain control, according to a recent Congressional Research Service (CRS) report. The Clean Air Act assumed that power plants had a useful life of 30 to 40 years. Those built after 1970 would have to meet strict emission requirements, leading to a gradual reduction of emissions as clean new plants replaced dirty old ones. The report found, however, an industry trend toward overhauling old plants, extending their life 20 to 30 years. The clean coal technology program "run[s] a significant risk of developing acid rain control technology which no one will use absent new legislation or regulatory action," the report said.[27]

---

[25] The law (HJ Res 372 — PL-177) mandates a balanced federal budget by 1991. Chief sponsors were Sens. Phil Gramm, R-Texas; Warren B. Rudman, R-N.H.; and Ernest F. Holling, D-S.C.

[26] Bagge sharply attacked the Department of Energy for proposing that companies receiving federal funds under the program should be required to repay the money. Sen. Robert C. Byrd, D-W.Va., told the conference that Congress intended for the money to be distributed as grants, not loans.

[27] Larry B. Parker and Alvin Kaufman, "Clean Coal Technology and Acid Rain Control: Birds of a Feather," Congressional Research Service, Oct. 23. 1985, p. 43.

Recommended Reading List

Books

Brown, Lester R., et al., *State of the World 1985,* Worldwatch Institute, 1985.
Pawlick, Thomas, *A Killing Rain,* Sierra Club Books, 1984.

Articles

Braunstein, Leslie, "Clean Coal Technology: Just in Time," *Electric Perspectives,* Fall 1985.
Haines, L. Wayne and James N. Woodman, "Air Quality and Forest Health: The Forest Industry View," *The Environmental Forum,* November 1985.
Hawkins, David G., "The Benefits and Costs of Acid Rain Control," *Journal of the Air Pollution Control Association,* March 1985.
Trisko, Eugene M., "The Clean Air Act and Acid Rain," *Electric Perspectives,* Summer 1984.

Reports and Studies

"Acid Rain, Answers to Your Questions," Edison Electric Institute, 1985.
Driscoll, Charles, et al., "Is There Scientific Consensus on Acid Rain?" Ad Hoc Committee on Acid Rain: Science and Policy, Institute of Ecosystem Studies, The New York Botanical Garden, Mary Flagler Cary Arboretum, October 1985.
Editorial Research Reports: "Environmental Conflicts in the 1980s," 1985 Vol. I, p. 121; "Acid Rain," 1980 Vol. I, p. 443.
General Accounting Office, "An Analysis of Issues Concerning Acid Rain," U.S. Government Printing Office, Dec. 11, 1984.
Katzenstein, Alan W., "Understanding Acid Rain," Edison Electric Institute, 1983.
Lewis, Drew and William Davis, "Joint Report of the Special Envoys on Acid Rain," U.S. Government Printing Office, January 1986.
National Clean Air Coalition, "The Clean Air Act, A Briefing Book for Members of Congress," April 1985.
Natural Resources Defense Council, "Tall Stacks, A Decade of Illegal Use; A Decade of Damage Downwind," March 1985.
Office of Technology Assessment, "Acid Rain and Transported Air Pollutants," U.S. Government Printing Office, June 1984.
Parker, Larry B., and Alvin Kaufman, "Clean Coal Technology and Acid Rain Control: Birds of a Feather?" Congressional Research Service, U.S. Library of Congress, Oct. 23, 1985.
Roth, Philip, et al., "The American West's Acid Rain Test," World Resources Institute, March 1985.
Sheffield, Raymond M., et al., "Pine Growth Reductions in the Southeast," U.S. Department of Agriculture, Forest Service, U.S. Government Printing Office, November 1985.

Graphics: Cover illustration by Assistant Art Director Robert Redding; maps by Staff Artist Kathleen Ossenfort, adapted from EPA and OTA data.

WILDLIFE MANAGEMENT

by

Tom Arrandale

Aug. 2
1 9 8 5

Editor's Update: Congressional legislation to renew the Endangered Species Act *(see p. 24)* had been passed by the House but not the Senate when the lawmakers returned from their 1986 Easter recess. Both chambers had voted to renew the Clean Water Act *(see p. 28)* but final passage awaited a reconciliation of differences between the two versions.

The Supreme Court Dec. 4, 1985, *(U.S. v. Riverside Bayview Homes Inc.)* broadly interpreted the meaning of navigable waterways, thus strengthening the Clean Water Act's Section 404 requirement for developers to obtain permits before filling in wetlands *(see p. 27)*.

Congress in 1985 enacted "sodbuster" and "swampbuster" legislation that would penalize cultivation of highly erodible land and conversion of wetlands *(see p. 182)*.

WILDLIFE MANAGEMENT

IN PLACES, the United States still abounds with fish and wildlife. All over the country, sportsmen take to the wilds each summer and fall to fish for trout and bass or hunt deer, grouse, ducks and other game. Backpackers, photographers and bird watchers explore the nation's forests, deserts and shorelines in growing numbers, on the lookout for a fleeting glimpse of North America's rich and varied wildlife heritage.

On visits to their ranch near Santa Barbara, Calif., President and Mrs. Reagan "enjoy seeing the hawks, the blacktailed deer, and raccoons and possums," Reagan told *National Wildlife* editor John Strohm in a recent interview.[1] Black bear and mountain lions have also been spotted in the Southern California mountains where Reagan's ranch is located. Whitetailed deer have reoccupied forests that have reclaimed abandoned farms in the South and East, while the adaptable coyote, the "song dog" of the Western plains, has extended its range from the Los Angeles suburbs to the sheep-farming country of New England. For the time being at least, a 1972 ban on the pesticide DDT may have saved the bald eagle, peregrine falcon and brown pelican. Lake trout are back in the Great Lakes, and Atlantic salmon spawn in New England rivers where they disappeared more than a century ago. The buffalo are gone from the Great Plains, but beaver, elk, wild turkey and pronghorn antelope have been brought back from the brink of extinction.

But other American wildlife is in deep trouble. The California condor may be about to vanish *(see box, p. 25),* and the whooping crane remains in peril. Stream-blocking dams and overfishing have depleted Pacific salmon runs, and state and federal officials in 1984 imposed a moratorium on harvesting the declining Atlantic striped bass. Despite protection under the Endangered Species Act, it may be too late to preserve the red wolf, black-footed ferret, Florida panther, Wyoming toad, dusky seaside sparrow and a host of other birds, mammals, insects and plants in the wild. The grizzly bear, gray wolf and bighorn sheep have retreated to a few last strongholds in the lower 48 states or Alaska and Canada. "What I'm effectively doing," U.S. Fish and Wildlife Service biologist Charles J. Ault

[1] John Strohm, "President Reagan Gives His Views on Wide-Ranging Conservation Issues," *National Wildlife*, June-July 1985, p. 16.

lamented, "is documenting the demise of wildlife resources." [2]

Before the 1970s, state and federal wildlife programs concentrated on managing remnant big-game herds and stocking fish to provide recreation for hunters and fishermen. The national environmental movement of the last two decades has forced government wildlife managers to pay more attention to protecting "non-game" species and salvaging lands that provide critical wildlife habitat. But with federal budget cutbacks crimping wildlife programs, environmental groups, sportsmen, farmers, ranchers, land developers, industrialists and anti-hunting activists are competing to influence the direction of wildlife management policies. Rarely are the debates dispassionate. "Of all environmental concerns, wildlife issues are the most evocative," observed Santa Fe, N.M., environmentalist Brant Calkin, a former Sierra Club national president.

Endangered Species Law Up for Renewal

With the Endangered Species Act up for renewal in 1985, Congress now is reviewing what probably is the federal government's most controversial wildlife program. Under the 1966 law, strengthened in 1973, government biologists have listed about 350 species of wild plants and animals in the United States as in danger of extinction.[3] Another 4,000 species are considered in trouble, and conservationists charge that the Reagan administration has been dragging its feet on granting them formal protection. Last summer, for the first time, a listed endangered species — the Palos Verdes blue butterfly — probably went extinct when the city of Rancho Palos Verdes, Calif., rototilled its last remaining habitat to make way for a ball field.[4]

One of the most controversial parts of the amended Endangered Species Act received little attention when it was approved in 1973. It ordered all federal agencies to make sure that government-funded or approved projects would not jeopardize protected wildlife or disrupt habitats critical to their survival. Seizing on that language, environmental groups turned to the courts to block federal dams and other construction projects. In the most controversial case, the U.S. Supreme Court in 1978 barred the Tennessee Valley Authority from finishing its Tellico Dam in Tennessee because it would destroy critical habitat for

---

[2] Ault and others quoted in this report were interviewed by the author unless otherwise indicated.

[3] Under the law, a species is considered endangered if it faces immediate extinction in most of its range. A threatened species, including the grizzly and the wolf, is considered likely to become endangered in the foreseeable future. The 1973 amendments directed the Interior Department's Fish and Wildlife Service and the Commerce Department's Marine Fisheries Service to list and draft plans for preserving habitat for both endangered and threatened species.

[4] See Defenders of Wildlife, "Saving Endangered Species, Implementation of the U.S. Endangered Species Act in 1984," May 1985, p. 15.

California Condor Setbacks

The California condor, a living relic from the Pleistocene Age, is perilously close to extinction in the wild. In 1984 biologists counted only 15 free-flying condors, including five breeding pairs. This spring, however, biologists at the Condor Research Center in Ventura, Calif., had yet to observe three of the breeding pairs return to their territories; one member of a fourth pair was missing. An emaciated male condor died in April after a rancher found it and turned it over to center biologists.

Since 1982, a controversial program sponsored by the U.S. Fish and Wildlife Service, the California state government and the National Audubon Society has been attempting to build a condor breeding flock in captivity to supplement or replace the remaining wild population. Researchers have taken eggs from condor nests for incubation at the San Diego zoo; breeding pairs often produce a second egg after a first egg is removed.

In 1984 there were 16 condors in captivity, including 10 females and five males that had yet to reach maturity. The agencies hope to establish five captive breeding pairs whose offspring could be released to the wild.

The project is controversial. In 1980 a wild condor chick died while researchers were removing it from the nest. Some environmentalists charge that the effort can only artificially prolong the species, with no assurance that condors bred in captivity would find enough habitat left to survive if they are ultimately freed.

the snail darter, a three-inch fish then listed as endangered.[5] Congress responded to the Tellico ruling by exempting the project from the endangered species law and setting up a Cabinet-level board with power to let future federal projects proceed despite potential threats to endangered animals or plants.

Developers and other business interests quickly began to press for changes in the law. In 1981 the Reagan administration directed the U.S. Fish and Wildlife Service (FWS) to consider possible economic impacts before listing a species for protection, and Reagan's first secretary of the interior, James G. Watt, officially slowed the pace of listing new species, contending that

[5] Biologists have subsequently found several new snail darter populations, and Fish and Wildlife Service officials have downgraded the snail darter from endangered to threatened status.

the FWS instead should focus limited resources on preserving plants and animals already listed. But Congress, renewing the act in 1982, overruled the administration's policy of weighing economic impacts in listing species. Watt's successor, William P. Clark, accelerated the process, and officials in 1984 designated 41 species for protection.

Conservationists credit the Reagan administration for progress in drawing up species recovery plans, but they contend that budget cutbacks prevent the FWS from following through on those blueprints. Just since the Endangered Species Act was renewed in 1982, seven or eight candidate species have disappeared, Environmental Defense Fund attorney Michael Bean noted, providing "a rather serious indication that all is not working as it should be."

This year the Reagan administration and business interests are backing a simple extension of the endangered species law. Conservationists generally find few structural problems with the law, Bean said, but they maintain that funding levels proposed by the administration "fall far short of what is needed to make the act work." The House July 29 approved a three-year extension that made few changes in the law and kept funding at current levels. The Senate has yet to act on the reauthorization.

Desert bighorn sheep

Recent court decisions could force Congress or the Supreme Court to confront other controversies over endangered or threatened species. In January the 8th U.S. Circuit Court of Appeals ruled that Indians taking bald eagles for their feathers on the Yankton Sioux reservation in South Dakota were exempt from the 1973 law. Ruling on a Sierra Club lawsuit in February, the same court said that the Interior Department could not permit sportsmen to trap threatened wolves in Minnesota if there were other means of controlling their numbers. Montana game managers fear that the wolf decision could set a precedent for court action barring Montana's carefully controlled hunting of grizzly bears *(see box, p. 33).*

The National Audubon Society has urged Congress to close an exemption to the Endangered Species Act that permits falconers to keep peregrines reared from captive stock. The law already prohibits the capture of wild peregrines. The National Wildlife Federation and Western water developers meanwhile have been sparring over FWS rulings on proposed dams that could eliminate Colorado River habitat for three rare fish and divert water flows from the Platte River Valley in Nebraska, a critical region for whooping cranes, bald eagles and waterfowl.

Critical Need to Preserve Wildlife Refuges

The Endangered Species Act has spurred federal and state officials to search out surviving species and encouraged captive breeding programs to replenish depleted wild populations. Its primary benefits, however, may stem from setting aside new wildlife refuges and preserving habitat critical to species' survival. "The Endangered Species Act is really a habitat conservation act," said Alan Wentz, director of the National Wildlife Federation's fisheries and wildlife program. "Without the law, the habitat of an animal like the grizzly bear would be infringed on even more than it has been." [6]

But habitat for non-endangered animals continues to disappear. Each year, housing developments, highways, shopping centers, power lines and other urban developments sprawl across thousands of acres of farm lands, seashores or lakeshores. Intensive agriculture exposes soils to erosion and converts diverse vegetative cover to row after row of the same crop. In mountains and deserts, mining, logging, petroleum exploration, ski resorts and other activities tear up valleys and meadows, driving wildlife further into the back country. "Overall, the picture for wildlife is darker due to continuing habitat loss," Wentz has noted.[7]

One important, and endangered, habitat is wetlands — swamps, bogs, coastal salt marshes, river bottoms, prairie "pothole" depressions and other low-lying, moisture-laden lands. As the countryside filled up, farmers and developers drained and filled wetlands to make way for fields, resorts and housing developments. In the process they destroyed nutrient-rich ecosystems offering prime habitat for fish, shellfish, waterfowl, beavers, hawks, bobcats, alligators, songbirds and other forms of wildlife. The lower 48 states once held an estimated 215 million acres of wetlands. Less than 100 million acres remain, and a 1982 FWS study found that losses have accelerated in recent decades to 458,000 acres a year.[8] Loss of wetlands may account for the steep decline in the number of ducks migrating south from Canada this fall. Officials project a 22 percent drop from last year.

---

[6] Quoted by Sam Iker, "Can We Live Up to the Law?" *National Wildlife,* April/May 1985, p. 13.

[7] "1985 Environmental Quality Index, Nagging Problems Still Ahead," *National Wildlife,* March 1985, p. 34.

[8] U.S. Fish and Wildlife Service, Office of Biological Services, "Status and Trends of Wetlands and Deepwater Habitats in the Coterminous United States, 1950s to 1970s," September 1982. For background see "America's Disappearing Wetlands," *E.R.R.,* 1983 Vol. II, pp. 613-632.

The federal government has contributed to the loss of wetlands by draining millions of acres itself, turning lands over to the states for reclamation and helping farmers convert wetlands to food production. At the same time it has since 1929 bought wetlands for waterfowl refuges. In 1934, Congress provided a steady source of funds for wetlands purchases by requiring waterfowl hunters to buy federal "duck stamps" each year. Now priced at $7.50 each, the stamps raise revenues of roughly $16 million a year.

But wetlands, which once went for $1 an acre, now may cost as much as $1,000 an acre; and conservationists contend that more federal purchases are needed to preserve surviving wetlands from development before prices go even higher. A bill (HR 1203) is pending before Congress that would provide up to $75 million a year over 10 years for wetlands purchases by state and federal agencies.[9]

Wildlife groups are also pressing Congress to force the U.S. Army Corps of Engineers to tighten regulation of dredge-and-fill operations under the Clean Water Act of 1977, which is up for renewal this year. Expanding the corps' traditional power to supervise navigable waterways, Section 404 of the law requires developers to obtain permits before filling in wetlands throughout the nation. Environmentalists maintain that the Corps of Engineers has consistently tried to narrow the scope of wetlands development subject to federal review.

Slowing the Loss of Farm-Land Habitat

In many parts of the country, farms offer wildlife its best surviving habitat. But during the agricultural boom years in the 1970s, farmers plowed up marginal soils, cut down windbreaks, and planted "fencerow to fencerow" to expand crop production. Soil erosion accelerated, and wildlife was driven from fields and pastures. By 1984, noted M. Rupert Cutler, a former assistant secretary of agriculture, ". . . neither the wildlife associated with America's farms nor our farmers themselves have ever been in worse shape." [10]

Farm-land wildlife has suffered severe damage across the nation, especially in the Midwestern and Great Plains Farm Belt states. Between the late 1950s and the late 1970s, populations of the ring-necked pheasant, a common game bird on the plains, fell 96 percent in Ohio, 85 percent in North Dakota, 70

---

[9] The bill's sponsor is John B. Breaux, D-La., chairman of the House Merchant Marine Subcommittee on Fisheries and Wildlife Conservation.
[10] M. Rupert Cutler, "Integrating Wildlife Habitat Features in Agricultural Programs," *Transactions of the 49th North American Wildlife and Natural Resources Conference,* Boston, Mass., March 23-28, 1984, p. 132. For background, see "Soil Erosion: Threat to Food Supply," *E.R.R.,* 1984 Vol. I, pp. 229-248.

percent in Colorado and more than 60 percent in five other states, according to a survey by the Association of Midwest Fish and Wildlife Agencies. Quail, grouse, songbirds, cottontail rabbits and other species also declined in those states during that period.

Conservation groups fault U.S. Department of Agriculture subsidy and erosion control programs for often ignoring wildlife values. Farmers idled millions of acres under the Reagan administration's 1983 Payment-in-Kind (PIK) program, for instance, but a survey by the private, non-profit Wildlife Management Institute found that only about 11 percent of the retired lands in 12 Midwest states had been seeded with cover suitable for wildlife.[11]

Whooping crane

Some states now lease marginal lands from farmers for wildlife habitat or offer incentives for landowners to plant native grasses or other suitable wildlife cover. But conservation experts view the current crisis in the U.S. farm economy as perhaps the best chance to improve conditions for wildlife. "Our overproduction has been caused by bringing a lot of marginal crop land into production," Robert J. Gray, director of policy development for the American Farmland Trust, commented. "We want to take 30 to 50 million acres out of production. . . ." [12]

The House and Senate Agriculture committees have approved legislation that would create a "conservation reserve" to pay farmers for taking highly erodible land out of production. The committees have also approved "sodbuster" provisions that would disqualify farmers who cultivate highly erodible land from receiving federal price-support benefits. Congress debated but could not reach agreement on similar legislation in 1984. Sen. Edward Zorinsky, D-Neb., and Sen. Bob Kasten, R-Wis., are proposing similar "swampbuster" penalties to discourage the conversion of prairie potholes, river bottoms and other wetlands to agricultural production. Wentz, the National Wildlife Federation official, has predicted that a multi-year program

[11] Wildlife Management Institute, "PIK Program Shorts Conservation," *Linking Agriculture and Resource Conservation Programs,* Oct. 7, 1983, cited by Cutler, *op. cit.*
[12] The trust is a national membership organization dedicated to protecting farm land from conversion to non-agricultural uses and soil erosion.

to prod farmers to set aside lands and plant protective cover "would be at least as important, if not more important, than the entire National Wildlife Refuge System." [13]

Government Role

H UMANS HAVE influenced North American wildlife since the Ice Ages, when hunters followed game across the Bering Strait land bridge from Asia. Spear points have been uncovered with mastodon bones, and some scientists have suggested that skilled hunters with specialized weapons may have helped wipe out woolly mammoths, giant sloths, camels and other mammals that vanished from the continent as glaciers retreated. Native American tribes depended on game for food, clothing and shelter but were too few in numbers to seriously harm overall wildlife populations.

Early European explorers and colonists in the New World were astonished by the sheer numbers of American wildlife. They came from a continent where most forest had been cut and meat was scarce, and they quickly recognized the economic potential of harvesting fish and furs for export. Barely a decade after Columbus' first voyage, Spanish, French, English and Portuguese ships were fishing the North Atlantic coast for cod, carrying cured and salted fish back to European markets. While Spanish conquistadores searched for gold, French explorers penetrated to the Great Lakes, upper Mississippi Valley and eventually across the Great Plains to trade for beaver pelts and other furs.

By the mid-1800s beaver had been trapped out of many American rivers. Over the rest of the 19th century, expanding settlements and hunting pressure took a relentless toll on other wildlife. The great auk, a flightless bird once common on North Atlantic coastlines, in 1844 became the first species native to North America to be extinguished as the result of human impacts. The passenger pigeon had largely vanished by the 1890s, victim of overhunting and the cutting of Eastern woodlands.

By then, buffalo hunters had eliminated the mighty bison herds from the plains; homesteaders and hunting for market had reduced pronghorns from more than 30 million to 13,000 and driven the elk into the mountains. "Perhaps never before in human history had so many animals, of different species, been

---

[13] Quoted by Sam Iker, "A Plot to Plant for Wildlife," *National Wildlife*, April-May 1984, p. 23.

killed in so short a time," wrote former National Wildlife Federation President Thomas L. Kimball and a colleague.[14]

Even in colonial times, Americans began to recognize that uncontrolled slaughter was depleting valuable wild populations. In 1639, Newport, R.I., established the nation's first closed season on deer hunting; and 12 of the 13 original colonies had enacted wildlife protection laws by the time of the American Revolution. In the 19th century, naturalists, artists, and writers such as John James Audubon and James Fenimore Cooper decried the loss of wildlife; their demands to protect remaining wild animals helped fuel the American conservation movement.

Massachusetts set up the first state game agency in 1865. By 1880 every state and territorial government had enacted some form of fish or game law; and the U.S. Supreme Court in a series of rulings upheld their authority to regulate hunting and fishing. But states often were unable to enforce hunting laws vigorously, and some protected species continued in decline. At the same time, states continued to offer bounties for killing wolves, mountain lions and other predators that threatened livestock — sometimes with unintended consequences. In one famous example, the systematic elimination of livestock predators on the Kaibab Plateau north of the Grand Canyon in Arizona allowed the region's mule deer population to multiply far beyond habitat capacity. Their browsing severely damaged the land's ability to produce more forage, and thousands of deer starved in the mid-1920s.

It was only gradually that biologists and other natural resource experts recognized that game populations could be increased by improving habitat conditions. Aldo Leopold, a professionally trained forester, pioneered scientific management techniques during the 1920s. Even today, Leopold's 1933 book *Game Management* is considered the bible for wildlife biologists.[15] Building on Leopold's teachings, state game managers in the last 50 years have saved threatened game animals and expanded wildlife habitat. Elk, pronghorns, wood ducks, beaver, and even a few scattered bands of wild bison reoccupied parts of their range. By the mid-1930s all 50 states had restricted deer-hunting to specific seasons, while 43 states had restored or introduced wild turkey populations. Game managers now recognize the role predators play in the ecological balance. Many

---

[14] Thomas L. Kimball and Raymond E. Johnson, "The Richness of American Wildlife," in *Wildlife and America*, Council on Environmental Quality, 1978, p. 8.

[15] Leopold was one of the founders of what became the U.S. environmental movement. In 1924, he was responsible for creating the Gila Wilderness Area in New Mexico, the first unit of the national forest wilderness system. After retiring from the U.S. Forest Service in 1933, Leopold took a chair in wildlife management at the University of Wisconsin, the first such academic position in the nation.

predators are no longer considered "varmints" to be shot and trapped without restriction. In most areas, states classify mountain lions and black bears, which are not protected by the Endangered Species Act, as game animals, protected by hunting seasons and bag limits.

Conservation Management on Public Lands

Ever since the conservation movement began, the U.S. government has assumed a growing role in managing the nation's wildlife. Through treaties and legislation, Congress has asserted federal authority to manage migratory waterfowl, combat illegal wildlife trade across state lines and preserve endangered species. And as the nation's largest landowner, the federal government controls more than 600 million acres of land — in national parks, forests, military bases and public range lands — that comprise most of the country's best unspoiled habitat.

Congress took a first step toward federal protection for wildlife when it created Yellowstone National Park in 1872. Applying its power to regulate commerce between states, Congress in the Lacey Act of 1900 prohibited interstate transportation of wild animals or birds that had been killed in violation of state law. President Theodore Roosevelt, an enthusiastic hunter and founder of the Boone and Crockett Club, an influential sportsmen's organization, expanded national parks and forests and in 1903 proclaimed the first national wildlife refuge, on Pelican Island off the Florida coast, for herons and egrets that were being intensively hunted for plumes to decorate women's hats. Congress in 1909 authorized the government for the first time to buy lands for wildlife protection when it established a National Bison Range in Montana.

In 1916, the federal role expanded when the U.S. Bureau of Biological Survey, under pressure from farm and ranch interests, began taking over predator control efforts. Federal laws and treaties protecting migratory waterfowl set the stage for enlarging the refuge system. In the Migratory Bird Treaty Act of 1918, Congress drew on its treaty-making powers to give the Biological Survey power to set strict limits for state waterfowl hunting seasons.[16]

The Fish and Wildlife Service, formed in 1939 by merging the Biological Survey and the Commerce Department's Bureau of Fisheries, within the Interior Department, now manages more than 400 refuges in 49 states and five trust territories,[17] along with waterfowl production areas, research stations and fish

---

[16] The Supreme Court upheld this use of Congress' treaty-making power in the case of *Missouri v. Holland* (1920).

[17] Congress more than doubled the national wildlife refuge system in 1980 to 89 million acres when it designated 53.8 million acres of Alaskan lands for new or expanded refuges.

Yellowstone Grizzly Management

The great silver-backed grizzly bear probably has stirred more fear and awe among men than any other American wildlife. Today, no other wild animals pose more difficult problems for federal and state wildlife managers than grizzlies still roaming Wyoming and Montana mountains and forests around Yellowstone National Park.

Between 40,000 and 50,000 grizzlies now live in Alaska and western Canada. Only 800 to 900 survive in the Lower 48 states, virtually all in northern Montana, northwestern Wyoming and the Idaho panhandle. Of those, 400 to 600 bears live around Glacier National Park in Montana, while another 200 or so range through the Yellowstone National Park back country and onto surrounding national forests and private lands. The northern Montana grizzlies fare relatively well, and Montana state game officials grant hunting licenses for  sportsmen to harvest up to 25 a year, depending on the number of deaths from other causes.

In the Yellowstone ecosystem, on the other hand, the grizzly population has been falling since at least the mid-1960s; and there is disagreement over what to do about it. The Park Service in the early 1970s closed garbage dumps where bears had been feeding for 50 years. Some critics argue that the move forced the bears to roam out of the park and kill ranchers' sheep. Grizzlies have killed several campers in recent years, and wildlife officials have had to destroy them.

Some Forest Service officials want to set up feeding stations to supplement grizzlies' diets and manage habitat to keep them from roving so far. The Park Service and Fish and Wildlife Service prefer to prevent encounters with humans by temporarily closing parts of Yellowstone and to designate lands outside the park where grizzly habitat needs are given preference over logging, grazing or other activities.

Some recreation groups question whether protecting Yellowstone grizzlies is worth the cost and effort, especially when the species has a better chance to survive in Alaska and Canada. Others defend preserving the Yellowstone grizzlies as a test of the nation's ability to live in harmony with wilderness and the creatures it contains. The grizzly "has such prowess, history and reputation that he isn't only of the wilderness but also makes wilderness on the ground and in our heads," *Sports Illustrated* contributing editor Bil Gilbert has written.

hatcheries. The agency lists and drafts plans for protecting endangered and threatened species, distributes federal funds to state game programs, sets overall seasons and limits for hunting migratory birds and advises other federal agencies on potential impacts from proposed government projects.

The national park system, nearly 75 million acres in 48 parks, also provides wildlife with the equivalent of natural refuges. The National Park Service tries to preserve native ecosystems with as little interference as possible. Federal law prohibits hunting in most parks, and Park Service officials generally let predators, disease and other natural forces keep numbers in balance. State wildlife laws regulating hunting and fishing apply to most other federal lands, but federal agencies are responsibile for maintaining wildlife habitats. Although national forest wilderness areas and the federal Wild and Scenic Rivers system contain some of the country's last unspoiled habitat, the U.S. Forest Service and the Bureau of Land Management (BLM) manage most other federal lands under multiple-use policies that make wildlife habitat protection only one of several objectives.[18]

In 1976 Congress gave the BLM and Forest Service new powers to preserve wildlife values along with other uses. Both agencies beefed up their staffs with wildlife biologists as they drafted long-term plans for managing lands for lodging, mining, oil and gas exploration, recreation and environmental protection. But the Forest Service is still administered by foresters trained primarily in timber production, while BLM remains reluctant to challenge livestock interests that have always dominated public land management policy in Western states. Environmentalists charge that the Reagan administration has prodded the Forest Service and BLM to step up logging and mining on public lands regardless of the costs to wildlife.

Extending Protection to Non-Game Species

Since the 1920s state wildlife agencies have relied on revenue from hunting and fishing licenses to fund their game management programs.[19] As a consequence, state game departments traditionally have devoted most of their attention to increasing big-game mammal and fish populations to provide more targets for sportsmen. But game species hunted for sport make up less than a fifth of the 3,700 vertebrate species in the United States and its coastal waters.

---

[18] For background on the National Wilderness Preservation System, see "Protecting the Wilderness," *E.R.R.*, 1984 Vol. II, pp. 589-608.

[19] Federal excise taxes on sporting arms and fishing tackle are used to aid state management programs. These taxes generated $114 million to be distributed to the states in 1985. Congress in 1984 approved additional taxes and import duties on motorboat fuel and fishing equipment which are expected to generate another $83 million a year for fish management and boating safety programs.

With broadly based environmental groups taking more interest in wildlife protection, state agencies have been under pressure to preserve songbirds, shorebirds, small mammals, reptiles and amphibians. "Non-game wildlife species are the forgotten stepchild of wildlife management," National Wildlife Federation Executive Vice President Jay D. Hair maintained. ". . . [B]etter management of the non-game resource could prevent many species from declining to the point where they may face extinction."

Most states now devote some resources to non-game species, and 33 states augment game department budgets with state income tax "checkoffs" permitting taxpayers to contribute annual tax refunds to wildlife conservation programs. Congress in 1980 authorized federal assistance to state non-game program's but never has appropriated funds for the purpose. State game officials, worried that declining license sales will dry up their budgets, have been searching for additional revenue sources. Missouri now designates a portion of its state sales tax receipts for wildlife programs, and other state game departments receive part of their funds from annual legislative appropriations. Non-game tax checkoffs produce substantial revenues but face growing competition from checkoffs for other causes.

Game department officials, reluctant to depend on annual appropriations from legislatures subject to political pressures, talk about asking non-consumptive users of wildlife — backpackers, photographers, birdwatchers — to contribute to wildlife management through taxes on equipment they frequently buy. "Someday, wildlife people are going to wake up to the fact that there is a broader constituency than sportsmen," noted Jennifer Lewis, staff biologist for the Humane Society of the United States. "A lot of non-consumptive users don't like the idea of paying equipment taxes," Lewis added, "but that would allow them a voice in the process that they don't have now."

Continuing Threats

THE NATION'S population growth and steady habitat loss have complicated the task of managing American wildlife. Biologists, game managers, sportsmen and ecologists alike recognize that the fate of wildlife is intimately connected to the quality of the nation's air, water and soil. Industrial pollution and toxic chemicals not only threaten human health, but wildlife populations as well. "We're finding out every day how environmental contaminants are affecting fish and wildlife as well as us," Ault commented.

President Nixon in 1972 banned most uses of DDT, once a common pesticide, after FWS researchers linked its residues to thin egg shells that threatened the ability of bald eagles, peregrine falcons, brown pelicans and other birds to reproduce. Since the ban went into effect, eagle and peregrine numbers have been increasing, and officials in 1984 removed the brown pelican from the endangered species list. But DDT spraying to fight malaria and agricultural pests continues in Central and South American nations where some U.S. migratory birds winter. DDT residues washed from previously sprayed fields, old pesticide manufacturing plants and dump sites continue to concentrate in U.S. river basins and turn up in waterfowl tissue samples. Sediments from a closed DDT manufacturing site at the U.S. Army's Redstone Arsenal have produced heavy concentrations downstream at Wheeler National Wildlife Refuge in Alabama, wintering grounds for up to 90,000 ducks and geese. Researchers still have not found the source of DDE, a DDT matabolite, that is contaminating fish, starlings and mallards in cotton-growing regions of the Pecos River and Rio Grande valleys of New Mexico and Texas and along the Gila River in Arizona.

Immature peregrine falcon

Meanwhile other pesticides and toxic chemicals have found their way into wildlife populations. In the summer of 1981, 17 states along the central flyway followed by migrating birds considered canceling waterfowl hunting seasons after the insecticide endrin contaminated game birds feeding in Montana and Wyoming wheat fields. In New York and New Jersey duck hunters in 1981 and 1982 were advised against eating wild waterfowl from the Hudson and Niagara rivers potentially contaminated with PCBs, chemicals formerly used in electrical equipment, that were banned in 1979.

Polluted water even threatens national refuges. FWS officials have found toxic water in 121 national refuges, more than one-quarter of the total.[20] In March Interior officials began driving birds away from the 5,900-acre Kesterton National Wildlife Refuge in California's agricultural San Joaquin Valley after toxic farm-land drainage caused deaths and deformities in fish and waterfowl. Biologists attributed the damage to high concentrations of selenium, a naturally occurring element, washed into the refuge by an 82-mile-long irrigation drainage canal that the U.S. Bureau of Reclamation opened in 1981.

Renewed Debate Over Coyote Poisoning

Another long-running debate is heating up now that the federal government has partially lifted a 1972 ban on poisoning coyotes on Western range lands. President Nixon that year issued an executive order barring the use of coyote poisons on federal lands, and the U.S. Environmental Protection Agency (EPA) by regulation halted use of strychnine and sodium monofluoroacetate (compound 1080) baits after finding that eagles, hawks, bobcats, foxes and other wildlife were consuming them and dying.

Although the FWS Animal Damage Control Division continued coyote control efforts, sheep ranchers throughout the West continue to blame the 1972 ban for heavy lamb losses. The Reagan administration, sympathetic to livestock industry demands, in 1982 resumed limited use of "denning" — the incineration or fumigation of coyote pups in their dens — and expanded use of M-44 "coyote getters," spring-loaded devices that inject lethal sodium cyanide doses when a coyote tugs at the bait with its teeth. Reagan in 1982 lifted Nixon's 10-year-old ban on using compound 1080 on federal lands, and, as of July 18, the EPA has allowed ranchers to fit sheep with collars containing compound 1080 to poison coyotes that usually attack by biting them in the necks. Predator control researchers maintain that only coyotes will consume the toxicants.

Environmentalists object to resuming compound 1080 use, arguing that ranchers could protect lambs by hiring herders, building electrified fences or keeping guard dogs on the range. But many sheepmen could not afford the costs, and federal researchers say that non-lethal methods have yet to prove effective in keeping predators away from sheep.

Drives to Ban Lead Shot, Stop Poaching

Both federal and state officials are now debating controversial steps to prevent the inadvertent lead poisoning of waterfowl and other birds, including bald eagles. In a dispute that has split sportsmen across the nation, environmental groups have been

---

[20] See Philip Shabecoff, "Toxic Water Threatens Many Wildlife Refuges," *The New York Times,* April 30, 1985, p. A16.

Controversy Over Sport Hunting

Conservation groups often differ among themselves on game management issues, especially sport hunting. The National Wildlife Federation represents 4.2 million members, many of them sportsmen, but its local affiliates sometimes take more conservative stands than the federation's national staff.

Groups like the Sierra Club and Defenders of Wildlife focus on preserving overall wildlife populations and view hunting as an acceptable management tool to keep numbers in line with habitat capacity. Many of their supporters, on the other hand, are personally opposed to sport hunting. National Audubon Society members wrote in protest after the group's magazine published an article in March 1985 defending Indiana's decision to open a hunting season on mourning doves.

Maintaining that sport hunting inflicts needless cruelty, the Humane Society has filed suit against the U.S. Fish and Wildlife Service to block hunting on national wildlife refuges. The group contends that state game commissions and departments set hunting limits to cater to hunters' demands, not to keep wildlife numbers in balance. "We feel most animals, including deer, are capable of controlling their own populations if you let them alone," said Jennifer Lewis, staff biologist for the organization.

Many state game officials, who themselves hunt and fish, contend that Americans should enjoy that right so long as they don't damage wildlife resources. With few predators left and habitat steadily eroding, sportsmen play a vital role in controlling game populations, they maintain.

urging the FWS and state game commissions to ban lead shot, forcing hunters to load shotguns with steel shot that many consider less effective ammunition.

Lead poisoning in waterfowl has been documented since the 1890s. By one estimate, 2 or 3 percent of the nation's waterfowl die from lead poisoning each year. Diving for food on lake or stream bottoms, ducks, geese and other birds often ingest lead pellets scattered by shots fired by hunters drawn by concentrations of birds during hunting season. Concern over lead poisoning has grown with evidence that endangered bald eagles, picking up pellets themselves or eating waterfowl killed or crippled by toxic lead levels, have been dying in growing numbers.[21]

In 1984, 21 bald eagles were found dead from lead poisoning, according to FWS reports obtained by National Wildlife Federation officials. In the mid-1970s, the federal agency proposed designating certain areas where waterfowl hunters would be required to use steel shot. But the National Rifle Association

---

[21] See Oliver H. Pattee and Steven K. Hennes, "Bald Eagles and Waterfowl: The Lead Shot Connection," *Transactions of the 48th North American Wildlife and Natural Resources Conference*, March 19-24, 1983, Kansas City, Mo., p. 230.

and hunting groups protested the lead-shot ban, contending that steel shot causes guns to misfire and kills less effectively, increasing the numbers of injured and crippled birds. Starting in 1979, Congress amended annual Interior Department appropriations bills to prohibit the FWS from enforcing steel-shot zones in any state unless state game officials gave their consent. Environmentalists fault Reagan administration officials for moving slowly to impose lead-shot restrictions, even on federal wildlife refuges.

By 1984, the service had established steel-shot zones in 32 states. The National Wildlife Federation, although it represents hunters, has been pushing for more aggressive action. The federation contends that failure to impose more steel-shot zones violated the Endangered Species Act requirement to protect bald eagles. The organization filed suit June 14 seeking to force the Interior Department to bar lead shot in 22 counties in five states or to close hunting seasons.[22]

Illegal hunting also threatens valuable, often endangered, species. Across the nation, poachers take game and fish illegally out of season. Hunters, guides and collectors also conduct a lucrative trade in wild animals; the government has estimated that illegal wildlife trade nets its participants as much as $100 million a year.

Federal and state game wardens have stepped up the fight against illegal shipments of live animals, pelts and other parts of the animals across state lines or to other nations. In the last few years FWS investigators have mounted several controversial "sting" operations against reptile collectors, Indians selling bald eagle feathers, grizzly and big horn sheep poachers and falconers who allegedly sell peregrines and other rare birds of prey taken from the wild.

The operations have had some success. Just recently a Montana court sentenced a poacher to 15 years in federal prison for attempting to sell a grizzly carcass to an undercover wildlife agent. But some organizations, including groups who have played an important role in re-establishing endangered birds in the wild, have protested the government's tactics as illegal entrapment.

---

[22] The five states are California, Oregon, Missouri, Illinois and Oklahoma. Trial is scheduled for Aug. 13 in federal district court in Sacramento.

Selected Bibliography

Books

Cadieux, Charles, *These Are the Endangered*, Stone Wall Press, Washington, D.C., 1981.

Leopold, Aldo, *Game Management*, Charles Scribner's Sons, New York, 1933.

_____ , *A Sand County Almanac*, Sierra Club/Ballantine Books, New York, 1949.

Leopold, A. Starker, Ralph J. Gutierrez and Michael T. Bronson, *North American Game Birds and Mammals*, Charles Scribner's Sons, New York, 1981.

Matthiessen, Peter, *Wildlife in America*, Viking Press, New York, 1959.

Reed, Nathaniel P., and Dennis Drabelle, *The United States Fish and Wildlife Service*, Westview Press, Boulder, Colo., 1984.

Yaffee, Steven Lewis, *Prohibitive Policy, Implementing the Federal Endangered Species Act*, MIT Press, Cambridge, Mass., 1982.

Articles

Audubon, published by the National Audubon Society, selected issues.

Defenders, published by Defenders of Wildlife, selected issues.

Field & Stream, selected issues.

National Wildlife, published by the National Wildlife Federation, selected issues.

Outdoor News Bulletin, published by the Wildlife Management Institute, selected issues.

Reports and Studies

Editorial Research Reports, "America's Threatened Coastlines," 1984 Vol. II, p. 819; "America's Disappearing Wetlands," 1983 Vol. II, p. 613; "Troubled Ocean Fisheries," 1984 Vol. I, p. 429.

Environmental Law Institute, "The Evolution of National Wildlife Law," prepared for the U.S. Council on Environmental Quality, 1977.

International Association of Fish and Wildlife Agencies, annual convention proceedings.

U.S. Council on Environmental Quality, "Wildlife and America," 1978.

Wildlife Management Institute, "Transactions of the North American Wildlife and Natural Resources Conference," published annually.

TROUBLED OCEAN FISHERIES

by

Richard C. Schroeder

June 15
1 9 8 4

Editor's Update: The World Fisheries Conference July 6, 1984, outlined a "Global Strategy" calling on the U.N. Food and Agriculture Organization to develop five special action programs for 1) planning, management and development of fisheries; 2) development of small-scale fisheries; 3) development of aquaculture; 4) international trade in fish and fisheries products; and 5) promotion of fisheries for alleviating undernutrition. The conference also called for FAO annual investments of $15.6 million for these programs over the next five years. The figure was exceeded in the first year in contributions to the FAO plus multilateral and bilateral programs.

TROUBLED OCEAN FISHERIES

THE PRICE of fish is on the rise, not just in seafood stores and supermarkets in the United States but around the world, in rich and poor countries alike. The world's oceans, once thought of as an inexhaustible source of protein-rich food, are beginning to show the strains of overfishing, pollution and the ever-increasing demand for food by a human population that is expanding by nearly 80 million persons a year.

"Three tremendous shocks have hit the world fishing industry in the past 15 years, affecting every individual fish consumer," said a spokesman for the Food and Agriculture Organization (FAO) of the United Nations. "First, the ocean fish catch, after rising 5 to 7 percent a year since 1950, suddenly trailed off to under 1 percent in the mid-1970s. That is about half the population growth, so fish is scarcer and dearer every year. Second, the great oil price rises in the 1970s affected fishing much harder than other industries, because fuel is the biggest cost component after the purchase of a boat. This hits both the small fisherman with an outboard motor and the big Russian factory ship, and both very hard. And third, during the negotiations for the new Law of the Sea Convention nearly all coastal countries adopted the 200-mile exclusive economic and fishing zone, radically altering rights of access to fishing banks that have been open to all throughout history.... What you have, in short, is the world's oldest and biggest industry after farming in complete ferment." [1]

The FAO is convening a World Fisheries Conference in Rome June 27-July 6 to assess what is happening to the fish catch and to plan a strategy for better management and development of ocean fisheries. The conference, the FAO spokesman said, "is the first global attempt since the triple shock to take an in-depth look at what comes next."

The rise and fall of the ocean fisheries industry happened quickly. In the 25 years following World War II, the worldwide catch of ocean fish increased dramatically, rising in some years by nearly 9 percent, well above the rate of population growth. Technological improvements in fishing gear and government-

---

[1] Nicholas Raymond, FAO Fisheries Conference information officer, letter to the author dated March 12, 1984.

backed investment in new equipment enabled fishermen to take more fish from traditional fishing grounds and to move into previously unexploited areas, such as the frigid waters of Antarctica. By 1970, the worldwide catch averaged nearly 40 pounds (18 kilograms) a person a year, although people in some affluent industrialized countries consumed twice that average while those in some landlocked Third World countries ate virtually no fish.[2] In that period, several developing countries moved to the forefront of the world fishing industry, Chile and Peru in the Western Hemisphere among them.

The rate of growth in the fish catch peaked in the early 1970s, however. After more than doubling in just 12 years, from 28 million metric tons in 1958 to 62 million tons in 1970, the global catch has grown very slowly in the past decade. Between 1981 and 1982, the last year for which complete data are available, the world catch (excluding whales) rose only slightly from 74.6 million tons to 75.0 million tons.[3] The world catch of food fish, at about 52.5 million tons, did not increase at all in 1982. The catch of non-food fish grew by 2 percent to 22.5 million tons.

Uncertain Prospects for Future Growth

The prognosis for the future of ocean fisheries is cloudy. Experts are divided on how much the yield can be expanded, or whether any significant increase in the fish catch is possible. The most optimistic estimate is given by the World Bank, which predicts that the yield can increase to 120 million tons a year. According to bank estimates, about half of this new yield can come "from rebuilding and better management of currently depleted or heavily fished stocks (especially anchovetas and herring) and the remainder from intensified fishing of those stocks now only lightly or moderately harvested. Beyond this, there are also some prospects for expanded production of unconventional species . . . which until now have been caught only in very limited quantities. . . ."[4]

The FAO estimates are smaller but still on the optimistic side. "Excluding aquaculture [fish farming], the final yield from currently exploited species is unlikely to be much more than 110 million tons," FAO officials predict. "Production could eventually be increased above this limit, however, by catching so-called unconventional species such as the shrimp-like Antarctic

    [2] Estimate by Lester Brown in *Building a Sustainable Society*, W. W. Norton, 1981, p. 40. The estimate includes fish processed into meal, which is generally used for animal feed or fertilizer, and indirectly consumed by humans. Direct human consumption of fish products was about 27 pounds a person a year in 1972-74, according to "Fishery Sector Policy Paper," World Bank, December 1982, pp. 16-17.
    [3] *The State of Food and Agriculture 1983*, Food and Agriculture Organization, August 1983, p. 15. A metric ton equals 2,204.6 pounds.
    [4] Fishery Sector Policy Paper," *op. cit.,* p. 12. Anchovetas are small anchovies used mainly for fish meal.

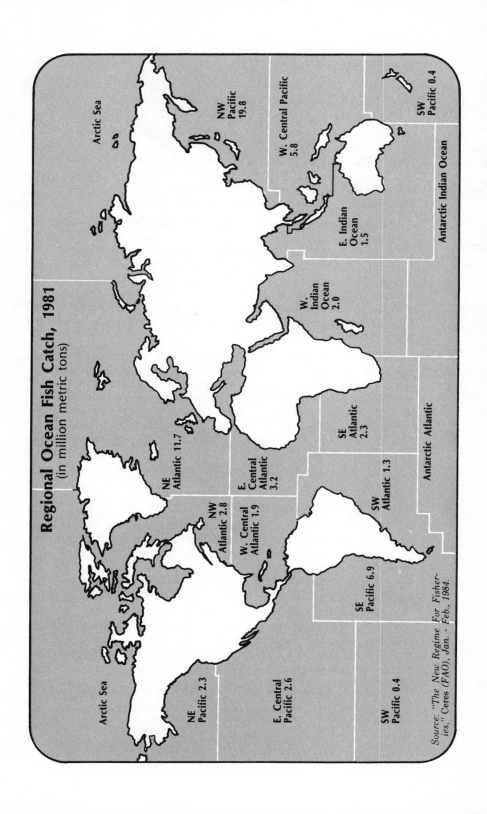

Regional Ocean Fish Catch, 1981
(in million metric tons)

Arctic Sea

NW Pacific 19.8

W. Central Pacific 5.8

SW Pacific 0.4

E. Indian Ocean 1.5

Antarctic Indian Ocean

W. Indian Ocean 2.0

NE Atlantic 11.7

E. Central Atlantic 3.2

SE Atlantic 2.3

Antarctic Atlantic

NW Atlantic 2.8

W. Central Atlantic 1.9

SW Atlantic 1.3

SE Pacific 6.9

Arctic Sea

NE Pacific 2.3

E. Central Pacific 2.6

SW Pacific 0.4

Source: "The New Regime For Fisheries," Ceres (FAO), Jan. - Feb., 1984.

krill, lantern fish, oceanic squid and small pelagic [ocean-going, surface] fish." [5]

But one of FAO's own experts, Francis T. Christy Jr., the organization's senior fishery planning officer, is much less sanguine. "In general terms, the picture is bleak," he wrote in early 1984. "The natural limits to the yields of many stocks have been reached. . . . Large numbers of individual stocks of fish are now being fished at, or close to, their maximum sustainable yields, and some are being fished beyond that level." [6]

Lester Brown, the head of the Washington-based Worldwatch Institute, supports the more pessimistic assessment and cites *The Global 2000 Report,* prepared under the auspices of the Council on Environmental Quality and published in 1980. That report, Brown wrote, concluded "that the generally accepted annual potential of 100 million tons of traditional marine species probably cannot be achieved *on a sustained basis.* More likely, says *Global 2000,* the sustainable oceanic catch is close to the present catch. . . ." [7]

Whether the global fish catch expands significantly or remains about the same, the upward pressure on fish prices is expected to continue into the foreseeable future. The World Bank forecasts that per capita fish consumption will increase to an estimated 33 pounds annually by next year. Rising per capita consumption together with population growth will push total demand to between 114 and 125 million metric tons by the year 2000, FAO's Christy says. [8] Even using the FAO's optimistic projection of a catch of 110 million tons, supply would fall short of demand.

Impact of Overfishing on Ocean Production

Two technological developments spurred the extraordinary boom in ocean fisheries in the 1950s and 1960s. One was the introduction of huge "factory trawlers," with on-board fish processing facilities and freezing capability. The other was the adoption of synthetic fiber fishing nets and mechanical gear-hauling systems that permitted the use of larger fish nets. Together the two developments briefly revolutionized the fishing industry and, by increasing the catch well beyond the maximum sustainable yields of numerous species, nearly destroyed it. By the mid-1970s, the so-called "distant water fleets" had nearly denuded the rich North Atlantic fishing grounds of the

---

[5] "Fisheries Development in the 1980s," Food and Agriculture Organization, undated, p. 4.

[6] Francis T. Christy Jr., "Fisheries for Food: Global Developments and Special Needs," unpublished paper prepared for the Right to Food Conference, Montreal, May 1984. The paper carries a disclaimer reading: "The views expressed in this paper are those of the author and do not necessarily reflect the views of FAO."

[7] Brown, *op. cit.,* p. 53.

[8] Christy, *op. cit.,* p. 17.

most prized species of demersal (bottom feeding) fish, such as cod, haddock and halibut, and had spread out to other major fishing grounds in the South Atlantic, the North Pacific and the Indian Ocean.

William W. Warner, a noted author on fishery topics, describes the factory ships in this way: "In the mid-1950s a new kind of fishing vessel began to cross the Atlantic. It was very large, it fished from the stern, and it quickly processed and deep-froze nearly all the fish it caught. Its operations were continuous, all around the clock and in all but the worst weather. 'They're fishing out there with ocean liners!' is the way astounded Canadian and American fishermen who first saw these vessels described their arrival." [9]

The adoption by the coastal nations of 200-mile fishing zones and the signing of the United Nations Convention on the Law of the Sea *(see p. 53)* has brought effective regulation to 95 percent of the world's prime fishing grounds and is making the factory ship obsolete.[10] In the assessment of the Inter-American Development Bank, "The era of large factory ships designed to exploit resources in the waters of far away countries is coming to an end." [11]

With the gradual withdrawal of the giant factory ship fleets, there is hope that some of the depleted species can be restored to optimal levels. Between 1973 and 1978, for example, the world catch of bottom-feeding fish fell from 26.1 million tons to 10.7 million tons. But even at that level, some experts believe that the current catch is very close to the maximum sustainable yield.[12] And when a species is fished at a level beyond the maximum sustainable yield, calamity can follow, as happened off the coast of Peru a dozen years ago:

Around February 1972, at the height of its glory and with little warning, the Peruvian anchoveta quietly collapsed. It was one of the greatest disasters in fishing history. Over the previous decade, Peru had built up the world's biggest single-species fishery on the humble anchoveta, hauling in catches of up to 12 million tons a year from the cool, upwelling coastal waters. Production was still peaking in late 1971 when the weather began to change. Warm water moved closer to shore, forcing the anchoveta into concentrated shoals where they were fished with even greater intensity. Then, early in 1972 — for reasons still unclear — young fish spawned the year before failed to appear as new

---

[9] William W. Warner, *Distant Water: The Fate of the North Atlantic Fisherman*, Penguin Books, 1984, pp. vii-viii.
[10] "The New Regime for Fisheries: Prospects, Policies, Practices," *Ceres* (Magazine of the FAO), January-February 1984, p. 26.
[11] "Fishery Resources," Chapter V of *Economic and Social Progress in Latin America*, Inter-American Development Bank, August 1983.
[12] Christy, *op. cit.*, p. 12

"recruits" into the stock. Overfished and under-replaced, the anchoveta biomass began to disintegrate — and Peru's fishing boom went bust. The catch plummeted to 4.4 million tons in 1972 and less than 1.5 million tons the year after. The mid-1970s saw a partial recovery, then another slump, and latest reports indicate that 1983's anchoveta haul will be the smallest in two decades.[13]

Even before the great collapse, a team of international biologists in 1970 had estimated the maximum sustainable catch of Peruvian anchovetas at 9.5 million tons a year. Depletion of the anchoveta stock was accomplished not by a fleet of ultramodern factory trawlers but by a relatively unsophisticated national fleet of modest size, showing that even in the absence of distant water fleets the danger of overfishing remains high. Among species currently in danger, according to the FAO, are sardines off the coast of Mexico, shrimp in the Bay of Bengal, blue-fin tuna in the Northwest Atlantic and off Australia, and blue and bowhead whales in the North Pacific.

Pollution Damage; Disappearing Wetlands

Pollution is also eroding fish stocks. Much attention has been focused on oil spills and the discharge of toxic metals into the oceans. But according to *The Global 2000 Report,* the more important effects stem largely from chronic low-level pollution. For centuries, humans have made the seas the world's garbage dumps, pouring thousands of waste products into vast oceans seemingly unaffected by the intrusion of chemicals, organic wastes from humans and animals, pesticides, detergents and junk metal.

"The long-term biological effects of polluting the ocean with industrial, military, municipal, and agricultural wastes are not fully known," Erik P. Eckholm, an American environmentalist, wrote in 1976. "Both the quantity and variety of ocean pollutants are growing faster than our ability to collect information about them and about their individual and synergistic consequences for the marine biosphere. The natural instability of many fish populations sometimes makes it difficult to tell whether overfishing, pollution or a natural environmental change is responsible for a stock's collapse. It is certain, however, that oceanic pollution is now global in scale, and that it poses a serious threat to marine food resources." [14]

The Chesapeake Bay, the United States' largest estuary and one of the world's richest, is an example of the harmful impact of pollution and other human activity on marine resources. In recent years the catch of oysters, blue crabs, shad, striped bass

---

[13] "The New Regime for Fisheries," *op. cit.,* p. 29.
[14] Erik P. Eckholm, *Losing Ground: Environmental Stress and World Food Prospects,* W. W. Norton, 1976, p. 160.

World Fish Catch, Selected Species
(In thousands of tons)

	Potential	Catch 1966	Catch 1977	% of Potential 1966	% of Potential 1977
Salmon	650	453	480	70	74
Flounder, cod	6,700	4,692	3,786	70	57
Herring, anchovies	15,600	13,709	1,801	88	12
Shrimp, lobster	1,670†	830	1,542	50	92
Tuna	2,260	1,031	1,592	46	70
Other demersal*	37,100	9,628	17,097	26	46
Other pelagic**	40,200	13,045	28,655	32	71

* Bottom feeding fish in coastal areas of developing countries
** Surface fish in coastal areas of developing countries
† Estimate

Source: The World Bank, United Nations Food and Agricultural Organization

and other prized sources of seafood has declined precipitously in the bay. Its rich marine life is falling victim to years of discharge of industrial and human waste from the big cities that lie within its drainage basin — Baltimore, Washington and Richmond — and from fertilizer and pesticide runoff from the basin's farms and suburbs. Construction near streams that feed into the bay causes a buildup of sediment that covers submerged aquatic plants on which the bay's marine life depends. The federal government and the surrounding states of Maryland and Virginia are mounting cleanup efforts, but the estimated price of restoring the bay to full health — between $1 billion and $3 billion — makes success questionable.[15]

Estuaries like the Chesapeake Bay may be the most biologically productive areas on earth. Of the 10 kinds of fish that are most valuable commercially, only tuna, lobsters and haddock are not dependent on estuaries. The Chesapeake Bay alone accounts for 33 percent of the U.S. oyster catch and half of the blue crab haul. But the shores of estuaries and other valuable wetlands around the oceans' fringes are under multiple assault not only from polluters and builders, but also from would-be reclaimers of the half-drowned lands for agricultural and industrial uses. According to one estimate, more than 11 million acres of American wetlands, an expanse twice the size of New Jersey, have been drained for farmland, homesites, roads and other uses in the past 30 years. Ten times that amount has been lost since

---

[15] See William W. Warner, *Beautiful Swimmers: Watermen, Crabs and the Chesapeake Bay,* Penguin Books, 1977. Also see Peter McGrath, "An American Treasure at Risk," *Newsweek,* Dec. 12, 1983, pp. 68-72.

the first European settlers arrived here. Each time a wetland is drained and "rehabilitated," the world's oceans lose yet another spawning ground for fish.[16]

Impetus for Change

THERE ARE two strong incentives for finding solutions to the declining fish catch. Fishing makes a significant contribution to the economies of the industrialized and developing countries alike, and fish is an important nutritional element for an ever-growing world population.

The commercial value of the world fish catch now exceeds $50 billion a year. Of that, about one-third ($16.7 billion in 1981) finds its way into international trade. While the top five fish exporters are industrialized countries — Canada, the United States, Norway, Denmark and Japan — the fishing industry accounts for more than 5 percent of the gross national product of several developing countries, such as Indonesia, Malaysia, the Philippines, Senegal and Thailand.[17] The fishing sector also stimulates development and employment in related industries including transport, shipbuilding, repair and maintenance, processing, ice-making, cold storage and freezing activities, and animal-feed production and packaging.

In the leading fishing nations, the industry tends to be either export or import-oriented, but two of the leaders, the United States and Japan, are near the top in both categories *(see table, p. 51)*. The total catch of fish is divided nearly evenly between the industrialized and developing countries; in 1982, the developing countries caught 36.7 million tons of fish, while the developed countries caught 38.3 million tons. The developed countries, however, are more dominant in the international fish trade, accounting for 56.4 percent of the export market in 1981. The ratio could change dramatically, though, as more and more developing coastal nations begin to exploit the marine resources within their 200-mile fishing zones.

To assist them in doing so, international agencies plan to increase their spending on the fishery sector in coming years. The FAO has been providing about $30 million a year for fishery projects ($33.8 million in 1979, for example) and, in cooperation with the UN Development Program and other do-

---

[16] See "America's Disappearing Wetlands," *E.R.R.*, 1983 Vol. II, p. 613.
[17] "Fishery Sector Policy Paper," *op. cit.*, p. 35.

Top Ten Fish Exporters, Importers

Exporters (1981)	Value (In Millions)	Importers (1981)	Value (In Millions)
Canada	1,267	Japan	3,737
United States	1,142	United States	2,988
Norway	1,002	France	1,051
Denmark	940	United Kingdom	997
Japan	863	Federal Republic of Germany	819
Republic of Korea	835	Spain	749
Iceland	713	Italy	720
Taiwan	623	Hong Kong	362
Mexico	538	Belgium	348
Netherlands	512	Netherlands	339

Source: Ceres (FAO), Jan.-Feb., 1984, p. 38.

nors, expects to increase its funding by a minimum of $15.6 million a year for a five-year period beginning in 1985.[18] Between 1964 and 1981, the World Bank lent member countries in the developing world $259 million for fisheries projects worth nearly $470 million in all. At present, 20 new projects involving $540 million in bank funds are planned between 1982 and 1986.[19] Regional banks, such as the Inter-American Development Bank and the African Development Bank, are also increasingly active in their support of the fisheries sector.

Fisheries are also a major source of employment in the Third World, providing jobs, some of them part-time or seasonal, to an estimated 16 million people. Many more are engaged in related activities such as processing and marketing. By far the largest part of the fishery work force in the developing countries is employed in small-scale fishing. By the end of the 1970s, Third World countries were earning some $11.2 billion a year from exports of fish and fish products.

Population Growth and Need for Protein

Recognition that the capacity of ocean fisheries is finite and that the present catch may be near its outer limits coincides with another startling trend, this one having to do with population growth. Although the *rate* of the world's population growth has been declining slowly over the past decade, the *number* of people added to the population each year is on the rise.

The U.N. Fund for Population Activities (UNFPA) shows that the world population increased from 3.99 billion in 1974 to

---

[18] "Draft Strategy for Fisheries Management and Development and Associated Programmes of Action," FAO, April 1984.
[19] "Fishery Sector Policy Paper," *op. cit.*, pp. 47, 53.

4.76 billion by 1984. The annual rate of growth fell from an estimated 2.02 percent in 1974 to 1.67 percent 10 years later. Despite that decline, about 78 million people were added to the population in each year of the decade, and the UNFPA expects that number to increase to 89 million by 1995-2000.[20]

Although the rate of population growth was higher 10 years ago than today, the world economy was expanding at a more rapid rate than population, and the food supply was also increasing faster. The opposite is true today; economic growth rates and food supply increases are lagging behind population growth. Similarly, the growth in the ocean fish catch is about one-half that of the population growth rate. Simply put, less food — and especially less protein food — is available per capita than 10 years ago.

The UNFPA hints strongly of an impending world food shortage. "Even in a situation of low economic growth, the increase in demand for food will exceed the rate of growth of population and given the fact that an increase in food production depends on a number of complicated institutional and technical factors and often involves considerable time lags, the tendency for the emergence of a food-population imbalance is ever present if anticipatory long-term planning is not undertaken.... In the long term, it will not only be necessary to raise supplies of resources such as food to take into account the increases in population, but population itself [must] be planned to match the limited available resources, because it is one of the variables on the demand side of the equation involving these relationships." [21]

Population pressures on ocean fisheries are particularly acute because fish are a prime source not only of protein but also of iron and iodine, both critical to human health. Fisheries contribute about 6 percent of the world supply of protein and about 24 percent of protein derived from animals, taking into account the use of fish meal in animal feed. For most of the developing world, however, fish plays an even more important nutritional role. In Southeast Asia, for example, 55 percent of the animal protein is derived from fish. In Africa the figure is 19 percent, compared with 11.8 percent in Europe and only 5.3 percent in North America.[22] In some of the poorer parts of the developing world, fish is often the only source of "meat."

---

[20] "Mexico and Beyond," United Nations Fund for Population Activities, p. 1. The UNFPA prepared this material for an international population conference the United Nations has scheduled for August 6-13 in Mexico City, the first such meeting since a previous U.N. population conference was held in Bucharest, Romania, in 1974.

[21] *Ibid.,* pp. 10-11.

[22] "Fisheries Development in the 1980s," *op. cit.,* p. 5.

Protein deficiencies, compounded by vitamin and mineral deficiencies, contribute to the deaths of nine million children a year in the developing countries. Seven million are afflicted by marasmus or kwashiorkor, both protein-deficiency diseases, and one million by nutrition-deficiency blindness. Some 600 million people in the developing world suffer from iron-deficiency anemia and 150 million from iodine-deficiency goiter.

Establishment of Exclusive Economic Zones

These incentives to find ways to maintain or expand the worldwide fish catch come at a time when coastal countries are beginning to operate under new international laws regulating national fishing rights. Negotiations on an international sea regime began more than a quarter of a century ago, in 1958. Little progress was made in two separate negotiating rounds conducted under United Nations auspices during the 1960s. But by the early 1970s, it had become apparent that the lack of internationally accepted rules defining jurisdiction over ocean fisheries was leading to disaster. Under pressure from increased catching capacities, a number of important fish stocks were over-exploited, and some had collapsed.

It was in this sobering climate that a third round of sea law negotiations got under way in 1973. Nine years of arduous bargaining followed, culminating with the completion of a Convention on the Law of the Sea on April 30, 1982. The treaty, which was signed by 130 nations, officially recognized "exclusive economic zones" already unilaterally proclaimed by more than 100 coastal countries. These nations claimed exclusive control over fishing and exploitation of natural resources in the zones, which generally extended 200 miles from shore.

The United States and three other nations voted against the Convention. The United States supported the provisions regarding regulation of fishing, but balked over arrangements for mining the deep-sea bed in waters beyond national jurisdiction.[23] The United States has claimed a 200-mile economic zone, but enforcement is a matter of national law rather than international treaty obligation. Under U.S. law, the National Oceanic and Atmospheric Administration (NOAA) allots a portion of the total allowable catch of fish in U.S. waters — currently 30 percent — to foreign fishermen, sets quotas by species and collects licensing fees to support enforcement efforts.

The establishment of the 200-mile exclusive economic zones will permit more rational management of ocean fisheries and could help halt the decline of several food fish stocks. But,

[23] For background, see "Oceanic Law," *E.R.R.*, 1974 Vol. I, p. 403; "Deep-Sea Mining," *E.R.R.*, 1978 Vol. II, p. 721.

ironically, the economic zones will benefit only a relatively small number of Third World developing countries. Two-thirds of the total value of the ocean's fish catch, excluding the ocean pelagics, have been taken off the coasts of the industrial countries, and most of the distant water fleets have come from these countries, the exceptions being the Republic of Korea, Thailand, Cuba and, to some extent, Ghana. The other third of the catch has come from waters where only a few Third World countries claim jurisdiction. More than half of the Third World portion has been taken off the west coast of Africa and a significant amount has been taken off the west coast of Latin America. The rest of the developing world has jurisdiction over waters that are the source of just 4 percent of the worldwide ocean fish catch.[24]

The developing countries, such as Mauritania, Morocco, Senegal, Angola, Namibia and Argentina, that stand to gain the most from establishment of the exclusive economic zones are already members of the various regional fishery commissions that have been set up to regulate fishing in designated ocean areas. (Other fishery commissions have been established to regulate fishing for particular species such as whales and tuna.)

The Law of the Sea Treaty has had a significant impact on these commissions. Members generally included the nations whose coastal waters were being fished and those countries doing the fishing. The bulk of ocean fishing came under the jurisdiction of one or another of these bodies. But because they lacked enforcement powers, the regional groups exercised little effective control over ocean fishing. A participating nation could escape jurisdiction merely by withdrawing from the organization. In certain cases, countries could put teeth into international controls by denying fishing privileges in their own waters to countries that ignored international arrangements. When the International Whaling Commission, for example, voted in 1982 to suspend all whaling operations in 1986, Japan, the Soviet Union, Norway, Iceland, Brazil, Peru and South Korea said they would defy the ban. The United States, in turn, is threatening to cut off fishing rights and import privileges from any nation that does not comply.

The establishment of exclusive economic zones has prompted many coastal states to seek renegotiation of previous conventions. The first regional commission to revise its framework was the Fishery Committee for the Eastern Central Atlantic, which has jurisdiction in the waters of West Africa between Morocco and Zaire. Under the revised rules, a management subcommittee with membership open only to the nations along that coast-

---

[24] Christy, *op. cit.*, p. 16.

line will supervise fishing in the zone and will coordinate its own rules with measures in effect beyond the 200-mile limits. Member states of the South Pacific Forum Fisheries Agency recently signed a pact providing for closer coordination of control of fishing by foreign vessels. Known as the Nauru Agreement, it establishes uniform terms and conditions for licensing, catch reporting and monitoring and surveillance within the exclusive economic zones.

Increasing the Catch

TWO DIFFERENT fishing industries, in effect, exist side-by-side around the world. In recent years the development of large-scale, or industrial, fishing received most of the attention. The major investments and technological improvements went into the big oceangoing stern trawlers, their sophisticated seine nets and winches, and their fish-processing and freezing plants. But the decline in the fish catch and the new law of the sea are compelling fishery experts to focus on the other fishing industry, the small-scale, or "artisanal," fishermen. An FAO publication reports that small-scale fisheries account for about 25 percent of the world catch and 40 percent of all food fish.[25]

The World Bank says that large- and small-scale fisheries can complement each other, although it agrees that a potential for conflict between the two exists. The bank is concentrating more assistance on artisanal fishing in the belief that "the potential for expanding large-scale operations is extremely limited" in most developing countries and that the development of artisanal fisheries "entails fewer constraints."[26] On the one hand, says the bank, large-scale fisheries resemble the agribusiness firms of the developed countries: They are relatively more capital intensive; they provide higher incomes for both owners and crews; they supply most of the canned and frozen fish consumed around the world as well as most of the fish meal. Artisanal fisheries, on the other hand, are largely based in rural areas, are heavily labor-intensive and, aside from small motors, have little sophisticated gear. Small-scale fisheries employ primitive methods for handling and processing, and they supply most of the fish intended for direct human consumption.

Development of artisanal fisheries in Third World countries

---

[25] "Fisheries Development in the 1980s," *op. cit.*, p. 10.
[26] "Fishery Sector Policy Paper," *op. cit.*, pp. 28, 31.

presents enormous organizational and managerial challenges because fishing communities are often dispersed over extensive coastlines. Yet the advantages of small-scale development appear to outweigh the inherent difficulties. Artisanal fishing uses much less energy than industrial fishing and provides relatively more employment per unit of catch. Moreover, the requirements for expanding the sector are modest: small amounts of credit for the purchase of boats and motors, improvement of marketing and processing facilities and the upgrading of rural roads leading from the dockside to urban areas. Best of all, from the standpoint of fisheries experts, the artisanal fisherman presents little threat to existing fish stocks, and considerable expansion of the sector is possible before the point of over-fishing is approached.

Alternative Means to Expand Fish Supply

Fishing is a notoriously wasteful industry. Better handling of the existing fish catch could dramatically increase the amount of fish protein available to the growing populations of the poor countries. The FAO estimates that 1.5 million tons of fresh fish and 2.7 million tons of dried fish are lost each year through spoilage, although the technology for minimizing or preventing the losses is available. The World Bank's estimate of waste is even greater; 10 million metric tons are lost each year, the bank claims, due to improper handling, processing and marketing. Of that amount, five million tons are lost or discarded as "by-catch" *(see below),* three million tons are destroyed by insect infestation, and the remainder through spoilage. These losses, the bank asserts, equal nearly 20 percent of the world's catch allocated for direct human consumption.

"By-catch" losses refer to unwanted fish taken along with a desired species. The by-catch, sometimes referred to as "trash fish," is often discarded at sea, usually dead. In some cases the by-catch is sold to low-income consumers as food or processed into fish meal. The shrimp industry is a prime offender in this category of waste. By some estimates, the by-catch represents as much as 80 percent of the total haul of shrimpers' nets.[27] Alternatives suggested to discarding the by-catch at sea include limits on shrimp-fishing at times of high by-catch and requirements that the by-catch be retained and either placed in expanded storage on shrimp trawlers or transferred to cargo vessels stationed on or near the fishing grounds.

Many experts have suggested programs to improve the utilization of the small pelagic fishes, such as sardines and anchovies. The small pelagics make up almost 45 percent of the

---

[27] Christy, *op. cit.,* p. 21.

total world catch, but of the 33.5 million tons taken in 1981, almost half was converted into fish meal for animal feed. Fish meal is in great demand as a source of protein for animals and poultry, but handling problems appear to account for the relatively large portion of the pelagic catch that is converted into meal. The fish are very oily and spoil rapidly. With the present methods and equipment, it is more economical for fishermen to pump sardines into fish meal factories than to process them for human consumption. Extensive research is being conducted, however, on ways to produce fish meal products that are edible by humans and taste good.

Attention is also turning to the use of unconventional species of fish that, for one reason or another, are currently fished at levels well below their maximum sustainable yields. Among the species frequently mentioned are oceanic cephalopods (squid and octopus), Antarctic krill, and mid-ocean mesopelagics, such as lantern fish. The cephalopods are highly prized as food fish in parts of Asia and processing methods are available for preparing them in ways attractive to other palates as well, but the technology for catching the species is still relatively undeveloped. Present fishing methods also make the cost of catching the mid-ocean mesopelagics uneconomically high. Most interest is concentrated on the krill of Antarctica, small, delicate,

World Bank Photo by Yosef Hadar, 1984

shrimplike creatures that swim in huge masses in the frigid polar waters. Commercial harvesting of krill has begun; the 1981 catch totaled 450,000 tons, most of it made into meal. Marketing and processing constraints — the fish must be processed within three hours of the catch if they are to be consumed by humans — have kept the yield well below its estimated potential of 50 million tons a year.

Promising Potential of Coastal Aquaculture

Of all the available alternatives, aquaculture, or fish farming, may prove the most viable method for increasing the supply of food fish for human consumption. According to David James, a fishery industry officer for FAO, "Aquaculture now produces more than eight million tons of fish yearly, mainly in Asia. But with a shift from freshwater to coastal aquaculture, plus adequate investment and training, production could be as high as 30 million tons by the turn of the century." [28]

Experts claim that only 10 percent of the eggs laid by sea fish reach sexual maturity while the maturation rate is 90 percent in fish farms. Unlike dry-land farming, fish farming can more easily adjust its harvest to demand, minimizing distribution problems and spoilage losses and maximizing profits according to market conditions. Moreover, advances in technology have broadened the range of species that can be farmed successfully. The Inter-American Development Bank notes that: "African tilapia are being raised in Asia and tropical America with excellent results. Trout, a species that originates in the rivers and lakes of Europe, has been successfully introduced into the streams and rivers of the Andean mountains in South America. Fresh water shrimps from Asia have begun to be cultured in Central America and the Middle East. Salt water shrimp is being grown in captivity in ponds or coastal lagoons of Asian and Latin American countries by means of natural environment adaptation works that make use of favorable geographic conditions." [29]

Other species being commercially farmed include carp, freshwater catfish, oysters, mussels and salmon. A relatively new approach is the use of mangrove swamps for aquaculture. In Northeast Brazil, mangroves have been used for raising crabs for several years, but the technique is only now beginning to be developed on a commercial scale.

There are several million fish farmers worldwide, most of whom live in Asia, but as an industry, aquaculture is still in its infancy. The FAO reports that of an estimated 30 million to 40 million hectares suitable for aquaculture, fewer than one-tenth are presently used.[30] In its Fishery Sector Policy Paper, the World Bank said: "Various natural resources exist such as wastelands and flood control areas, now idle, that could be utilized for aquaculture and, at the same time, could be used to enhance other development activities. For example, fish ponds can be used simultaneously to produce aquatic vegetables and flowers and as a means of purifying sewage water. In fact, mixed cropping can substantially increase rice yields, since fish excreta fertilize the paddies and fish eat weeds."

On balance, the bank concluded, "the advantages of aquaculture — the relatively low consumption of fuel, the lack of

---

[28] "The New Regime for Fisheries," *op. cit.,* p. 29.

[29] "Fishery Resources," *op. cit.,* p. 75.

[30] "Fisheries Development in the 1980s," *op. cit.,* p. 12. A hectare is equal to 2.471 acres.

dependence on a fixed resource base, and the potential for integration with agriculture — are substantial."

Five-Point FAO Plan of Action for Fisheries

All these issues are likely to figure prominently in the deliberations of the FAO World Fisheries Conference that convenes in Rome later this month. More than 150 countries are expected to participate in the conference, with up to 70 international agencies attending as observers. FAO experts have been working for several months on a five-part draft program for fisheries management and development that will guide FAO strategy in the fishery sector for the next five years. The draft plan covers small-scale fisheries, aquaculture, international trade and alleviation of under-nutrition.

The FAO meeting takes place as the governments of coastal nations and of the major fishing powers are trying to map out a *modus vivendi* within the changed circumstances brought about by the Convention on the Law of the Sea and the new 200-mile exclusive economic zones it codifies. Many of the developing coastal countries lack the financial and technical capacity to exploit the marine life and other resources within their 200-mile limits. One aim of the FAO action program is to help to "develop industrial fishing capacities in countries which wish to phase out foreign operations." For the coastal countries that opt for continued licensing of foreign vessels within national waters, the program will provide assistance to harmonize fisheries legislation and to establish control procedures for foreign vessels within the exclusive economic zones.

There is a strong emphasis throughout the proposed program on strengthening small-scale fisheries. The FAO intends to help governments formulate project proposals in small fishery development and will enlist support for "global loans" from lending agencies, which will then be divided among small-scale fishery projects. The organization also plans to provide training assistance and technical advice for small-scale fishery projects. In aquaculture, the FAO will utilize an existing network of six regional centers in Brazil, China, India, Nigeria, the Philippines and Thailand to provide research and training.

An FAO spokesman said it is difficult to predict what concrete results will come from the Rome meeting, since nothing of its kind has been held since the Law of the Sea Convention revolutionized regulation of the oceans. Perhaps the conference will have served its purpose if it dispels one illusion — that oceans are vast and illimitable reservoirs of fish waiting to be caught to feed hungry people.

Selected Bibliography

Books

Brown, Lester R., et al., *State of the World 1984, A Worldwatch Institute Report on Progress Toward a Sustainable Society,* W. W. Norton, 1984.
——, Building a Sustainable Society, W. W. Norton, 1981.
Christy, Francis T. Jr., and Anthony Scott, *The Common Wealth in Ocean Fisheries,* The Johns Hopkins Press, 1965.
Dumont, Rene, and Bernard Rosier, *The Hungry Future,* Frederick A. Praeger, 1969.
Eckholm, Erik P., *Losing Ground: Environmental Stress and World Food Prospects,* W. W. Norton, 1976.
Sebenius, James E., *Negotiating the Law of the Sea,* Harvard University Press, 1984.
Warner, William W., *Beautiful Swimmers: Watermen, Crabs and the Chesapeake Bay,* Penguin Books, 1977.
——, *Distant Water: The Fate of the North Atlantic Fisherman,* Penguin Books, 1984.

Articles

"Law of the Sea — How Effective?" *The Vision Letter,* Jan. 15, 1983.
McGrath, Peter, "An American Treasure at Risk," *Newsweek,* Dec. 12, 1983, pp. 68-72.
"The New Regime for Fisheries: Prospects, Policies, Practices," *Ceres,* January-February 1984, pp. 25-38.
"Trouble in Ocean Fisheries," *The Vision Letter,* May 15, 1984.

Reports and Studies

Editorial Research Reports: "America's Disappearing Wetlands," 1983 Vol. II, p. 613; "Deep-Sea Mining," 1978 Vol. II, p. 721; "Oceanic Law," 1974 Vol. I, p. 403.
Inter-American Development Bank, "Fishery Resources," Chapter V of *Economic and Social Progress in Latin America, 1983,* August 22, 1983.
United Nations Food and Agriculture Organization: W. C. MacKenzie, "An Introduction to the Economics of Fisheries Management," 1983; "Case Studies and Working Papers Presented at the Expert Consultation on Strategies for Fisheries Development," May 1983; "Draft Strategy for Fisheries Management and Development and Associated Programmes of Action," April 1984; "Fisheries Development in the 1980s," undated; "Report of the Expert Consultation on Strategies for Fisheries Development," 1983; "The State of Food and Agriculture 1983," August 1983.
World Bank: "Fishery Sector Policy Paper," December 1982; "Rethinking Artisanal Fisheries Development: Western Concepts, Asian Experiences," October 1980.

Graphics: Cover, p. 49 illustrations by Assistant Art Director Robert Redding; p. 45 map by Staff Artist Belle Burkhart.

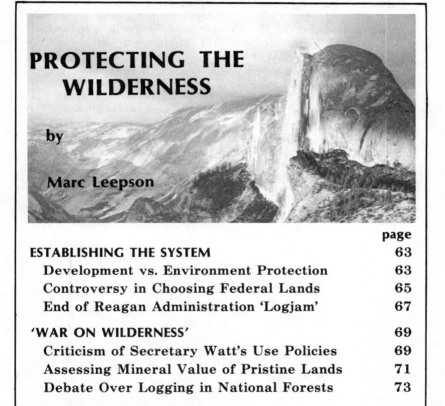

PROTECTING THE WILDERNESS

by

Marc Leepson

Aug. 17
1 9 8 4

Editor's Update: The 98th Congress added 8.6 million acres to the National Wilderness Preservation System, bringing the national total to 88.6 million acres.

The Roadless Area Review and Evaluation (RARE) process for evaluating potential wilderness areas *(see p. 65)* has been incorporated in the U.S. Forest Service's development of long-range plans under the National Forest Management Act of 1976.

A federal district court in California on April 18, 1985, ruled that the Interior Department had acted illegally in removing from wilderness consideration 1.5 million acres of Bureau of Land Management lands *(see pp. 73, 79)*.

PROTECTING THE WILDERNESS

THERE IS wilderness and then there is Wilderness. According to the dictionary, wilderness is any uncultivated and uninhabited tract of land. Wilderness with a capital "W," on the other hand, is something more. Some 82.3 million acres in the United States — about 3.5 percent of the total land area in the nation — are part of the National Wilderness Preservation System, which means they are protected from development. Under the terms of the Wilderness Act of 1964, which President Johnson signed into law 20 years ago on Sept. 3, 1964, no roads, dams or permanent structures may be built on these government-owned lands; motorized vehicles are forbidden; no timber may be cut. Lands in the wilderness system must be "administered for the use and enjoyment of the American people in such manner as will leave them unimpaired for future use and enjoyment as wilderness," the 1964 law says. The statute defines wilderness as "an area where the earth and community of life are untrammeled by man, where man himself is a visitor who does not remain."

The United States was the first nation to preserve wilderness lands and the effort was a long and controversial one. But passage of the wilderness law in 1964 did not put an end to the controversy. Today, two decades later, the issues of how much and which land should be added to the wilderness system remain hotly contested. As in the past, the arguments basically follow a development vs. conservation pattern. Environmentalists say that putting lands into the National Wilderness Preservation System is one of the few ways to stop timber, minerals, oil and gas developers from destroying ecosystems, wildlife habitats, watersheds and the other environmental qualities of undeveloped wilderness areas. Development interests, on the other hand, argue that legislation setting aside wilderness areas closes — or "locks up" — land forever without taking into consideration current economic conditions or the nation's future resource needs.

Wilderness areas add up to "a very sizable amount of land being set aside which does lock up the land base," said Scott Shotwell, vice president for congressional relations with the National Forest Products Association. Shotwell said that protecting wilderness forests from development has added to the enormous problems of the timber industry at a time when high interest rates have held down housing construction. And, Shotwell said, "when the demand comes back for housing, then there's going to be a problem because the land base [for timber] may not be there." [1]

Instead of designating areas as wilderness, Shotwell and others favor "multiple-use" management, which permits both conservation and developmental uses. Under the Federal Lands Policy and Management Act of 1976 most federal non-wilderness lands are managed in this way. "Lands managed for true multiple use are a national treasure, providing recreation and water, energy and minerals, and grass for cattle and sheep," said Vincent Carroll, assistant editorial page editor of the *Rocky Mountain News*. "Wise policy shouldn't nurture the fantasy that all human encroachment is permanently scarifying, that rehabilitation is everywhere a myth." [2]

Conservationists consider the term "multiple use" a euphemism for unchecked exploitation of the wilderness. Those who talk about multiple use "are the true proponents of single use," said Charles M. Clusen, director of conservation for the Wilderness Society.[3] "Logging and especially mining is the ultimate single use. If you mine something, it's not available for recreation; it's not available for wildlife habitats, for watershed purposes or anything else.... It's true of timbering, too. How many people want to have their picnic next to a clearcut?"

Warding off development on pristine lands is a main goal of conservationists. "The pressure on development is getting stronger and stronger," said Rep. John F. Seiberling, D-Ohio, chairman of the House Subcommittee on Public Lands and National Parks. "The fact that this land has stayed pristine and wild up to now doesn't mean it's going to stay that way forever." [4] Clusen said that wilderness preservation also entails being "the stewards of that which we have inherited and that which we must pass on, to retain productivity of the land and to keep natural systems in balance and not to destroy the earth, either through pollution or toxicity or mere destruction by physical means."

The National Wilderness Preservation System is made up of lands under the jurisdiction of four government agencies: the National Forest Service, the National Park Service, the Fish

---

[1] Persons quoted in this report were interviewed by the author unless otherwise indicated.

[2] Writing in *The Wall Street Journal*, May 15, 1984.

[3] The Wilderness Society, which was founded in 1935, is a Washington-based, non-profit conservation group that conducts programs to preserve and assure proper management of the nation's public lands. Former Democratic Sen. Gaylord Nelson of Wisconsin is the group's chairman.

[4] Quoted in *The New York Times*, July 15, 1984.

Island Lake, Bridger Wilderness, Wind River Range, Wyo.

and Wildlife Service and the Bureau of Land Management *(see chart, p. 595)*. More than three-fourths of the system is administered by the Department of Agriculture's U.S. Forest Service (27.6 million acres) and the Interior Department's U.S. Park Service (35.3 million acres, of which more than 91 percent is in Alaska). The 1964 Wilderness Act brought 9,139,721 acres of national forest lands in 13 states — mostly in the West — into the new wilderness system.[5] The act further required the Forest Service to review within 10 years areas in its jurisdiction to determine their suitability for preservation as wilderness. The Forest Service recommended hundreds of thousands of acres, and by 1970 Congress had passed laws increasing the system by more than one million acres.

Controversy In Choosing Federal Lands

But environmentalists criticized the Forest Service for not considering tens of millions of acres of *de facto* wilderness lands — roadless lands that were not classified as pristine, but still had most of the characteristics of wilderness. Under pressure from conservationists and Congress, the Forest Service in 1971 began an inventory of the *de facto* lands within its 191-million-acre system. The review, known as the Roadless Area Review and Evaluation (RARE), recommended wilderness designation for 12 million acres out of the 55.9 million acres inventoried. Conservationists criticized these recommendations, however, charging that many potentially qualifying wilderness areas were

---

[5] Arizona, California, Colorado, Idaho, Minnesota, Montana, Nevada, New Hampshire, New Mexico, North Carolina, Oregon, Washington and Wyoming.

ignored and that criteria for selection varied greatly. To head off logging and other development in roadless areas, which would disqualify the land for classification as wilderness, the Sierra Club challenged the Forest Service's RARE recommendations in U.S. District Court in San Francisco. The suit *(Sierra Club* v. *Butz)* was settled out of court in 1972 when the Forest Service agreed to file environmental impact statements, as required by the National Environmental Policy Act of 1969, before permitting any road building, logging or other development in roadless areas, including the acreage inventoried under RARE.[6]

According to government officials, the settlement cut back the amount of potential wilderness land that the Forest Service leased for logging operations in subsequent years. "Because of the requirement that we do an environmental impact statement, the rate at which we made [timber] sales in the roadless areas for basically the last decade has been substantially less than was originally planned," said George Leonard, the Forest Service's director of timber management.

Still, conservationists continued to criticize what they considered the slow pace with which the Forest Service was recommending additions to the wilderness system. In 1977, President Carter's first year in office, the Forest Service began a second roadless area inventory designed to stand up in court as well as to provide a final allocation of all forest system lands. The RARE II study, as it became known, was completed in 1978 and covered 62 million acres of roadless forest areas. Based on RARE II, the Carter administration recommended that Congress immediately designate 15.4 million acres as wilderness and study more closely 10.6 million acres of potential wilderness areas. The administration recommended that some 36 million acres be released for multiple use, including timber harvesting.

Once again conservationists were unhappy and filed suit to block development in roadless areas. "Although an improvement over the first RARE study, RARE II had major shortcomings," commented a Wilderness Society publication. "Some *de facto* forest wilderness areas were not included in the review, and far too little allocated to the further planning category." [7]

One aspect of the RARE II recommendations did please wilderness advocates. Congress began using the recommendations — as well as recommendations from conservationist groups that often extended wilderness beyond RARE II areas — to pass laws adding land to the wilderness system on a state-by-state basis. During Carter's term, the National Wilderness

[6] See "Wilderness Preservation," *E.R.R.*, 1975 Vol. I, pp. 394-398.
[7] The Wilderness Society, "Wilderness Lands in the United States," 1984.

National Wilderness Preservation System*

Agency	Acres	Percent**
National Forest Service	27,635,962	33.6
National Park Service	35,342,822	42.9
Fish and Wildlife Service	19,332,522	23.5
Bureau of Land Management	31,458	.2
TOTAL	82,342,764	

* Includes land set aside by legislation cleared by Congress through July 2, 1984.
** Does not add up to 100 because of rounding.

Preservation System grew by 64.4 million acres. Included in that figure were more than 56 million acres set aside in Alaska under the landmark Alaska National Interest Lands Conservation Act passed in 1980. That legislation more than tripled the size of the wilderness system.[8]

End of Reagan Administration 'Logjam'

The Alaska lands bill was the last major piece of wilderness legislation enacted until the summer of 1984. After his inauguration in January 1981, President Reagan and the Republican-controlled Senate slowed the pace of wilderness legislation to a trickle. In his first three years in office Reagan signed laws adding only 342,000 acres in three states, West Virginia, Indiana and Missouri, to the wilderness system. The president also vetoed a wilderness bill for Florida. "Since Ronald Reagan got elected until just a few months ago we essentially had a wilderness stalemate," Clusen of the Wilderness Society said in a July 5 interview. Before the 1980 elections, Clusen said, Congress passed several bills based on the RARE II recommendations, and others were pending. But after the election, Clusen said, Sen. James A. McClure, R-Idaho, became chairman of the Energy and Natural Resources Committee through which most wilderness bills must pass, and McClure "blocked [nearly] all remaining bills. . . . "

The main sticking point was the fate of the 36 million acres of *de facto* wilderness lands the RARE II study recommended against including in the wilderness system. Sen. McClure, the Reagan administration and the logging, mining and energy industries wanted these roadless lands released from all future reviews for their suitability as wilderness and opened for development. Conservationists wanted the Forest Service to

---

[8] The Alaska lands act set aside a total of 104.3 million acres into various types of conservation areas. The new wilderness lands consisted of 5.4 million acres of Forest Service land, 32.4 million acres in national parks and 18.7 million acres in national wildlife refuges. For background, see *Congressional Quarterly Weekly Report*, Aug. 13, 1983, pp. 1661-1662 and "Alaska: 25 Years of Statehood," *E.R.R.*, 1983 Vol. II, pp. 928-929.

review the 36 million acres periodically for possible designation as wilderness. Lawsuits filed in various states prevented the Forest Service from releasing the land for development. Then, on Feb. 1, 1983, the Reagan administration announced that the Forest Service would throw out the RARE II recommendations and start a third roadless area survey.[9]

Meanwhile, wilderness bills were piling up in Congress. More than two dozen measures calling for nearly 10 million acres of new wilderness in 21 states were pending when Congress reconvened on Jan. 23, 1984. Within weeks administration officials began meeting with congressional leaders to try to work out a compromise. After months of bargaining — primarily between Sen. McClure and Rep. Seiberling — an agreement was announced on May 2. The compromise language, which is to be added to all future wilderness legislation, calls for the Forest Service to reconsider *de facto* wilderness areas at least every 15 years for possible inclusion in the wilderness system. The agreement also authorizes the Forest Service to allow logging and other development on those lands in the interim. Under the compromise, each new wilderness bill passed by Congress "in addition to designating areas for wilderness, also will release many millions of acres for other uses," said Peter C. Kirby, coordinator of the Wilderness Society's forest management program. "The bills will both protect land and release land."

Both the Wilderness Society and the National Forest Products Association expressed satisfaction with the settlement. Association spokesman Shotwell said the compromise would give the timber industry the certainty it sought over how much federal forest will be available for logging. "To have it resolved was very helpful," he said. Wilderness Society spokesman Peter D. Coppelman said, "The Senate took a giant step toward fulfilling the potential of this Congress for being one of the most important Congresses for wilderness preservation in our history. . . . I think we have a good chance for getting at least 20 wilderness bills this year." [10]

As if to underscore the success of the compromise, the Senate Energy Committee May 2 unanimously approved six single-state wilderness bills. Congress went on to pass, and the president signed, seven wilderness bills — for Missouri, New Hampshire, North Carolina, Oregon, Vermont, Washington and Wisconsin — by the time Congress recessed July 2. The seven

---

[9] The announcement followed an October 1982 decision by the 9th U.S. Circuit Court of Appeals, which ruled that the Forest Service failed to file the required environmental impact statements in the California RARE II studies. RARE III studies have not yet been completed. For background, see Joseph A. Davis, "Wilderness Issues Erupting Again in Congress," *Congressional Quarterly Weekly Report*, Feb. 12, 1983, p. 335.

[10] Shotwell and Coppelman were quoted in *Congressional Quarterly Weekly Report*, May 5, 1984, p. 1007.

bills added more than two million acres to the National Wilderness Preservation System. Before recessing Aug. 10 for the Republican National Convention, Congress cleared a wilderness bill for Arizona. Senate-passed bills for Arkansas, California, Florida and Utah await action in the House when Congress reconvenes after Labor Day. The stage is thus set for the 98th Congress before its scheduled October adjournment to add more acreage to the National Wilderness Preservation System in the contiguous 48 states than any other Congress since the Wilderness Act was passed two decades ago. All is not clear sailing, however. Capitol Hill analysts say that serious disagreements between conservationists and development interests are threatening the passage of wilderness bills for at least three states: Idaho, Montana and Wyoming.

'War on Wilderness'

DESPITE CONSERVATIONISTS' satisfaction with the compromise, they remain extremely critical of the Reagan administration's wilderness policies. "This is an historical year for wilderness preservation," William A. Turnage, executive director of the Wilderness Society, said June 19, the day President Reagan signed four wilderness bills. "But the truth is, this administration was brought to this point kicking and screaming.... A lot of people deserve credit for today's additions to the wilderness system. Unfortunately they are not in this administration."

Conservationists say that the administration is waging a two-part "war on wilderness." First, they say, the administration has fought against expanding the wilderness system. Second, they say, it has worked to open already designated wilderness lands to energy and mineral development and to expand logging operations on pristine lands being considered for designation as wilderness.

If, indeed, there has been a war on wilderness, the opening salvos were fired in 1981 by then Interior Secretary James G. Watt, an outspoken champion of energy and mineral development on federal lands. Environmentalists raised an outcry when they intercepted an internal May 7, 1981, memo from Watt to his top aides listing as one of his key goals to "open wilderness areas." [11] As president of the Mountain States Legal Foundation from 1977 until he took over the Interior Department, Watt

---

[11] For background, see Congressional Quarterly's *1983 Almanac*, pp. 327-331.

had attacked "extreme environmentalists" for opposing resource development projects on federal lands.[12] He also vowed
to "swing the pendulum back to center" from preservationist
policies of previous administrations, not only in wilderness areas, but throughout much of the approximately 510 million
acres of land the Interior Department administers for the federal government. "The key to conservation is management,"
Watt said in a March 23, 1981, speech. "Conservation is not the
blind locking away of huge areas and their resources because of
emotional appeals." [13]

Many of Watt's early initiatives drew fire from conservationists. These actions included several that did not directly
affect wilderness lands, such as a plan to lease areas off the
northern California coast for oil drilling and a program to halt
land purchases for expansion of national parks and wildlife
refuges and use the funds to maintain existing parks instead. At
least three major proposals would have affected wilderness directly: Watt's plan to allow oil and gas leases on Bureau of Land
Management (BLM) lands being studied for possible inclusion
in the wilderness system; his call for adopting a deadline by
which Congress would either have to add areas to the wilderness
system or release them for development;[14] and his decision to
institute oil, gas and mineral leasing throughout lands already
designated as part of the wilderness system.

The latter plan, which was announced Feb. 21, 1982, brought
heated reactions from environmentalists and members of Congress. After the Interior Department granted leases for oil drilling in the Capitan Wilderness in New Mexico, Capitol Hill
reaction was so negative that Watt agreed to suspend all leasing
action until the end of 1982. On Dec. 18, 1982, just before Watt's
self-imposed moratorium on leasing was about to expire, Congress passed a measure prohibiting until Sept. 30, 1983, any
Interior Department funds from being used to issue oil and gas
leases in designated wilderness areas, as well as in areas being
considered for protection. Twelve days later Watt agreed not to
allow oil and gas leasing in the wilderness system or in BLM

---

[12] See "Access to Federal Lands," *E.R.R.*, 1981 Vol. II, pp. 693-712.

[13] Watt resigned his Cabinet post Oct. 9, 1983, rather than face an almost certain no-
confidence vote in the Republican-controlled Senate. His support had eroded badly following a Sept. 21 speech in which he characterized his appointees to a federal commission as "a
black, ... a woman, two Jews and a cripple." President Reagan named national security
adviser William P. Clark to succeed Watt. For background see *Congressional Quarterly
Weekly Report*, Oct. 15, 1983, pp. 2120-2123.

[14] Watt supported a bill sponsored in 1981 by Sen. S. I. "Sam" Hayakawa, R-Calif. (1977-
83), that would have set deadlines of Jan. 1, 1985, and Jan. 1, 1983, for Congress to act on
designating wildernesses on Western and Eastern lands respectively. The bill would have
authorized the lands to be released for other uses if Congress had not acted by the
deadlines. Once lands were released, the bill would have barred the government from
studying their suitability for wilderness or from managing them to protect their suitability
for wilderness designation. The bill received little support in Congress and was never
enacted into law.

Private Preserves

In addition to the 82 million acres of land in the federal wilderness system, there are about 10 million acres — much of it meeting the qualifications of wilderness — being held in pristine condition by individual states and private groups. The private conservation group with the largest holdings is the Nature Conservancy, which has brought more than two million acres under preservation in the United States, Latin America and the Caribbean since it began independent operations in 1951.

The Arlington, Va.-based group, the only national organization that buys land for conservation purposes, cooperates with colleges, other conservation organizations and government agencies to acquire and preserve lands. The Nature Conservancy today manages 800 preserves and owns more than 637,000 acres throughout the United States.

wilderness study areas from Oct. 1, 1983, until Jan. 1, 1984, when a permanent ban would take effect under the terms of the 1964 Wilderness Act.

Watt capitulated on the leasing issue, but at the same time he announced that the Interior Department would remove certain BLM lands from study for possible wilderness designation. Under the 1976 Federal Land Policy and Management Act, BLM had set aside 24 million acres for potential wilderness designation (see p. 606). Under the law those lands were to be preserved in pristine condition until Congress decided whether to include them in the wilderness system. Watt's new policy took away lands in three categories: parcels smaller than 5,000 acres, areas where the surface is federally owned but the underground mineral rights are privately owned, and areas bordering on federal wilderness or wilderness candidate areas. By August 1983, a total of some 1.5 million acres of BLM lands had been removed from study. A coalition of six environmental groups filed suit in Federal District Court in California to block the BLM action.[15] The case has yet to come to trial, but a temporary restraining order has been issued to prevent development of the 1.5 million acres until the case is decided.

Assessing Mineral Value of Pristine Lands

The Wilderness Act of 1964 contained a provision allowing mining companies to file minerals claims on wilderness lands until Dec. 31, 1983. The law also permitted mining companies with valid claims to explore, drill and produce minerals in wilderness areas so long as the companies followed Forest Service guidelines designed to protect "the wilderness character of

---

[15] The six organizations were the Environmental Defense Fund, National Audubon Society, National Wildlife Federation, Natural Resources Defense Council, Sierra Club and Wilderness Society.

the land." But in the 20 years since the act became law, only a handful of mining operations have been conducted on wilderness lands. One reason is that many of the wilderness areas are remote and inaccessible, making mining operations extremely costly and difficult.

Another reason is that conservation groups and, in some cases, the Forest Service have successfully opposed individual mining claims. "Almost from the outset there was conflict over [minerals] development, or even exploration inside the statutory wilderness," Howard Banta, the director of the Forest Service's minerals and geology division, said. "Industry saw the handwriting on the wall. They were simply not going to be allowed — even though the law permitted it — from the standpoint of public opinion to really explore. And there was very little certainty of being able to develop anything they would find. As a consequence . . . there was very little exploration done in statutory wilderness in the 20-year period."

Conservationists argue against mineral exploration and mining on wilderness lands because many of these operations permanently scar the land. Wilderness proponents also say that the issue is something of a red herring because very few official wildernesses contain significant amounts of minerals. The mining industry, on the other hand, says that wilderness areas are potentially rich with minerals.

Preliminary studies have failed to put the issue to rest. The Wilderness Act charged the U.S. Geological Survey (USGS) and the Bureau of Mines with surveying wilderness lands on a "planned, recurring basis" to determine their mineral values. USGS teams began studying the mineral potential of the wilderness system in 1965. A preliminary report covering about 45 million acres of the system published late in 1983 found that "about 65 percent of the areas we examined had evidence of mineralization," said Gus Goudarzi, USGS's wilderness coordinator. "Out of those, only about 20 percent of the actual area was involved. We found everything from sand and gravel . . . to limestone and dolomite and strategic metals." Goudarzi said the report was based on geochemical laboratory research, geophysical surveys and geologic mapping, but not on deep exploratory drilling. The report's results, therefore, assess only the mineral potential of wilderness areas. "That means the probability of it being there," Goudarzi said. "There is a lot more needed to be discovered through drilling, and we didn't do that." [16]

---

[16] The 1964 Wilderness Act calls for USGS to make recurring surveys on Forest Service wilderness lands, but Congress did not appropriate any USGS funds to do the job in fiscal year 1984. There are funds, however, for an ongoing minerals assessment on potential wilderness lands under the jurisdiction of BLM. That money has been appropriated under a 1976 law that added BLM lands to the list of potential wilderness areas.

Logging in National Forests
(billions of board feet)

Fiscal Year	Timber Cut	Timber Sold
1983*	9.2	11.1
1982	6.7	10.0
1981	8.0	11.4
1980	9.2	11.3
1975	9.1	10.8
1970	11.5	13.4
1965	11.2	11.5
1960	9.4	12.2

* Preliminary data

Source: U.S. Forest Service

Wilderness proponents and mining interests interpret the USGS findings differently. The Wilderness Society, for example, points to other studies, including one released by the Oak Ridge National Laboratory, which together with the USGS findings shows that "wilderness areas do not contain significant amounts of energy or minerals that could make any meaningful contribution to the needs of industry...." [17] Industry spokesman Tom Nelson, on the other hand, said the survey shows "there is a great deal of mineral potential [in wilderness areas]. We feel there is."

Debate Over Logging in National Forests

Another wilderness resource issue in which conservationists and the Reagan administration do not see eye to eye is the way in which the U.S. Forest Service manages logging operations in the national forests. The government has been selling timber on Forest Service lands since 1941. Of the 191 million acres managed by the Forest Service today, about 86 million acres are commercial timberland, capable of economic wood production. Timber cutting on the 27.6 million acres of Forest Service lands already designated as wilderness is not at issue; commercial logging is prohibited on those lands. The controversy concerns the fate of the 36 million acres of Forest Service lands under study for possible preservation (see p. 66).

Conservationists argue that much of this land should be kept free of roads and logging operations until Congress has decided which lands to include in the National Wilderness Preservation System. They maintain there is a glut of timber on the depressed lumber market and that there is consequently no need

---

[17] "Wilderness Lands in the United States," 1984.

to log lands that otherwise would retain their wilderness character. Reagan administration officials and timber industry spokesmen contend that valuable timber reserves in *de facto* wilderness lands are being kept out of production needlessly while Congress debates the eventual makeup of the wilderness system. They note that in some national forest areas permission to log may be of life-or-death importance to the livelihood of local loggers and sawmill workers.

The debate over choosing wilderness areas has kept nearly a third of national forest acreage "in a planning limbo of studies, lawsuits and repeated studies," said John B. Crowell Jr., the assistant secretary of agriculture for natural resources and environment who administers the Forest Service.[18] Crowell, a former general counsel for Louisiana Pacific Corp., the nation's second-largest timber company and the leading purchaser of government timber, has been an outspoken proponent of expanding timber operations throughout the national forests, including some *de facto* wilderness areas. Crowell and the timber industry favor doubling the timber harvest on Forest Service lands and accelerating the cutting of never-before-harvested old-growth stands of trees in the national forests.

Environmental groups and some Democratic members of Congress have been extremely critical of Crowell and his policies. *Environmental Action* magazine, for example, has characterized Crowell as a "long-time enemy of wilderness and forest preservation" who "has opposed the 'concept' of wilderness." [19]

Clusen of the Wilderness Society charged that under Crowell's leadership the Forest Service has worked "at a very rapid pace to basically road and log" *de facto* wilderness lands to "essentially prevent them from being designated" as wilderness. The society claims that since 1981 the Forest Service has sold more than three billion board feet of timber and built more than 3,000 miles of roads in previously roadless forest areas, thus disqualifying those areas from consideration as wilderness.

Clusen's assertion is "absolutely false," said George Leonard, the Forest Service's director of timber management. "The sale program has been virtually stable for the last 20 years," Leonard said *(see chart, p. 601)*. "Basically since 1972 we have cleared very few of the roadless areas with environmental impact statements. As a result, we just haven't been doing much work in those areas." Leonard also rejected charges that the

---

[18] Testifying before the House Interior and Insular Affairs Committee's Subcommittee on Public Lands and National Parks, June 12, 1981. For background, see Tom Arrandale, *The Battle for Natural Resources* (1983), pp. 131-154.

[19] "TIMMM-BERRR!," *Environmental Action*, June 1984, p. 4. The organization is a citizens' interest group that conducts research and provides information on many environmental issues.

Forest Service is anti-wilderness. "We are advocating substantial additions to the wilderness system," he said. Even though demand for timber currently is low, Leonard said, "there are more demands for use of the National Forest System than we're able to satisfy. So we try to carve a path that gives some reasonable balance between preservation and use.... If you could have all the wilderness that everybody wanted and still have all the timber, we wouldn't have a problem. But that's not true and so we've got to figure out some balance."

Management Challenge

THE 1964 LAW did not close wilderness areas to all human activity. Although the law stipulated that wilderness areas be preserved in pristine condition, it also required that the system "be devoted to the public purposes of recreational, scenic, scientific, conservation and historical use." These often conflicting mandates have set unique management challenges for the agencies that administer the system — primarily the Forest Service and the National Park Service.

Millions of people hike, backpack, hunt, fish and take part in other outdoor activities in wilderness areas every year *(see chart, p. 77).*[20] This large influx of humans has created problems in some wilderness ares. "We're trying to manage [wilderness areas] so that people can use and enjoy them in a manner that will leave them essentially unimpaired for the coming generations," said Bill Swenson, a Forest Service recreation staff officer. "A lot of the work we do as far as management is concerned is trying to protect the wilderness, to keep it from being loved to death."

The problem is expected to worsen in some areas in the next few years as more acreage is added to the system and more visitors are attracted to newly designated wildernesses. "As soon as you put a name to something, it becomes instantly more popular," Swenson said. Stanley E. Allgeier, assistant director of recreation for the Rocky Mountain region of the Forest Service, agreed. "Hang that big 'W' on an area and watch out," Allgeier said. "Sierra Club or someone will get hot on it and the next season it'll look like Fifth Avenue." [21]

---

[20] Sports hunting is not permitted in national parks. Hunting and fishing are not permitted in parts of or all of some wildlife refuges.

[21] Quoted by Dyan Zaslowsky, "Managing the Dream," *Wilderness*, summer 1984, pp. 27-28.

The large number of visitors streaming into wilderness areas in recent years has adversely affected the system in some places. Among other things, visitors have damaged fragile high-country flora, depleted firewood around campsites, polluted water through bathing and dishwashing, scattered litter along trails and attracted wild animals to food caches and buried garbage. A good deal of the environmental damage has been done on the extensive system of trails that snakes through the wilderness system.

The Forest Service budget for the current fiscal year includes $5.2 million for trail construction and $9.3 million for trail maintenance throughout all unroaded national forest land.[22] But agency officials maintain that they need much more funding to keep the trails properly maintained. Agency officials have been forced in recent years to rely heavily on help from unpaid volunteers for trail building and maintenance, as well as for other wilderness management tasks.[23] Last year nearly 2,500

"We're trying to manage [wilderness areas] so that people can use and enjoy them in a manner that will leave them essentially unimpaired. . . . A lot of the work we do . . . is trying to protect the wilderness, to keep it from being loved to death."

Bill Swenson, U.S. Forest Service

---

persons did volunteer work in wilderness areas maintained by the Forest Service. Aside from working on trails, the volunteers also helped rehabilitate overused campsites, provide information for visitors, build signs, survey historical sites, post boundaries, and conduct inventory and condition surveys. "We've been pretty successful in getting volunteers, especially in trails," Swenson said. "A lot of trail clubs have donated an incredible number of man years of work. . . ."

The Forest and National Park services have instituted permit systems to gather statistics on wilderness use as well as to limit the number of visitors in heavily used areas. The Forest Service requires entry permits in most areas; in others a voluntary registration system is in force. Wilderness rangers in national

---

[22] The National Park Service does not maintain a separate account for the wilderness areas it manages. The total management budget for the Park Service in the current fiscal year is $601 million. About $250 million is used for maintenance, including trail reconstruction.

[23] Some volunteers receive small per diem payments.

Visiting the Wilderness

Year	Overnight Stays in NPS Backcountry*	Visitor Days in NFS Wilderness** (in millions)
1983	2,579,716	9.9
1982	2,424,227	11.2
1981	2,329,845	11.4
1980	2,395,236	9.3
1979	2,397,098	9.6
1978	2,589,858	8.6
1977	2,569,502	8.0
1976	2,608,862	n.a.
1975	2,346,384	7.5
1974	2,172,196	n.a.

* Includes National Park areas not officially designated wilderness.
** Includes visits to primitive areas in the National Forest System not officially designated wilderness.

Sources: National Park Service, National Forest Service

forests also use permit and registration system information to keep track of visitors in case of emergencies. "It can help us if we get a call that somebody's overdue," Swenson said. "We'd have an idea of where they'd planned to go." Even though the Wilderness Act prohibits the use of motorized equipment or vehicles in the wilderness, the law does allow the use of four-wheel drive vehicles or helicopters to rescue stranded, endangered hikers.[24]

Permit information has been used as part of a wilderness education program in the Eagle Cap Ranger district on the Wallowa-Whitman National Forest in Oregon. In addition to working directly with visitors in the wilderness, Eagle Cap rangers and volunteers use the registration data to find out where most wilderness users live and then present educational pro-

[24] The law also permits the use of motorized equipment "in the control of fires, insects and diseases." Some conservation groups, including the Wilderness Society, oppose the idea of fighting natural fires in wilderness areas. According to the Wilderness Society publication, "The Wilderness Act Handbook," the group "generally supports a policy of allowing natural fires to play their ecological role in wilderness, with due regard, of course, for public health, safety and welfare in surrounding non-wilderness areas."

grams in schools and shopping centers to teach the proper use of the wilderness. "We call what we do here the human approach to wilderness management," said Eagle Cap administrator Tom Glassford. Visitors are handled with "warmth and sensitivity," he said, chiefly using "education, persuasion, hospitality, personal contact and volunteerism." [25]

The Outlook for Future Expansion of System

As federal agencies work out how best to manage the wilderness, attention is being focused on 1985, the beginning of the third decade following passage of the Wilderness Act of 1964. "The first decade [1964-74] was basically arguing about how you do things, how to manage them and what qualifies as wilderness," said Clusen of the Wilderness Society. "The second decade dealt with the *de facto* wilderness issue, particularly with forest lands — the Forest Service, RARE I, RARE II and now the congressional acts designating these lands." Clusen predicted that the third decade will bring a "conclusion" to the designation of Forest Service lands as wilderness. He also sees the intensification of an ongoing debate focusing on potential wilderness lands under the jurisdiction of the Bureau of Land Management.

BLM was formed in 1946 when President Truman merged the U.S. Grazing Service with the Interior Department's General Land Office. The agency's primary job was to dispose of land by lease or sale and manage the rest for multiple use, primarily livestock grazing, mining and oil and gas drilling. But even though BLM was funded by Congress, the agency operated without clear congressional authority, relying mainly on thousands of public land statutes, many left over from the homesteading era. That situation changed in 1976 when Congress enacted and President Ford signed into law the Federal Land Policy and Management Act — the first piece of legislation that granted BLM permanent authority to manage public lands not designated for special purposes. Included in the law was a provision directing the bureau to review and identify roadless areas under BLM jurisdiction for possible wilderness designation.

BLM today administers 397 million acres of federal lands — double the total of Forest Service land — scattered throughout Alaska and the West. The BLM lands include millions of acres of deserts, swamps and barren flats, areas that traditionally had been thought of as undesirable wastelands. That is one reason BLM lands were not included in the 1964 Wilderness Act. But many conservationists believe BLM lands have wilderness potential. The Wilderness Society, for example, states that

[25] Quoted by Zaslowsky, *op. cit.*, p. 33.

BLM lands are regions of "rare scenic beauty, unique natural values, and historical and archeological importance." [26]

An initial review of BLM lands for wilderness potential covered 174 million acres outside Alaska and was completed in 1980.[27] The review classified 24 million acres (about 13 percent of BLM lands in the West) as areas that would be intensively studied for potential inclusion in the wilderness system. Under terms of the 1976 law the agency has until 1991 to make its final recommendations to Congress. Meanwhile, the 24 million acres, called Wilderness Study Areas, are to be preserved in wilderness condition until Congress acts to include or exclude them from the National Wilderness Preservation System. However, under policies initiated by former Interior Secretary Watt and being challenged in court, some 1.5 million acres would be removed from further study (see p. 599).

Analysts say that Congress will begin dealing with the BLM lands soon after it takes care of the various pieces of legislation needed to finalize the designation of Forest Service lands. Congress is expected to enact legislation this year adding as much as 10 million acres of National Forest lands to the wilderness system. In addition, about 3.5 million acres of wildlife refuges are awaiting congressional designation. "Attention's going to turn to BLM full strength in 1985 or '86," said Gary Marsh of the bureau's wilderness branch. Wilderness advocates do not give a precise acreage figure when asked about their ultimate goals for the wilderness system. "Our concern is with the quality of those lands, much more than an acreage figure...," Clusen said. "What is the right amount in the year 1984 may not be the right amount in 2000."

---

[26] The Wilderness Society, "Wilderness Lands in the United States," 1984.

[27] Under the terms of the Alaska lands act of 1980 *(see p. 595)* BLM lands there were exempted from the wilderness review.

Selected Bibliography

Books

Arrandale, Tom, *The Battle for Natural Resources*, Congressional Quarterly, 1983.

Fox, Stephen, *John Muir and his Legacy*, Little, Brown, 1981.

Frome, Michael, *Battle for the Wilderness*, Praeger, 1974.

Leopold, Aldo, *A Sand County Almanac*, Oxford University Press, 1949.

Nash, Roderick, *Wilderness and the American Mind*, revised edition, Yale University Press, 1973.

Articles

Davis, Joseph A., "Wilderness Issues Erupting Again in Congress," *Congressional Quarterly Weekly Report*, Feb. 12, 1983.

Foreman, David, "It's Time to Return to our Wilderness Roots," *Environmental Action*, December 1983-January 1984.

Frome, Michael, "Promised Land," *National Parks*, January-February 1984.

Mosher, Lawrence, "Wilderness System is Under Siege by Oil, Gas, Mineral and Timber Interests," *National Journal*, Nov. 21, 1981.

Runge, Carlisle Ford, "Energy Exploration on Wilderness: 'Privatization' and Public Lands Management," *Land Economics*, February 1984.

Sierra (bimonthly magazine of the Sierra Club), selected issues.

Wilderness (quarterly magazine of the Wilderness Society), selected issues.

Reports and Studies

Editorial Research Reports: "Alaska: 25 Years of Statehood," 1983 Vol. II, p. 921; "Access to Federal Lands," 1981 Vol. II, p. 693; "Wilderness Preservation," 1975 Vol. I, p. 385.

Raeder, Joseph, "Wilderness Bills Released by the Seiberling-McClure Compromise," Environment and Energy Study Conference, May 7, 1984.

U.S. Forest Service: "Twentieth Annual Report of the Secretary of Agriculture on the Status of the National Forest Units of the National Wilderness Preservation System," 1984; "National Forest Timber Cut and Sold," Jan. 20, 1983.

Wilderness Society: "Wilderness Lands in the United States," 1984; "The Wilderness Act Handbook," 1984.

FEEDING A
GROWING WORLD

by

Mary H. Cooper

Oct. 26
1 9 8 4

Editor's Update: In 1985 rain brought improved harvests to much of hunger-stricken Africa, but some regions are still suffering from drought and need emergency food relief. Efforts to avoid repetition of the famine through early warning systems, emergency food stocks and improved coordination of relief are still in preliminary stages of development. Underlying problems of severe malnutrition remain.

The Reagan administration at the end of 1984 cut off U.S. funds for the International Planned Parenthood Federation, a private agency active in 119 countries, because some if its affiliates provide counseling to women seeking abortions. The administration Sept. 25, 1985, reaffirmed an earlier decision to reduce from $46 million to $36 million the U.S. contribution to the United Nations Fund for Population Activities because of its participation in Chinese family planning programs termed "coercive" by U.S. anti-abortion groups.

FEEDING A GROWING WORLD

H UNDREDS of thousands of people in Africa are dying from starvation or diseases related to malnutrition, victims of the worst drought in a decade. The toll could surpass the drought of the early 1970s when an estimated half million Africans died. In the intervening 10 years, the population in many African countries has increased more rapidly than food production, forcing them to rely on foreign sources for food.

Even when food is available in sufficient quantities, much of it never reaches the people in need. In Chad, where millions of people need immediate food relief, there is no rail or paved road system to transport food. There, as in Ethiopia, political unrest and civil war make distribution even more difficult.

The drought may also spell catastrophe for some of the few African nations that have viable economies. Kenya, one of the few drought-stricken nations to have accumulated sizable currency reserves from its exports to the developed world, is facing widespread hardship. The East African country's food needs far outstrip its production capacity, largely because of its 4 percent annual population increase.

Across the world, another food emergency threatens the lives of thousands of Indonesians left stranded when a recent typhoon destroyed roads and housing. Relief workers complain that promised food aid has not materialized. Supplies that have been delivered are not reaching the people for whom it was intended. Again, lack of adequate distribution channels, as well as inadequate government interest, are blamed. Again, local food production comes nowhere near meeting the emergency.

These emergency situations reveal the precarious state of food supplies in a growing world. Although the overall rate of population growth has slowed from about 2 percent to about 1.7 percent in the last 10 years, the total number of people is increasing steadily. The United Nations, which estimates global population to be 4.6 billion today, predicts it will reach 6 billion by the end of the century and 11 billion by 2025 if present trends continue. The Population Reference Bureau projections are somewhat lower; it estimates that population will be 8.1 billion by 2020 *(see box, p. 85)*. And while there is an aggregate food surplus in the world, the demand for food is already outstripping agricultural production in many countries, particularly in Africa *(see map, p. 87).*

The greatest increases in population are occurring in areas of the world that are least capable of supporting them. Indeed, some of the wealthier developed countries are witnessing a trend in the opposite direction. Some, such as France, are attempting to reverse their declining populations and the potential decline in their own economic and political power.

By contrast, the World Bank estimates that the populations of the developing nations are increasing by more than 2 percent a year. The average couple in these countries has at least four or five children. Ironically, it is in the very countries where industrial development and agricultural "carrying capacity" are lowest that population increase is highest. Of the 80 million children born each year, the United Nations estimates, 73 million are born to poverty-stricken parents in Africa, South Asia and Latin America.

New U.S. Approach to Population Growth

The first concerted effort to address world population growth was made a decade ago, when the United Nations sponsored the World Population Conference in Bucharest, Romania. The 136 government delegations attending the conference in 1974 approved unanimously a "World Population Plan of Action," which stressed the importance of including family planning projects in each nation's economic development plans. The statement set no targets for family size and declared that "all couples and individuals have the basic right to decide freely and responsibly the number and spacing of their children and to have the information, education and means to do so." [1]

The Bucharest meeting reflected the growing sense of urgency over the "population explosion." Typical of the period was a widely cited study prepared for the Club of Rome entitled *The Limits to Growth,* which concluded: "If the present growth trends in world population, industrialization, pollution, food production, and resource depletion continue unchanged, the limits to growth on this planet will be reached sometime within the next one hundred years." [2] This concern was quickly channeled into family-planning programs in developing countries. During the last 10 years, 39 developing countries — accounting for three-quarters of the world's population — have adopted

[1] "World Population Plan of Action," adopted by the World Population Conference, Bucharest, 1974. For background, see "World Population Year, *E.R.R.,* 1974 Vol. II, pp. 581-600.
[2] Donella H. Meadows *et al., The Limits to Growth: A Report for the Club of Rome's Project on the Predicament of Mankind* (1974), p. 24. The Club of Rome is an international association of scientists, economists and other professionals who study issues related to global resources.

Population Growth Projections

(in millions)

	Mid-1984* (Est.)	Natural Increase**	2000	2020
World	4,762	1.7%	6,250	8,086
More developed	1,166	0.6	1,270	1,350
Less developed	3,596	2.1	4,980	6,736
Excluding China	2,561	2.4	3,676	5,191
Africa	531	2.9	855	1,405
Asia	2,782	1.8	3,680	4,646
Asia (excluding China)	1,748	2.1	2,377	3,101
North America	262	0.7	297	328
Latin America	397	2.4	562	798
Europe	491	0.3	510	510
U.S.S.R.	274	1.0	316	364
Oceania	24	1.3	29	36

** *The effects of migration are not included in the current annual rate of natural increase.*

Source: Population Reference Bureau

policies of some kind to slow population growth. Although foreign assistance is crucial to carrying out these policies, the 39 governments are assuming an increasing portion of the costs.[3]

The principles expressed in the World Plan of Action were endorsed again this summer in Mexico City, where 148 government delegations attended the second U.N.-sponsored population conference, held Aug. 6-14. The United States was a signatory to the resolution despite a controversial change in its approach to population growth. The United States has been the largest contributor to family planning projects in developing nations.[4] But at the Mexico conference, U.S. delegation head James L. Buckley presented a statement that departed significantly from prior U.S. policy.

While reaffirming the Reagan administration's support for "population strategies based on voluntary family planning," Buckley, a former Republican senator from New York, challenged the view that slowing population growth is essential to economic development. Citing Hong Kong and South Korea as

---

[3] See J. Joseph Speidel and Sharon L. Camp, "Looking Ahead," *Draper Fund Report*, June 1984.

[4] In fiscal 1984, which ended Sept. 30, the United States contributed $240 million to family planning programs overseas, or 44 percent of all such contributions by the industrialized nations.

examples of rapid economic growth amid teeming populations, he stated that "population growth is, of itself, neither good nor bad. . . . People, after all, are producers as well as consumers." Taking up Reagan's oft-stated theme of the benefits of capitalistic economic systems, Buckley added: "We believe it no coincidence that each of these societies placed its reliance on the creativity of private individuals working within a free economy."

The new U.S. position also allowed American contributions to be used only for programs that are "not engaged in" and do not "provide funding for abortion or coercive family planning programs." While the U.S. contribution to the U.N. Fund for Population Activities (UNFPA) — $46 million in fiscal 1985 — was assured after the organization stated it would comply with the new conditions, the prospects for continued U.S. support of private family-planning agencies are less certain *(box, p. 89).*

The United States is nearly alone in its assessment of population control. Ironically, its new position resembles the stance championed by some Third World nations a decade ago, when the industrialized world appeared to be more enthusiastic about controlling population growth than the countries experiencing the highest growth rates. "Development is the best contraceptive" was the slogan adopted by China and other developing countries where officials believed the Western nations wanted to halt Third World population growth to protect their own political dominance. Now, in the opinion of Arthur Haupt of the Population Reference Bureau, "the vast majority [of Third World countries] show at least a wariness of rapid population growth. The American view isn't held in its entirety by hardly any of the less developed countries." [5]

Sub-Saharan Africa's Declining Food Output

Many demographers say the overall decline in population growth over the last decade is illusory. If China — where a draconian birth-control program has produced a 10 percent fall in the birth rate — is excluded from the assessment of Third World population trends, the picture is far less rosy. Sub-Saharan Africa alone appears to be in a position to eradicate all progress toward reducing population growth and increasing development made in other parts of the world. "Of all the major regions of the developing world, sub-Saharan Africa has had the slowest growth in food production and the fastest growth of population during the past twenty years," a recent World Bank

---

[5] The Population Reference Bureau is a Washington-based non-profit research and educational organization concerned with population and demographic issues.

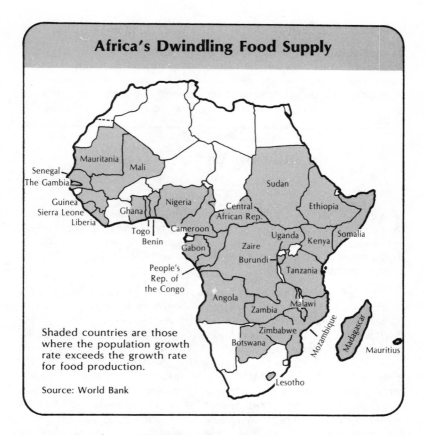

Africa's Dwindling Food Supply

Shaded countries are those where the population growth rate exceeds the growth rate for food production.

Source: World Bank

report pointed out. "It is the only region where food production is losing the race with population growth." [6]

Drought has undoubtedly exacerbated the continent's problems. The U.N.'s Food and Agriculture Organization (FAO) has identified 24 countries in need of emergency food aid — including several whose agricultural production normally meets food demand. The crisis seems certain to worsen. Of the 3.3 million tons of cereals the FAO estimates are needed in the area, only 2.3 million tons had been pledged by September. Inadequate storage facilities and the lack of means to transport and distribute the food once it arrives also hamper relief efforts.

But Africa's woes have longer-term roots as well. None, in the view of the World Bank, is more pervasive than the accelerating growth of population and inappropriate development programs that do not directly address the problems of improving food self-sufficiency. The population of sub-Saharan Africa is growing faster, at 3.1 percent a year, than that of any other continent. According to the World Bank report, the total population,

[6] World Bank, "Toward Sustained Development in Sub-Saharan Africa: A Joint Program of Action," September 1984, p. 14.

"which rose from 270 million in 1970 to 359 million in 1980, seems set to double by the turn of the century and significantly more than triple by the year 2020." [7] In addition, it continues, research has failed to improve the output and resistance to drought and pests of such local crops as millet and sorghum.

Population Growth Trends

OPINIONS VARY widely over which policies are best suited to slow world population growth, but most demographers agree on its principal causes and probable consequences. Rising birth rates occur both as a result of parental choice and a lack of contraceptive methods.

In most industrialized countries, the cost of raising each child is high, both in terms of additional family expenses and reduced family income for the parent who leaves the work force to care for the child. In most developing nations, however, each additional child represents a net family asset. Because mothers are paid little or nothing for their work, the time taken for child-rearing is far less costly than in the industrialized West. In rural areas, where women are better able to combine work with child care, more children mean more hands for agricultural work as well. In areas where schooling is not readily available for older children and teenagers, the incentive to have many children to contribute to family income remains high.

In areas of high infant and child mortality rates, young parents tend to have many children with the expectation that not all will survive. According to a World Bank report, one child in five dies in his first year in some areas of Africa, one in seven in parts of Bangladesh, India and Pakistan.[8] The close spacing of children often weakens mothers and children alike, worsening each baby's chances for survival. Parents also often see children as their sole source of support in old age, especially in poor countries lacking any type of state pension system or tradition of local support for the community's elderly. World Bank interviewers found that up to 90 percent of parents in Indonesia, Korea, the Philippines, Thailand and Turkey expected to turn to their children for support in old age.

Local customs can play an important role in determining a country's birth rate. Especially where women have little access to education and jobs outside the family, birth rates tend to

---

[7] "Toward Sustained Development in Sub-Saharan Africa," *op. cit.*, p. 26.
[8] World Bank, *World Development Report 1984*, May 25, 1984.

U.S. Policy on Population Control

Congress first began appropriating funds for family planning assistance to Third World nations in the early 1970s. Since then the United States has been the largest contributor to family planning programs administered by private agencies, multilateral organizations and the national governments themselves.

However, the new U.S. policy, which holds that economic development is the most efficient means of controlling population growth, has raised questions about the U.S. government's continued commitment to helping control the world's population growth.

One of the more controversial aspects of the new U.S. policy is its language on abortions, which are legal in most countries of the world. U.S. law already stipulates that all family programs receiving U.S. contributions must be voluntary and that U.S. contributions cannot be used for "forced or coerced" abortions or sterilizations. The new policy would ban aid to any private agency that "actively promotes" abortion, even if no U.S. funds are used directly for that purpose.

The main agency that could be affected by this language is the International Planned Parenthood Federation, which is active in 119 countries. Federation officials have said that eight of its affiliates have provided counseling to women seeking abortions. But at least one anti-abortion group in the United States has charged that the international organization has "aggresively promoted" abortions in developing countries. The private family planning agency is expected to discuss its response to the U.S. policy at a November meeting in London.

remain high. In many societies, particularly in Bangladesh and parts of Latin America and Africa, large families are regarded as an asset, and women are expected to marry early and have many children. Furthermore, the numerous family-planning programs introduced during the last decade have had differing results. In some countries they did not reach enough women to have an appreciable effect on rising birth rates.

Poverty is the biggest common denominator among countries experiencing high population growth. The World Bank, in fact, observes that "the higher a country's average income, the lower its fertility and the higher its life expectancy." [9] Accordingly, the regions with the lowest incomes — sub-Saharan Africa and India — also have the highest fertility and mortality levels — five to eight children per woman and life expectancies as low as 50 years. In the slightly more prosperous countries of East Asia and Latin America, life expectancy is some 10 years higher and women have an average of three to five children.

[9] *Ibid.*, p. 69.

There are some notable exceptions to this rule. China and Indonesia, for example, are relatively poor countries where fertility rates have fallen considerably in recent years. In contrast, some wealthier developing countries, including oil-exporting Mexico and Venezuela, have been less successful in reducing their birth rates than might have been expected. In these predominantly Catholic countries, Vatican opposition to all "artificial" means of birth control has undoubtedly hindered efforts to reduce population growth.

Consequences of Rapid Population Growth

Views on the consequences of rapid population growth have evolved considerably since 1798 when Thomas Malthus theorized that population increases geometrically and is slowed only by rising death rates caused by the resultant food shortages.[10] His observations were based on trends before the Industrial Revolution, when increases in population and therefore in the labor supply led to falling wages and thus reduced incomes. Over time population growth tended to contract. But this natural check on growth was largely removed with the dawn of the industrial age in the mid-1700s and improved living conditions. Mortality rates fell and overall fertility rates rose throughout most of Europe.

But birth rates in what is now the developed world soon leveled off and never approached the levels registered in the Third World during this century. In many countries today, the marked decline in infant mortality brought on by improved medical care has not been consistently offset by reduced birth rates. Since World War II, population growth has averaged 2 to 4 percent in the developing countries, far above the 1.5 percent level registered in Europe during the Industrial Revolution.

Furthermore, countries no longer have emigration outlets for their rising populations. Europe's growing numbers of the 1800s were largely absorbed by North and South America and Australia. And for those who did not emigrate, there were in most cases established national economic and political systems better equipped to cope with the pressures brought on by increasing populations than are offered in today's developing countries.

Although demographic trends have not conformed to Malthus' hypothesis, many observers agree with his central premise that population growth may eventually outstrip the Earth's ability to sustain its people. The Club of Rome study, for example, gave humanity at most a century to curb population growth.

---

[10] Malthus offered this theory in his *First Essay on Population*.

This view has been challenged not only by the Reagan administration in its Mexico City statement, but by some economists who see population growth as a positive contribution to world development. Julian Simon, a University of Maryland professor who is perhaps the best known advocate of this position, has emphasized the innovative force inherent in rising populations. While recognizing that famine and poverty may be among the short-term effects, he states that market forces and human ingenuity will in the long run correct any imbalances due to population increases. "The main fuel to speed our progress is our stock of knowledge, and the brake is our lack of imagination," Simon writes. "The ultimate resource is people — skilled, spirited, and hopeful people who will exert their will and imaginations for their own benefit, and so, inevitably, for the benefit of us all." [11]

Other demographic experts take a middle ground. In its 1984 *World Development Report*, the World Bank agrees that rising populations will not necessarily exhaust the world's finite resources but challenges Simon's assertion that more people automatically translate into technological advance. It paints a picture of poverty, illiteracy and population growth forming a vicious circle that requires a more complex solution than birth control alone. "...[R]apid population growth," it concludes, "is, above all, a development problem." [12]

In this way, the report distinguishes between the crowded but growing economies of Hong Kong and Singapore and the stagnating economies of Bangladesh and Kenya. The former have higher education levels and established economies, thanks to heavy investment by developed countries. Their population growth levels are also stabilizing. The latter have attracted comparatively little foreign investment, and their education levels are low and declining. At the same time, their populations are growing rapidly, ensuring that whatever resources are now used for education must increase significantly just to maintain existing educational services, let alone expand them. In addition to growing numbers of school-age children, high-fertility regions can expect large increases in the labor force. Lack of economic growth, however, means many people will not be able to find work, worsening poverty within these countries and further widening the gap between the world's rich and poor nations.

One troubling aspect of rapid population growth is urbanization. Big cities — once the result of industrialization — are increasingly found in the developing world (see table, p. 93).

---

[11] Julian L. Simon, *The Ultimate Resource* (1981), p. 348.
[12] *World Development Report 1984, op. cit.*, p. 80.

Hungry peasants are flocking to urban centers ill-equipped to accommodate them. Jobs, food, sanitation and housing are at a premium in Bombay, Mexico City, São Paulo and dozens of other Third World cities. But urbanization is only half the problem, according to the World Bank, which predicts that the rural population of all Third World countries, if unchecked, will grow by another one billion people by 2050. Instead of focusing on costly projects to redistribute the population away from the large cities, as the Mexican government has done in recent years, the bank suggests that rapidly urbanizing countries concentrate their meager resources on developing rural areas to stem the flow of people into the cities.

Results of Recent Family Planning Programs

By all accounts, the most effective program to curb population growth to date is China's "birth planning policy." First introduced in 1956, the program initially promoted late marriage and birth control. This effort was short-lived, however. Under the Great Leap Forward, begun in 1958, birth control was condemned as a ploy by the capitalistic nations to maintain their hegemony over the Third World. With the death in 1976 of Mao Tse-tung and the rise to power of China's "pragmatic" leadership, birth control again became a national priority.

Contraceptives, abortion and sterilization are available free of charge throughout China. Birth quotas are set at the commune, factory or neighborhood level by committees. Couples must apply to these committees for permission to have a child; permission is granted or denied according to a priority system. Since 1979 China has promoted an even stricter "one-child family" policy. Incentives in the form of bonuses, better jobs or housing, or access to further training or education are offered to couples that promise to have only one child. Those who fail to comply may be penalized.

The aggressive policy has been effective: China's birth rate has fallen by more than one half since 1965. But the price appears to be high. Press reports abound of forced abortions and a rising incidence of female infanticide, the result, critics say, of the one-child policy.

Other Third World nations have also reduced their birth rates, albeit to a lesser extent than China. When a city-based family planning program failed to have an appreciable effect on the birth rate in rural areas of Indonesia, the government decentralized the program to the village level and delegated responsibility for local family planning services and distribution of contraceptives to the traditionally powerful local leaders. Recent statistics suggest that peer pressure to conform at the

Projected Urbanization

(Cities with more than 10 million residents)

1950	(millions)		(millions)
New York, northeast New Jersey	12.2	London	10.4
2000			
Mexico City	31.0	Cairo, Giza, Imbaba	13.1
São Paulo	25.8	Madras	12.9
Tokyo, Yokohama	24.2	Manila	12.3
New York, northeast New Jersey	22.8	Greater Buenos Aires	12.1
Shanghai	22.7	Bangkok, Thonburi	11.9
Peking	19.9	Karachi	11.8
Rio de Janeiro	19.0	Bogota	11.7
Greater Bombay	17.1	Delhi	11.7
Calcutta	16.7	Paris	11.3
Jakarta	16.6	Tehran	11.3
Los Angeles, Long Beach	14.2	Istanbul	11.2
Seoul	14.2	Baghdad	11.1
		Osaka, Kobi	11.1

Sources: United Nations; World Bank

village level has reduced the birth rate in Java and Bali faster than in any other developing country except China.[13] The percentage of married women, aged 15 to 49, who use contraceptives ranges from 6 percent in sub-Saharan Africa to 25 percent in South Asia, 40 percent in Latin America and 65 percent in East Asia.[14]

Birth control efforts in Latin America have had varied results. Throughout the region, population growth remains high and is projected to increase by at least 2 percent a year, closer to 3 percent in Central America. This relatively poor performance is attributed to the persistence of the gap between rich and poor throughout the region. Mexico's family planning program has succeeded in reducing the average annual population growth from 3.2 percent between 1970 and 1980 to 2.4 percent in 1984. But, conceded Mexican President Miguel de la Madrid, "... [i]nternal financing was insufficient to meet the demographic pressures as they were translated into growing social demands for public expenditure and investment." [15] The coun-

---

[13] See Bruce Stokes, *Helping Ourselves* (1981). See also Martha Ainsworth, "Population Policy: Country Experience," *Finance and Development*, September 1984.

[14] "World Development Report 1984," *op. cit.*, p. 127.

[15] Miguel de la Madrid H., "Mexico: The New Challenges," *Foreign Affairs*, fall 1984, p. 66.

try's current fertility rate is still about twice that necessary to maintain its population level. Of particular concern to the Mexican government is the rapid internal migration of peasants to Mexico City, already a teeming metropolis unable to provide minimal services to its inhabitants, most of whom are relegated to the slums encircling the city.

As in Mexico, fertility fell by about one-third in Colombia during the 1970s. There, as in some other Latin American countries, doctors played an important role. "Doctors got it all started in the mid-1960s," Jean van der Tak of the Population Reference Bureau explained. "They got family planning going out of their concern over the number of women dying from illegal abortion." On the other hand, van der Tak blames doctors for obstructing effective programs in India. "Doctors *are* the problem in India," she said. "They are nominally responsible for family planning services, but they don't have the time. Most of them are men and there are not enough of them to do the job anyway. They want to keep their control over the services but they don't want to leave the cities and go to the countryside where family planning services are most needed."

Site of the world's first national family planning program, India saw its fertility rate fall rapidly, from 6.5 children per woman at the time the program was set up in 1952 to 4.8 in 1982, despite the country's low average income. Results vary markedly among India's states. By 1978, the state of Kerala, with its low infant mortality and high level of literacy among women, had seen its fertility rate sink to 2.7, while the rate in poorer Uttar Pradesh remained at twice that level. Despite India's successes, its population as a whole is rising by 16 million people a year, the fastest growth rate in the world.

Policy Implications of Country Experiences

Demographers and family planning experts see reason for both hope and despair from these experiences. Some, including Kingsley Davis of Stanford University's Hoover Institution, decry the lack of attention given to birth control in earlier years when there was a greater chance of averting the population explosion of the post-World War II period. Davis says recent efforts fail to address the root of the problem. "About all that a program of contraception, abortion, and sterilization can do is satisfy the demand [for birth control] quickly once that demand gets under way," Davis wrote. "But the purpose of population policy is to create the demand, not wait until something else creates it. As yet, except in China and Singapore, there is no anti-natalist policy worthy of the name." [16]

---

[16] Kingsley Davis, "Declining Birth Rates and Growing Populations," *Population Research and Policy Review*, no. 3, 1984, p. 73.

Others urge governments to act more aggressively to stem population growth. Speaking earlier this year in Nairobi, Kenya — a country whose birth rate has actually risen since 1965 — World Bank President A. W. Clausen emphasized the link between poverty and rapid population growth. "Economic and social progress helps slow population growth; but, at the same time, rapid population growth hampers economic development. It is therefore imperative that governments act simultaneously on both fronts. The international community has no alternative but to cooperate, with a sense of urgency, in an effort to slow population growth if development is to be achieved. But it must be slowed through policies and programs that are humane, non-coercive, and sensitive to the rights and dignity of individuals."

Clausen's predecessor, Robert S. McNamara, repeated this urgent call for action by both the countries involved and the international community. Citing the lack of political will by some governments to introduce and enact effective family planning programs, he predicted that "failure to act quickly to reduce fertility voluntarily is almost certain to lead to widespread coercive measures before the end of the century." For their part, he wrote, the developed countries should continue to provide technical and material assistance to birth control programs, conduct research in the effort to find safe and effective means of contraception and provide the results of their demographic research to high-fertility countries enabling them to institute programs best suited to their own goals.[17]

Implications for Food Policy

I N CONSIDERING the relationship between the rising world population and the availability of adequate food supplies, one must also consider whether a country is agriculturally self-sufficient. The fact that drought-stricken countries of sub-Saharan Africa are experiencing large-scale famine illustrates the difficulty of effectively channeling the world's food surpluses to areas of immediate need.

The United States is expected to produce bumper crops of corn and soybeans this year. Large wheat surpluses have already been harvested in the Common Market countries of Europe. At the same time, millions of people are dying of starvation or

[17] Robert S. McNamara, "Time Bomb or Myth: The Population Problem," *Foreign Affairs*, summer 1984, p. 1129. McNamara, defense secretary from 1961 to 1968, served as president of the World Bank from 1968 to mid-1981.

suffering from malnutrition. International response to appeals for emergency food relief has been far from adequate; only about one half of the requested food has reached the stricken countries.

The United States is the largest contributor of international food aid.[18] Through the Food for Peace program (PL 480, Title II), the U.S. government either provides food directly on a government-to-government basis or donates food to voluntary relief agencies, such as CARE or the Catholic Relief Service, which then transport it to targeted countries and may or may not help distribute it among the population. Under Food for Peace the U.S. government also contributes a quarter of the total food aid allocated through the World Food Program, administered by the U.N.'s FAO. The Food for Peace program has been faulted for indiscriminately dumping surplus grain and providing a disincentive for local food production in the destination countries.[19] But its supporters say the program should be more heavily funded.[20]

Unfortunately, Food for Peace and other food relief programs initiated in the grain-surplus nations can do little to improve distribution within the country of destination, one of the main obstacles to relief efforts. Many countries in need of immediate aid, such as Chad, lack seaports to receive food shipments. Once it arrives in city distribution centers, there is frequently no way to transport the food to the rural areas where it is needed. Food often spoils because of inadequate storage facilities. Internal strife often makes these distribution problems insurmountable. In both Ethiopia and Chad, civil war has made large parts of the country inaccessible to food relief.

Local Solutions to Chronic Food Shortage

Emergency relief efforts are no long-term substitute for agricultural self-sufficiency or, at the very least, the financial capacity to import food independently through foreign trade. "If the people of the Sahel had dollars to spend," said Haupt, editor of the monthly publication *Population Today*, "they would have international Safeways."

Many Third World nations have never recovered from the oil price shocks of the 1970s. Just as they were beginning to accumulate foreign reserves from the sale of agricultural products and minerals abroad, the oil crisis plunged the industrial nations into recession and demand for these commodities in the

---

[18] For background on U.S. agricultural policy, see "Farm Policy's New Course," *E.R.R.,* 1983 Vol. I, p. 233.
[19] See, for example, comment by James Bovard in *The Wall Street Journal,* July 2, 1984.
[20] The Reagan administration requested and Congress approved $1.4 billion for fiscal 1985 for Food for Peace. An additional $150 million in emergency food aid to the countries of sub-Saharan Africa was approved last summer.

Growth in Food Production
(Average Annual Percentage Change)

	Total		Per Capita	
	1960-70	1970-80	1960-70	1970-80
Developing countries	2.9%	2.8%	0.4%	0.4%
Africa	2.6	1.6	0.1	−1.1
Middle East	2.6	2.9	0.1	0.2
Latin America	3.6	3.3	0.1	0.6
Southeast Asia*	2.8	3.8	0.3	1.4
South Asia	2.6	2.2	0.1	0.0
Southern Europe	3.2	3.5	1.8	1.9
Industrial market economies	2.3	2.0	1.3	1.1
Non-market industrial economies	3.2	1.7	2.2	0.9
World	2.7	2.3	0.8	0.5

Does not include China.

Sources: Food and Agriculture Organization; World Bank

industrial nations dried up. Despite subsequent recoveries in the developed nations, demand for Third World products has not reached its former level. The fall in exports, together with rising external debt among many nations now experiencing food shortages, has reduced their capacity to meet food needs through foreign trade.[21]

Past efforts to improve the agricultural self-sufficiency of developing nations have yielded impressive results. The "Green Revolution" of the 1960s and 1970s successfully applied the research capabilities of the industrialized world to produce genetically modified plants — such as fast-maturing, dwarf varieties of rice, corn and wheat — that significantly increased agricultural output in areas of Latin America, India and South Asia.[22] As a result, most of the developing countries are today producing as much food per capita as they have in the past despite rapidly increasing population growth.

But many — including China and India — are barely keeping up, while others — including the majority of sub-Saharan African countries — are falling behind in per capita food production, making them ever more vulnerable to natural disasters. These countries present special geological and climatic problems that the Green Revolution did not address. Although sub-

---

[21] For background on the debt burden and trade problems among the developing nations, see *E.R.R.*, "World Debt Crisis," 1983 Vol. I, pp. 45-64, and "Global Recession and U.S. Trade," 1983 Vol. I, pp. 169-188.

[22] For background, see *E.R.R.*, "Green Revolution," 1970 Vol. I, pp. 219-238.

Saharan Africa abounds in uncultivated land, almost half of it is closed to livestock or cultivation because it is infested with tsetse flies, the carriers of sleeping sickness (trypanosomiasis). In addition, some countries in the region — 14, according to a World Bank estimate — lack sufficient land to sustain their growing populations if cultivated according to traditional, subsistence farming methods. In many the rough terrain and remoteness of tillable lands make it very expensive to introduce modern agricultural techniques. Much arid land can be cultivated only if costly irrigation networks are constructed.

Various international technical aid and training programs are focused on helping the African countries improve their agricultural productivity. The U.S. Department of Agriculture, in conjunction with the Agency for International Development (AID), conducts some 150 such projects worldwide, 30 of them in Africa. In most of these projects, Dr. Peter Koffsky of USDA's Africa program explained, surveys are conducted to assess the local agricultural conditions; it is then up to the national governments to act on the basis of these surveys. Other projects are more direct: Koffsky cited the example of the USDA's Dry Land Cropping Systems Research project undertaken in Kenya in conjunction with the FAO. "In the Kenya project," he said, "we work with farmers to assess which crops are best, such as drought-resistant maize. But long-term policy is hard to assess. The effectiveness of the projects varies considerably."

Many technical innovations have yet to be applied in much of Africa. Multiple cropping — harvesting more than one crop each year on the same plot — is one method used in some Asian countries to feed their growing populations. New plants better adapted to arid conditions and poor soil offer some promise to sub-Saharan Africa. The use of fertilizers, which has greatly increased agricultural productivity in the developed nations, could also improve self-sufficiency in this region, but they are expensive. The FAO estimates that seven sub-Saharan nations — Burundi, Kenya, Lesotho, Mauritania, Niger, Rwanda and Somalia — will be unable to feed their populations by the end of the century even if all these improvements are fully adopted.

Some observers say the main obstacle to agricultural self-sufficiency is political rather than technical. By holding down prices to make food affordable, it is said, the governments of many developing nations have discouraged local production, driving farmers off the land, encouraging migration to cities and pushing their countries into ever heavier dependence on external food assistance.

Urbanization is presenting its own food problems in many developing countries. When people migrate to urban centers, they become totally dependent on commercial sources of food and thus vulnerable to any breakdown in the distribution system. Slum dwellers, who may have migrated to the cities to escape starvation in the countryside, often become victims of severe malnutrition and disease related to poor sanitation.[23]

Prospects for Sustaining Future Growth

If conditions today are grim in many parts of the world, will future generations be able to feed themselves? Optimists like Julian Simon find little cause for concern. "...[T]here is little reason to believe that, in the foreseeable long run, additional people will make food more scarce and more expensive, even with increasing consumption per person," he wrote. "It may even be true that in the long run additional people actually *cause* food to be less scarce and less expensive, and cause consumption to increase." [24]

Stunted corn, Mozambique

If World Bank projections are correct, the Earth will have the capacity to feed its growing numbers. Because world grain production is projected to grow by 3.5 percent a year until the end of the century, while annual demand is expected to increase by only 2.6 percent, the World Bank expects food output to be adequate to meet the global demand over this period. Even in the 21st century, when the world's population is expected to level off at about 11.4 billion people, the World Bank predicts that the Earth will still be able to continue providing today's average per capita intake of food.

But quite a different picture emerges when individual regions, countries or population groups within countries are considered. Even barring further drought and technical or political obstacles to increased food production, two Third World regions — sub-Saharan Africa and Latin America — are identified as potential disaster areas because of their rapid population growth and slow income growth. Unless corrected, this combination promises eventually to produce widespread starvation.

---

[23] See James E. Austin, *Confronting Urban Malnutrition* (1980).
[24] Simon, *op. cit.*, p. 69.

Selected Bibliography

Books

Cuca, Roberto, and Catherine S. Pierce, *Experiments in Family Planning: Lessons from the Developing World*, Johns Hopkins University Press, 1977.

Eckholm, Erik P., *Losing Ground: Environmental Stress and World Food Prospects*, W. W. Norton & Co., 1976.

Gupte, Pranay, *The Crowded Earth: People and the Politics of Population*, W. W. Norton & Co., 1984.

Meadows, Donella H., *et al.*, *The Limits to Growth: A Report for the Club of Rome's Project on the Predicament of Mankind*, Universe Books, 1972.

Simon, Julian L., and Herman Kahn, eds., *The Resourceful Earth, A Response to 'Global 2000'*, Basil Blackwell, 1984.

Articles

Ainsworth, Martha, "Population Policy: Country Experience," *Finance & Development*, September 1984.

Davis, Kingsley, "Declining Birth Rates and Growing Populations," *Population Research and Policy Review*, no. 3, 1984.

Gilland, Bernard, "Considerations on World Population and Food Supply," *Population and Development Review*, June 1983.

McNamara, Robert S., "Time Bomb or Myth: The Population Problem," *Foreign Affairs*, summer 1984.

Mellor, John W., and Bruce F. Johnston, "The World Food Equation: Interrelations among Development, Employment, and Food Consumption," *Journal of Economic Literature*, June 1984.

Population Today, selected issues.

Shepherd, Jack, "Africa: Drought of the Century," *The Atlantic*, April 1984.

Reports and Studies

Berg, Alan, "Malnourished People: A Policy View," World Bank Poverty and Basic Needs Series, June 1981.

Brown, Lester R., "Population Policies for a New Economic Era," Worldwatch Paper 53, March 1983.

Brown, Lester R., and Edward C. Wolf, "Soil Erosion: Quiet Crisis in the World Economy," Worldwatch Paper 60, September 1984.

Editorial Research Reports: "Soil Erosion: Threat to Food Supply," 1984 Vol. I, p. 229; "World Food Needs," 1974 Vol. II, p. 825; "World Population Year," 1974 Vol. II, p. 581.

Winrock International, "World Agriculture: Review and Prospects into the 1980s," December 1983.

World Bank, "Toward Sustained Development in Sub-Saharan Africa: A Joint Program of Action," August 1984.

—— "World Development Report 1984," May 25, 1984.

Graphics: Cover illustration by Art Director Richard Pottern, cover photo and p. 815 photo by Sen. John C. Danforth, R-Mo. (Both photos were taken in Mozambique, Africa.) Map, p. 803, by Assistant Art Director Robert Redding.

AMERICA'S THREATENED COASTLINES

by

Roger Thompson

Editor's Update: Congress in March 1986 reauthorized the Coastal Zone Management Act for five years *(see p. 110)*. The reauthorization continued 1986 funding levels and provided for a gradual increase in state matching funds up to a 50-50 sharing in fiscal year 1989.

Congress rejected a block grant program to share federal revenues from offshore drilling with coastal states *(see p. 112)* but did resolve a longstanding dispute over oil and gas revenues covered by the Outer Continental Shelf Lands Act. The coastal states would receive 27 percent, and the federal government 73 percent, of revenues from wells situated between three and six miles offshore, including $6.4 billion already accumulated in escrow. The resolution of this conflict makes it less likely that the block grant program will be enacted.

The Environmental Protection Agency has begun a gradual shift of sludge dumping from the New York Bight Apex, 12 miles offshore, to a site 106 miles offshore *(see p. 116)*. All dumping at the 12-mile site will end by December 1987. The EPA is re-examining, after public comment, proposed new regulations for ocean burning of toxic wastes.

AMERICA'S THREATENED COASTLINES

LIVING BY THE SEA is an ancient desire — and a modern hazard of growing proportions. Western civilization evolved on the shores of the Mediterranean Sea. Generations later and a continent away, Americans in increasing numbers are building homes, setting up businesses and vacationing along the nation's coasts. But not without paying a steep price in lives lost and property damaged.

Hurricanes in this century have killed over 13,000 people living in states along the Gulf of Mexico and Atlantic Ocean. Most died in storms that struck before 1940. Improved weather forecasting since then has provided coastal residents with advance warning. But property damage has become far costlier, as more and more development takes place on the beach. Although free of hurricanes, West Coast residents share with Easterners the menace of winter storms. High tides and pounding waves gouged out huge sections of California's scenic coastal Highway 1 in January 1983. Damage to coastal property exceeded half a billion dollars.[1] From Cape Cod to the Carolinas, the same winter was also one of the worst on record.

Even without destructive storms, scientists believe that natural, relentless beach erosion eventually will endanger much of the development along the nation's coasts. Erosion averages two feet a year on the Atlantic Coast. Louisiana loses 40 square miles of its coastal marsh land to the Gulf of Mexico each year.[2] On the West Coast, dams on California rivers have deprived the state's beaches of their main source of replacement sand, causing severe rates of beach erosion.

The major problem is that the ocean level now is rising one foot or more a century, which some climatologists attribute largely to a long-term warming trend that is causing polar ice caps and glaciers to melt.[3] A prominent theory is that the

---

[1] National Environmental Satellite, Data, and Information Service, "Climate Impact Assessment 1983," p. 11

[2] For background, see "America's Disappearing Wetlands," *E.R.R.*, 1983 Vol. II, pp. 613-632. Also see George Getschow and Thomas Petzinger Jr., "Louisiana Marshlands, Laced With Oil Canals, Are Rapidly Disappearing," *The Wall Street Journal*, Oct. 24, 1984.

[3] Evidence of a warming trend is not universally accepted. Only a decade ago, the National Center for Atmospheric Research attracted public attention with data indicating the Earth gradually was cooling and that glacial retreat had halted about 1940. For background, see "World Weather Trends," *E.R.R.*, 1974 Vol. II, pp. 515-538, and "Ozone Controversy," *E.R.R.*, 1976 Vol. I, pp. 205-224.

warming is expected to accelerate early in the next century because of a"greenhouse effect," a rise in global temperature resulting from the buildup of carbon dioxide in the atmosphere. Carbon dioxide, which comes from burning fossil fuels such as coal and gasoline, traps the Earth's heat rather than allowing it to escape into space. The National Academy of Sciences and the Environmental Protection Agency (EPA) have estimated that greenhouse warming is likely to cause a one- to five-foot rise in sea level in the next century.[4] "If the sea level rises one foot, all the recreational beaches will erode in about 40 years," said James G. Titus, an EPA policy analyst and co-author of *Greenhouse Effect and Sea Level Rise* (1984).[5]

Coastal communities build sea walls and other barriers to preserve their shorelines. But scientists say that such efforts often hasten beach destruction. A popular way of rebuilding beaches is to pump sand from offshore, but it is costly and must be repeated in several years. The costliness and ultimate futility of fighting the sea persuaded Congress two years ago to end federal subsidies for new construction on undeveloped barrier islands on the Atlantic and Gulf coasts. Since 1972, the federal government has given states money to make and implement coastal zone management plans under provisions of the Coastal Zone Management Act. Twenty-three states and five territories now have federally approved plans. But many state officials say these programs will shut down if the Reagan administration succeeds in cutting off their federal funding.

Coastal-state officials also are critical of the administration's refusal to cooperate with them in planning for offshore oil and gas exploration. The states have filed numerous lawsuits to block the Reagan administration's accelerated lease-sale schedule. A sympathetic Congress has intervened on behalf of the states and declared sizable areas off the California and New England coasts off-limits.

Energy exploration is not the only source of conflict. For more than a decade, New York City and surrounding municipalities have fought federal regulations that seek to end their dumping of sewage sludge in the Atlantic 12 miles off of the Long Island shore. More recently, Gulf Coast states have protested experimental toxic waste-burning at sea. The EPA sanctioned the burning, then halted it at least temporarily, and now is expected to publish new regulations by the end of the year.

---

[4] See *Changing Climate,* Carbon Dioxide Assessment Committee, National Research Council, 1983; J. Hoffman, D. Keyes and J. Titus, "Projecting Future Sea Level Rise," U.S. Government Printing Office, No. 055-000-0236-3, 1983; and S. Seidel, D. Keyes, "Can We Delay a Greenhouse Warming?" U.S. Government Printing Office, No. 055-000-00235-5, 1983.

[5] Persons quoted in this report were interviewed by the author unless otherwise indicated.

These issues become more urgent and more difficult to re-solve as population swells in coastal areas. Fifty-three percent of the U.S. population lives within 50 miles of the Atlantic, Gulf, Pacific or Great Lakes coastlines, up from 46 percent in 1940. The average density per square mile ranges from a high of 414 along the Atlantic Coast to 134 along the Gulf of Mexico — still far greater than for the rest of the United States (43), even excluding Alaska and Hawaii.[6]

Effects of Relentless Shoreline Erosion

Relatively protected port cities such as Boston, New York, Baltimore, Charleston, New Orleans and San Francisco contrib-ute significantly to the population density figures. But these are not the areas most threatened by severe weather or coastal erosion. It is resort development along unprotected shorelines — whether in or near major cities like Miami Beach and San Diego or along relatively isolated beaches — that does head-on combat with the elements.

Before World War II, coastal development was generally sparse and beach cottages were relatively inexpensive, writes Orrin Pilkey Jr., a Duke University geologist, and colleagues in *Coastal Design* (1984).[7] When severe weather or erosion de-stroyed property, rebuilding was likely to take place farther inland to maintain the original distance from the shore. After the war, the affluent society blossomed and a building boom hit coastal areas. People rushed to the coasts to play on the beaches and soak up the sun. Increasing numbers of older Americans retired to coastal communities. Few who bought beach property had lived by the sea before. Even fewer understood the dynam-ics of coastal erosion or the hazards of severe weather.

A principal rule of beaches is that they are constantly chang-ing. The same beach typically has one profile in summer and another in winter. The waves whipped by winter storms tend to erode the beaches, making them narrower and steeper. Winter storms deposit enormous amounts of sand offshore, where it awaits gentler summer waves that will push it back to the beach. This explains why the summertime beach typically is broader and less steep. Erosion takes place when more sand is removed than replaced in the annual cycle of removal and rebuilding.

The shorelines of barrier islands present their own special problems. The 295 islands that stretch like a broken chain from Maine to Texas are narrow strips composed largely of sand and shells. They are generally characterized by a beach and dune on the ocean side, and salt marshes and estuaries on the mainland

---

[6] *Statistical Abstract of the United States, 1984,* Census Bureau, p. 10.
[7] *Coastal Design, A Guide for Builders, Planners and Homeowners* (1984), p. 17.

side. These islands were formed at the end of the last ice age, some 12,000 years ago, and have gradually migrated landward as the sea level rose due to glacial melting. Wind, waves and ocean currents constantly reshape the islands.

Shoreline erosion has gotten an extra push in recent decades from higher sea levels. By some calculations, the sea rose four to six inches in the last century and beginning about 50 years ago stepped up the pace. Pilkey thinks it has since been rising "at a rate of perhaps one foot per century." He believes most of the erosion taking place today on America's beaches is due to this increase, and estimates that 90 percent of America's coastline is eroding at a significant rate. For example, nearly half of North Carolina's 320 miles of island shoreline is eroding faster than the two-foot-a-year average for the East Coast.[8]

Methods for Halting the Sea's Advance

As coastal development intensified, soaring real estate investments seemed to justify the expense of trying to stop shoreline erosion. Engineers devised various types of barriers to "stabilize" the shoreline and protect property. While these measures may shelter property from the sea's landward advance, "erosion proofing" eventually destroys the beaches that brought people to the coast in the first place.

Barriers built parallel to the beach are called seawalls if they are constructed of concrete and steel, and bulkheads if they are made of wood. Revetments are boulders armoring the shoreline at the dune line. Bulkheads and revetments cost $100 to $300 or more a linear foot and are intended only for storm protection. Seawalls cost $300 to $800 or more a linear foot and may be in constant contact with the waves.

Pilkey calls such barriers "the absolute last resort of shoreline stabilization." Where beaches lie between seawalls and the low-tide level, the force of the waves rebounding from the seawalls during high tide eventually will narrow and destroy the beach. Wave energy normally absorbed by the beach is reflected seaward and carries valuable sand out to sea. In time, the shore in front of the seawall will erode and threaten to undermine the structure *(see illustration)*. Boulders, or rip-rap, may be used to stabilize the shore in front of the seawall. Continued erosion may require additional emplacements. Two rows of boulders protect the seawall at Galveston. And a third is being planned. Geologists call the spread of seawalls the "New Jerseyization" of America's coast. Like much of the shoreline of New Jersey, more and more seaside property is being protected by seawalls.

[8] See James G. Titus, et al., "National Wetlands Newsletter," September-October 1984, p. 4; Pilkey, *op. cit.*, p. 2; Neil Caudle, "The Ocean is Coming, The Ocean Is Coming," *Coast Watch* (University of North Carolina Sea Grant newsletter), January 1984, p. 2.

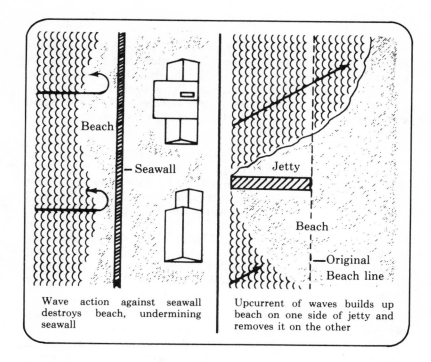

| Wave action against seawall destroys beach, undermining seawall | Upcurrent of waves builds up beach on one side of jetty and removes it on the other |

Trapping sand with groins, walls built perpendicular to the coast, is another common erosion control method. Groins may be built of steel, wood, concrete or sand-filled bags. They work because sand generally moves along the shore with ocean currents. Groins trap sand on the up-current side of sand flow. But they cause the down-current side to erode by eliminating its sand supply *(see illustration)*. Where a series of groins are used, the result is a scalloped or serrated shoreline that builds some portions of the beach and destroys others. Jetties are similar to groins, but are much larger and are most often used to prevent sand from filling boating and shipping channels. Robert Morton, a Texas geologist, estimates that about half that state's sand had been locked in place by jetties built to protect harbors.

Moving Sand to Badly Eroded Beaches

Many beaches have been restored by hauling sand from deposits that accumulate in channels or behind jetties, or by pumping it from underwater deposits offshore. Rebuilt beaches are a lure for tourism and a buffer against storms. Ocean City, N.J., Virginia Beach, Va., and Carolina and Wrightsville beaches in North Carolina are among those that have trucked in millions of cubic feet of sand over the years.

Restoration by pumping sand from offshore is relatively new, a method that became widely used during the early 1970s. It is used frequently in Florida, where more than 25 percent of that state's 782 miles of beaches are subject to severe erosion.[9] Delray Beach, 50 miles north of Fort Lauderdale, lost 100 feet of its three-mile beach front to erosion during the 1950s and 1960s. A huge revetment failed to stabilize the shoreline. During the summer of 1973, an offshore dredge pumped 1.6 million cubic yards of sand onshore to restore the 100 feet of beach. The project cost $2.1 million.

Miami Beach has been one of the latest beneficiaries of shoreline reconstruction. The resort city lost much of its original beach during a 1926 hurricane that devastated the island. By the early 1970s, erosion had claimed most of what was left. Groins provided the only beach sand for tourists. The U.S. Army Corps of Engineers in 1977 undertook to replenish the sand along 10.5 miles of beaches. Some 13.5 million cubic yards of sand were pumped in from 6,000 to 12,000 feet offshore, creating beaches up to 300 feet wide. The project was completed in 1982 at a cost of $52.4 million, most of it ($28.7 million) federally funded.

Aside from the high cost, the major problem for beach restoration is the maintenance required to replace the new sand once it erodes. Within two years, Wrightsville Beach lost 43 percent of the 1.6 million cubic feet placed on its shoreline in 1965.[10] Delray Beach lost an estimated 120,000 cubic yards of sand each year after restoration.[11] In both cases, expensive maintenance projects were required to again rebuild the beach. Pilkey estimates that the erosion rates of rebuilt beaches is 10 times that of natural beaches because they are steeper than natural ones, therefore more vulnerable to sand loss.[12]

While erosion works slowly, storms can wipe out almost overnight what it takes months to accomplish. Oceanside, Calif., spent over $3 million hauling sand to its beach in 1982, only to have it washed away by winter storms in 1983. Atlantic City pumped $9 million worth of sand to its depleted beach in the summer of 1983, but lost it all during storms last spring.

Artificial sea grass is the latest erosion-control method to gain widespread attention. Much of the optimism about its success in stabilizing beaches came from a test conducted at the Cape Hatteras, N.C., lighthouse, where the historic structure is in danger of falling into the sea *(see cover photo)*. Inventor William Garrett planted his artificial sea grass — gray polypropylene fronds rising up from tubes set parallel to the

[9] Thomas J. Campbell and Richard H. Spadoni, "Beach Restoration — An Effective Way to Combat Erosion on the Southeast Coast of Florida," *Shore and Beach*, January 1982, p. 11.
[10] U.S. Army Coastal Engineering Research Center, "Shore Protection Manual, Volume II," Corps of Engineers, 1977, pp. 6-28.
[11] Campbell and Spadoni, p. 12.
[12] Pilkey, p. 151.

Miami Beach before (left) and after restoration

beach — at the site and said measurements show the beach has held its ground or grown.[13] A team of scientists and engineers concluded in the fall of 1983 that his artificial sea grass had little to do with the reversal of erosion.[14]

Destruction From Hurricanes, Storms

While erosion is a relentless thief, coastal storms get most of the attention because of their sudden, dramatic impact. On the East Coast, some geologists contend that damage done by winter storms may increase in years to come because of a phenomenon known as beach "profile steepening." Studies have found that the unseen portion of beaches just offshore is eroding more rapidly than the visible beach. For example, the visible beach at Ocean City, Md., is eroding at a rate of two feet annually, while the underwater part is eroding seven feet a year.[15] The resulting sharper dropoff indicates that the beach will provide less protection during storms than when the profile was flatter.

The greatest storm threat comes from hurricanes. Twenty-seven of the hurricanes that struck American shores between 1900 and 1982 were destructive enough to cause $50 million or more in property damage.[16] Recent storms have been the most destructive. The 1926 storm that devastated Miami Beach de-

[13] See Susan Begley, "The Vanishing Coasts," *Newsweek*, Sept. 24, 1984, p. 77.

[14] See *Coast Watch*, p. 6.

[15] Michael Barth and James G. Titus, *Greenhouse Effect and Sea Level Rise: A Challenge for This Generation* (1984), p. 255. Atlantic winter storms, called northeasters for the direction of their winds, may have gale-force winds and linger over the coastline for days. The storms strike only during winter and spring, due to seasonal change in weather patterns. West Coast winter storms often have low winds but destructive waves generated hundreds of miles offshore.

[16] Paul J. Herbert and Glenn Taylor, "The Deadliest, Costliest, and Most Intense United States Hurricanes of This Century (And Other Frequently Requested Hurricane Facts)," National Hurricane Center, Miami, Fla., Jan. 1984.

stroyed $112 million in property. In contrast, Hurricane Frederick packed less force but destroyed a record $2.3 billion in property along the coasts of Mississippi and Alabama in 1979.

The deadliest storm hit Galveston in 1900, killing 6,000 people. Since then 30 other coastal storms have each taken at least 25 lives. Better forecasting has lowered the death toll by providing residents with more time to move inland. However, the increasing density of coastal development, especially in places like the Florida Keys, may one day make evacuation impossible, resulting in another catastrophe on the scale of Galveston, said Neil Frank, director of the National Hurricane Center in Miami.

Frank said recent studies indicate it would take 18 hours to remove people from vulnerable coastal areas around Tampa, Fla., 22 hours to evacuate Miami and Fort Lauderdale, and 30 hours to clear the Keys. That "assumes I'm going to be able to give 30 hours' lead time to evacuate the Keys, and that there aren't going to be any wrecks to stall traffic," he said. Though adding that most hurricanes proceed on a course that would allow such warning, he recalled a hurricane that struck the Keys in 1935, killing 500 people. It "left Andros Island [in the Bahamas] as only a tropical storm. Just 30 hours later it blew through the Keys and was one of the strongest hurricanes to hit the U.S. in this century."

Coastal Management

A S THE NATION started becoming much more aware of the environment in the late 1960s, the inadequacy of state and federal policies on coastal development drew more attention. An oil spill in 1969 off the coast of Santa Barbara, Calif., sharply defined the conflict between the nation's growing energy demand and the need for environmental protection.[17] In 1972, the same year Congress passed landmark clean water legislation, it passed the Coastal Zone Management Act. The act declared it was in the national interest to have wise management of the nation's coastline: some 12,383 miles of oceanside — 88,633 miles if the entire tidal shoreline of bays, estuaries and other inlets is included — plus 4,530 miles of Great Lakes' littoral.[18] The act provided federal guidelines for developing coastal management programs but made participation voluntary. The

---

[17] An estimated 235,000 gallons of crude oil escaped when a well being drilled erupted on Jan. 28, 1969, in the Santa Barbara Channel. The blowout was capped on Feb. 8. Oil blackened 30 miles of Southern California beaches.
[18] Figures from the National Oceanic and Atmospheric Administration.

Abuse of the Great Lakes

The Great Lakes have long suffered from the side-effects of civilization. Clear-cutting of climax forests during the last century caused massive erosion. Sediments filled the wetlands that served as spawning areas for fish and the habitat for birds and other wildlife. During the first half of this century, new species of marine life were introduced to the lakes. One, the eel-like sea lamprey, was a vicious predator that wiped out the trout.

In the second half of the century, public concern shifted to the effect of sewage and industrial wastes flowing into the lakes. Large portions of Lake Erie were declared "dead." Similar horror stories prompted the United States and Canada, in 1978, to sign the Great Lakes Water Quality Agreement to work jointly on water quality problems. Major efforts have been made by both nations to upgrade wastewater treatment plants. The focus today is on an accumulation of toxic chemicals in the waters.

35 states and territories bordering the Atlantic, Gulf, Pacific and Great Lakes had two powerful incentives for participating: the act provided two-thirds of the cost of developing a coastal management program, and it guaranteed that federal activities must be consistent with state plans "to the maximum extent practicable."

So far 23 states and five territories have obtained federal approval of their coastal management programs, beginning with Washington in 1976.[19] State programs often have evolved amid considerable controversy over controls on future shoreline development. A primary goal of most plans is to prohibit constructon too close to the eroding coastline. North Carolina's program, widely considered a model for others to follow, has imposed a controversial "setback" regulation since June 1979. New buildings must be 60 feet landward of the vegetation line or a distance 30 times the annual erosion rate — whichever is greater. The state's Coastal Resources Commission last fall doubled the setback for new multi-unit buildings such as hotels and condominiums. But pressure from developers caused the commission to cap the setback increase at 105 feet.

[19] Others in order of federal approval are: Oregon, California, Massachusetts, Wisconsin, Rhode Island, Michigan, North Carolina, Puerto Rico, Hawaii, Maine, New Jersey, Virgin Islands, Alaska, Guam, Delaware, Alabama, South Carolina, Louisiana, Mississippi, Connecticut, Pennsylvania, New Jersey, Northern Marianas, American Samoa, Florida, New York and New Hampshire.

David Watson, president of the Dare County (Nags Head) Board of Realtors, says the new setback will discourage hotel development, devalue beachfront property and shrink the county's tax base, thereby making it more difficult to provide public facilities for the thousands of tourists who flock there each summer. Nags Head Mayor Don Bryan disagrees: "My view is that the Coastal Area Management Act has furnished a tool with which we can make people aware of the problem. It helps us form rules that will benefit ocean-front property owners. . . ." [20]

Florida chose not to adopt the setback approach. Rather, it requires that all new buildings seaward of a "coastal control line" — frequently several hundred feet landward of the beach — must meet stringent construction standards for durability and storm resistance. States that have sidestepped tough development restrictions may find it harder to do so in the future. Congress amended the Coastal Zone Management Act in 1980 to expand and sharpen national objectives and reauthorize federal funding for five years — through Sept. 30, 1985. Among the nine new or strengthened objectives for state programs were: improve management of coastal development to minimize loss of life and property, and provide better protection for natural resources such as wetlands, estuaries, fish and wildlife habitats.

Uncertain Future for Guiding Legislation

Coastal states already are preparing for congressional hearings in the spring that will consider whether to extend the act beyond its expiration date next fall. The program's future is far from certain. Each year since 1981, the Reagan administration has proposed no funding. Federal officials argue that the states should take over program financing. But Congress has continued funding at a reduced level.[21] Arthur J. Rocque Jr., chairman of the Coastal States Organization, contends that a majority of the state coastal management programs will shut their doors if federal funds are withdrawn. "Coastal states, to a large extent, are financially unable, despite their willingness, to assume the full responsibility of acting as sole stewards of this nation's ocean and coastal resources," he said.[22]

To break the budgetary impasse, coastal states have asked Congress to set aside up to $300 million a year of the approximately $6 billion the Treasury gets from offshore oil and gas

---

[20] Quoted in *Coast Watch*, pp. 8-9.

[21] Funding reached an all-time high of $70 million in 1980. Under the Reagan administration, funding dropped to $41 million for the combined fiscal years 1982 and 1983, $21 million in fiscal year 1984 and advanced to $34 million for the present fiscal year, 1985.

[22] Testimony before the Senate Commerce, Science and Transportation Committee, March 17, 1983. The Coastal States Organization, an association of U.S. maritime states and territories interested in management of coastal and maritime resources, has offices at 444 N. Capitol St., Washington, D.C. 20001.

royalties. The money would be distributed among the states to fund coastal management programs. Revenues from offshore energy activities are the federal government's second largest source of income, after income taxes. Bills incorporating the revenue sharing idea passed the House last year and again this year with the support of the National Governors' Association, the Coastal States Organization and most environmental groups. But the Reagan administration opposes the idea, calling it a drain on the Treasury. The bill died on the Senate floor in October during the final days of the 98th Congress under threat of a filibuster from the Republican opposition. Proponents say revenue sharing will be a major issue during next year's debate over extension of the Coastal Zone Management Act.

Another big issue concerns federal cooperation with the states in developing offshore oil and gas resources. Cooperative ties that were formed during the early years of the Coastal Zone Management Act have been strained under the Reagan administration. Eight years ago, Congress enacted the Coastal Energy Impact Program to help states plan for new or expanded coastal refineries, pipelines, port expansion, public utilities and their environmental impact. The program allocated millions to states for planning purposes. But the Reagan administration, contending that the actual impact has been far less than anticipated, has eliminated new funding for the program.[23] The affected states hope to obtain new money for it through the proposed revenue sharing measure.

Offshore Oil Leasing; States vs. the Feds

Money is not the only federal-state issue. The states contend that the Reagan administration has forsaken its responsibility under the Coastal Zone Management Act to cooperate in carrying out offshore oil and gas exploration plans. The act assured the states that once their management plans were approved, any federal action "directly affecting" their coastal zones would have to be consistent with state plans, insofar as possible. This so-called consistency provision was the basis for California's unsuccessful attempt to stop federal offshore oil lease sales.

The dispute arose in 1981 when James G. Watt, then secretary of the interior, announced the sale of 115 tracts for oil exploration off the coast of central California. State officials said the sale posed a clear threat to endangered sea otters and would not be in concert with California's coastal management plan. It asked that the sale be canceled. When the Interior Department refused, the state filed suit to block the sale by invoking the consistency provision.

[23] Funds continue to be made available from unspent amounts allocated in previous years.

A federal district court and a federal appeals court upheld the state's protest. But on Jan. 11, 1984, the Supreme Court rejected its argument by a vote of 5 to 4.[24] Writing for the majority, Justice Sandra Day O'Connor said that "consistency" findings do not affect oil and gas lease sales. Such determiniations are required only later when actual drilling and production begin. The state contended that leasing and exploration cannot be neatly separated — that the time to say no to exploration is before oil companies sink millions into leasing.

A month after the court ruled, a bipartisan coalition in Congress introduced a bill to nullify the decision. The measure would require the federal government to make its oil lease sales consistent with state coastal management plans. Interior Secretary William P. Clark, who succeeded Watt, opposed the legislation and told congressional committees he would recommend that President Reagan veto it. The bill died at the end of the session, but supporters plan to reintroduce it next year.

Watt had fueled the consistency controversy when he implemented a five-year plan to accelerate federal lease sales of offshore tracts totaling one billion acres — about five times what the Carter administration had envisioned for the same period. The plan was put into effect July 21, 1982. Since world oil shortages and resulting increases occurred a decade ago, during the 1973-74 Arab oil embargo, every administration has proposed a significant increase in offshore exploration. But Watt's program was far bigger, and more controversial.

Protection for Undeveloped Barrier Islands

In contrast to the offshore oil dispute, the Reagan administration and the states worked together to enact the Coastal Barrier Resources Act of 1982. The act cut off federal subsidies for roads, bridges, utilities and flood insurance for 186 barrier island areas designated as "undeveloped." [25] The areas comprise about one quarter of the 2,685 miles of barrier-island shoreline along the Atlantic Ocean and Gulf of Mexico. The act does not prohibit landowners from building on their property. But it does shift costs and risks from the federal government to the private sector — or to state and local governments if they choose to step in. Enforcement of the act is projected to save the Treasury $5.4 billion over 20 years, plus significant amounts for state and local governments.[26]

The first legal test of the act ended with a victory for its

---

[24] *Secretary of the Interior et al. v. California et al.,* Jan 11, 1984.

[25] "Undeveloped" was defined as those areas which on March 15, 1982, contained less than one walled or roofed building per five acres or did not have fully developed roads, sewer and water systems.

[26] David R. Godschalk, "Impacts of the Coastal Barrier Resources Act," March 1984, p. 9. Federal infrastructure subsidies for undeveloped areas ended Oct. 18, 1982; flood insurance for new buildings ended Oct. 1, 1983.

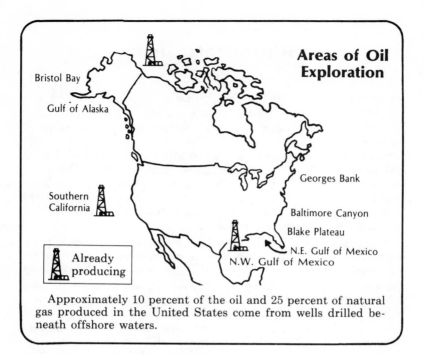

Areas of Oil Exploration

Bristol Bay

Gulf of Alaska

Georges Bank

Southern California

Baltimore Canyon

Blake Plateau

N.E. Gulf of Mexico

N.W. Gulf of Mexico

Already producing

Approximately 10 percent of the oil and 25 percent of natural gas produced in the United States come from wells drilled beneath offshore waters.

supporters. Eleven developers of Topsail Island, N.C., a 26-mile-long island adjacent to the Camp Lejeune Marine Base on the state's southern coast, joined in a 1983 suit to challenge the act. The plantiffs claimed that the act erred in designating their land "undeveloped." They pointed out that the area in question, the northern end of the island, already was under development and had access to sewer and water systems, and a state road. Withdrawal of federal flood insurance to the area would halt development and mean big financial losses unless the plantiffs could find a private insurer — a difficult feat at best. Federal Judge James C. Fox on Jan. 31, 1984, ruled that the maps designating undeveloped areas under the act had been approved by Congress and were beyond judicial review.[27]

David R. Godschalk, a professor of planning at the University of North Carolina at Chapel Hill, reviewed the act's early impact and found little evidence that private companies were stepping in to insure coastal property where federal insurance no longer applied. Without insurance, lenders are not likely to finance new building on undeveloped islands. Ironically, Godschalk speculated that developers eventually may have an easier time securing insurance for multifamily projects than individuals who want to build single beach cottages.[28]

---

[27] *M. F. Bostic et al. vs. United States of America et al.*, U.S. District Court, Eastern District of North Carolina, New Bern Division, No. 83-139-CIV-4.
[28] Godschalk, *op. cit.*, p. 27.

Environmental Strains

THE DEBATE OVER coastal issues does not stop at the shoreline. Federal and state officials are engaged in disputes involving the pollution of coastal waters and preservation of marine life. One such dispute involves New York City's 60-year-long practice of dumping sewage sludge — the blackish liquid left after treatment of raw sewage — in the Atlantic Ocean 12 miles south of Long Island. The site, known as the New York Bight Apex, is approximately 80 feet deep. New York City and eight surrounding municipalities dump nearly eight million tons of sludge in the area each year.

The practice has been under attack since 1976, when a massive bloom of algae plagued New Jersey coastal waters. The algae used up oxygen and killed thousands of fish that washed ashore. The same summer, beaches on the south shore of Long Island were coated with sewage, triggering accusations that waste had drifted ashore from the dumping area. Although it was later determined that the problem arose from a nearby wastewater treatment plant, the uproar did not go unnoticed by Congress. In 1977 it amended the Marine Protection Research and Sanctuaries Act of 1972 (commonly known as the Ocean Dumping Act) to ban ocean sludge dumping after Dec. 31, 1981.[29]

New York City challenged the deadline in federal court and won at least a temporary victory. On April 14, 1981, Judge Abraham D. Sofaer ruled that the ban applied only to dumping that would "unreasonably degrade the environment." He said no evidence had been offered to show how much, if any, harm had been done to marine life by sludge dumping at the New York Bight. Sofaer allowed the dumping to continue pending new Environmental Protection Agency regulations and designation of a new ocean site. The savings from dumping sludge at sea weighed in New York's favor. City officials argued that treating the sludge on land would require an initial expenditure of $250 million for facilities and an additional $45 million a year in operational costs. By contrast, the city spends about $3 million annually hauling sludge to the ocean dump site.[30]

In accordance with the court's ruling, the EPA held public hearings and conducted studies to reconsider use of the site. The agency announced last spring it favored moving the sludge dumping to a site 106 miles offshore in waters more than a mile deep. Final action is pending. Meanwhile, the House in October

---

[29] The law banned ocean dumping of radiological, chemical or biological warfare agents or radioactive wastes.

[30] R. L. Swanson and M. Devine, "Sludge Dumping Policy," *Environment*, June 1982, p. 16.

passed for the third year in a row a bill that would stop sludge dumping in the New York Bight Apex. The measure died in the Senate when Congress adjourned. "This bill has not become law largely because the Senate Environment and Public Works Committee has been overwhelmed with six or seven other major environmental bills needing attention," said Kenneth Kamlet, director of the Pollution and Toxic Substance Division of the National Wildlife Federation.

Issue of Burning Toxic Waste at Sea

A more volatile issue has arisen over the advisability of burning toxic wastes at sea. The practice is not new. The EPA first issued permits for experimental burning of hazardous chemicals in the Gulf of Mexico in 1974. Based on the reported success of the venture, the EPA issued permits for experimental burning in 1977, 1981 and 1982. In October 1983, the agency gave tentative permission to license the incinerator ship *Vulcanus* to burn toxic wastes 200 miles off the Texas coast. But vocal public opposition led the agency to withdraw its approval. Residents of Brownsville, Texas, and Mobile, Ala., feared their communities would become storage areas for millions of gallons of toxic waste to be loaded on incineration ships.[31]

An EPA official who reviewed the controversy recommended in a special report last spring that the agency issue permits for experimental incineration of 3.3 million gallons of polychlorinated biphenyl (PCBs) and DDT stored at an Alabama landfill. But Assistant EPA Administrator Jack E. Ravan rejected the recommendation and called for more study "to ensure that all legal, technical and operational issues are addressed."[32] Ravan said the agency also should consider proposals for incineration ships to operate from the East and West coasts, as well as the Gulf of Mexico. New regulations for ocean burning are not expected until the end of the year.

Chemical companies are pressuring the EPA to move forward with the ocean-burning program as the safest way to dispose of the bulk of 276 million metric tons of toxic chemicals generated each year in the United States. Many scientists and policy makers consider land disposal of toxic wastes unsafe. "Large amounts are put in pits, ponds or lagoons or injected into deep wells," Kamlet said. In contrast, land-burning is expensive and little-used. But it costs less to burn at sea. Kamlet said the National Wildlife Federation cautiously supports ocean burning, if the EPA enforces adequate regulations. "There haven't been too many other environmental groups to take this position," he said.

[31] Desmond H. Bond, "At-Sea Incineration of Hazardous Wastes," *Environmental Science Technology*, Vol. 18, No. 5, 1984, p. 149. For general background, see "Toxic Substance Control," *E.R.R.*, 1978 Vol. II, pp. 741-760.
[32] Quoted in *The Washington Post*, May 24, 1984.

Disposal of low-level nuclear waste at sea has not been permitted since passage of the Ocean Dumping Act in 1972. Before then, the United States had dumped about 107,000 oil drums of low-level radioactive waste.[33] Congress in 1982 renewed the law to head off expected Reagan administration efforts to resume the practice. The issue arose when the Navy in March 1982 announced it was considering sinking old radioactive submarines in the depths of the ocean, after removing their nuclear fuel. At the time, the Navy had been investigating sites in the Atlantic 17,000 feet deep and 200 miles southeast of Cape Hatteras, N.C., and a spot in the Pacific about 14,000 feet deep around 150 miles southwest of Cape Mendocino, Calif.

Chesapeake Bay Cleanup; Fishing Ban

In contrast to the bickering that marks the sludge and toxic waste issues, recent efforts to clean up the Chesapeake Bay have demonstrated that the states and federal government can work together. The bay is the largest estuary in the United States and one of the most productive shellfish and marine breeding grounds in the world. It covers 2,500 square miles and is fed by 150 rivers, creeks and streams that flow through six states. Concern over bay pollution prompted Congress in 1976 to direct the EPA to conduct a five-year study of the bay's water quality and resources. The $27-million study, released early this year, documented the decline in the bay's aquatic life and pinpointed the main sources of pollution.

Among its findings: excessive amounts of nutrients from agricultural runoff and urban wastewater have stimulated growth of undesirable plants, such as algae, that rob the water of oxygen needed to sustain marine life; and high concentrations of toxic organic compounds and heavy metals in sediments at the bottom of the bay. "[I]t is clearly established that nutrient loadings have substantially increased, and massive quantities of toxicants have entered this system, and that the unchecked increases of these pollutants threatens important resources," the report concluded.[34]

This year President Reagan endorsed the bay cleanup in his State of the Union message and during the summer made a quick tour of the area — a trip characterized in the press as an election-year attempt to counter environmentalist attacks on his record. The president said he supported a four-year federal commitment of $10 million annually to aid in cleanup activities. This is in addition to the roughly $200 million EPA will spend

[33] P. Kiho Park, et al. "Disposal of Radioactive Wastes in the Ocean," *Sea Technology,* January 1984, p. 66.

[34] "Chesapeake Bay Program: Findings and Recommendations," Environmental Protection Agency, September 1983, p. 24.

on upgrading sewage treatment plants in the bay basin in fiscal year 1985 — the same level of commitment the agency has made for the past several years.

The report spurred Maryland, Virginia, Pennsylvania and the District of Columbia to form a cooperative council to solve the bay's problems. Maryland Gov. Harry R. Hughes made the bay cleanup a priority of his administration and took the lead in persuading others to join in the effort. The Maryland General Assembly voted to spend $36 million this year on the bay, Virginia added $13.4 million and Pennsylvania $1 million. These sums are relatively small in comparison to $1 billion in specific recommendations in the EPA report. But they are an important start, said Virginia Tippie, technical coordinator of the federally funded Chesapeake Bay Program in Annapolis, Md.

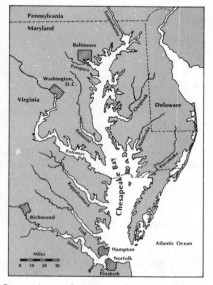

Before its adjournment in October, Congress approved $2.3 million for the National Oceanic and Atmospheric Administration to study bay fisheries. Oysters, blue crabs and soft-shelled clams are staples of the bay, and the basis of much of the area's family-dominated fishing industry. Pollution has reduced the catches of all three shellfish in recent years. No bay creature, however, has gotten more attention lately than its famed striped bass, also known as rockfish.

The fish, long prized by commercial and sports fishermen, have become so scarce that Maryland has decided to ban all striped bass fishing in its waters, beginning Jan. 1, 1985. Congress this fall passed legislation to prod all Atlantic Coast states to set a 24-inch minimum size for striped bass caught in the ocean and a 14-inch limit for those caught in state waters. If a state does not reduce its annual catch by 55 percent, the U.S. secretary of commerce could declare a moratorium on striped bass fishing in that state. Since 1973, catches of striped bass have dropped by nearly 90 percent, costing the Northeastern fishing industry more than 7,000 jobs and over $220 million in economic activity. While there is disagreement over what caused the decline, some point to pollution in the bay, the spawning ground for 90 percent of the East Coast striped bass.

Selected Bibliography

Books

Barth, Michael C., and James G. Titus, *Greenhouse Effect and Sea Level Rise, A Challenge for This Generation,* Van Nostrand Reinhold, 1984.

Pilkey, Orrin H. Sr., et al., *Coastal Design, A Guide for Builders, Planners, & Homeowners,* Van Nostrand Reinhold, 1984.

Articles

Begley, Sharon, "The Vanishing Coasts," *Newsweek,* Sept. 24, 1984.

Caudle, Neil, "The Ocean Is Coming, The Ocean Is Coming," *Coast Watch,* University of North Carolina Sea Grant, January 1984.

Harvey, Susan, "Federal Consistency and OCS Oil and Gas Development: A Review and Assessment of the 'Directly Affecting' Controversy," *Ocean Development and International Law,* Vol. 13, No. 4, 1983.

"Outer Continental Shelf Revenue Sharing Compromise," and "Consistency," Coastal States Organization fact sheets, 1984.

Reed, Phillip D., "Supreme Court Beaches Coastal Zone Management Act," *Environmental Law Reporter,* April 1984.

Reports and Studies

Godschalk, David R., "Impacts of the Coastal Barrier Resources Act," U.S. Department of Commerce, Office of Ocean and Coastal Resource Management, March 1984.

Editorial Research Reports: "America's Disappearing Wetlands," 1983 Vol. II, p. 613; "Troubled Ocean Fisheries," 1984 Vol. I, p. 429; "Offshore Oil Search," 1973 Vol. II, p. 537; "Coastal Conservation," 1970 Vol. I, p. 139.

Hoffman, J., D. Keyes and J. Titus, "Projecting Future Sea Level Rise," U.S. Government Printing Office, No. 055-000-023603, 1983.

National Advisory Committee on Oceans and Atmosphere, "The Exclusive Economic Zone of the United States: Some Immediate Policy Issues," May 1984.

National Planning Association, "Coastal Zone Management as Land Planning," October 1984.

Seidel, S., D. Keyes, "Can We Delay a Greenhouse Warming?" U.S. Government Printing Office, No. 055-0000-00235-5, 1983.

U.S. Department of Commerce, "Climate Impact Assessment United States, Annual Summary 1983," July 1984.

—— "Biennial Report to the Congress on Coastal Zone Management, Fiscal Years 1982 and 1983," Office of Ocean and Coastal Resource Management, September 1984.

U.S. Environmental Protection Agency, "Chesapeake Bay Program: Findings and Recommendations," September 1983.

U.S. House of Representatives, "Ocean and Coastal Resources Management and Development Block Grant," Report 98-206, 1983.

Graphics: cover photo of Cape Hatteras lihgthouse by Clay Nolen, North Carolina Travel and Tourism Division; p. 109 photo from City of Miami Beach; illustrations and maps by staff artists.

PREVENTING GROUNDWATER CONTAMINATION

by

Roger Thompson

July 12
1 9 8 5

Editor's Update: Congress on March 21, 1986, approved a two-month extension of the "superfund" waste-cleanup program *(see p. 130)* to gain time for settling differences between House and Senate bills to renew the program. For fiscal years 1986-90, the House would allot EPA about $10 billion; the Senate figure was $7.5 billion. The Reagan administration had requested between $4.5 billion and $5.3 billion.

Environmentalists hailed passage of the House version, which required stricter EPA standards and placed tax burdens primarily on the oil and chemical industries, but the Senate and the administration will press for compromise.

House and Senate conferees on March 17, 1986, reached tentative agreement on reauthorization of the 1974 Safe Drinking Water Act *(see p. 129)*. In a House-Senate compromise, the House bill's requirement that states submit underground drinking water protection plans for EPA approval was restricted to areas designated by the states as most likely to be contaminated. The Reagan administration expressed "serious reservations" about such federal involvement in "sensitive local land use and water rights decisions."

PREVENTING GROUNDWATER CONTAMINATION

FOR EVERY GALLON of fresh water flowing in the nation's rivers and confined by lakes, roughly 24 more are hidden underground — enough to fill the Great Lakes at least four times. Groundwater forms a vast natural resource that has grown in importance even as it has become increasingly endangered. U.S. consumption of groundwater rose from 34 billion gallons a day in 1950 to 88 billion gallons a day in 1980. Approximately half the nation now depends on groundwater — often untreated — for drinking water. Yet contaminated groundwater has been reported in every state. Household, farm and industrial wastes are being detected in the nation's underground water supplies with increasing frequency.

Groundwater protection is limited in part because there is no explicit national policy to protect its quality. There are, however, numerous federal and state laws that affect groundwater quality by regulating activities and substances that pollute it. At least 16 federal statutes authorize programs that in some way touch on groundwater protection. All 50 states have groundwater programs of some type; some have tougher regulations than those required under federal laws. Taken together, these programs have made significant strides in detecting, correcting and preventing groundwater contamination, particularly pollution caused by hazardous wastes.

Achievements under these programs have been significant but have not solved the problem. The federal "Superfund" program has cleaned up relatively few of the abandoned hazardous-waste sites scattered across the country. Instead of encouraging waste recycling and incineration, restrictions on land dumping have increased the use of deep-well injection to get rid of hazardous waste. But there is no guarantee that wastes pumped deep into the earth eventually won't pollute nearby groundwater supplies. And scientific uncertainty about the health consequences of waterborne chemicals has turned federal standard-setting into regulatory quicksand, leaving disposal of many known contaminants uncontrolled.

Nonetheless, Congress in recent years has attempted to strengthen hazardous-waste laws to prevent further ground water pollution. The House twice has approved measures that would require states to develop groundwater protection plans. Meanwhile, Sen. Dave Durenberger, R-Minn., is holding hearings on groundwater and intends to propose comprehensive protection legislation this fall. A House subcommittee has also announced that it will hold oversight hearings on groundwater pollution problems this fall.

There is some doubt in the environmental community, however, that separate legislation is necessary. "I'm not convinced that what is needed is a single, comprehensive bill vs. amendments to existing laws," said Velma M. Smith, director of the Environmental Policy Institute's groundwater protection project.[1] Strengthening current laws may meet less political resistance than developing a new groundwater package, she added.

Groundwater's Growing Importance to Society

Ninty-seven percent of all water on Earth is in the ocean, and 2 percent is frozen, leaving about one million cubic miles of fresh water available for human use. Roughly 4 percent of this is surface water contained in lakes, rivers and streams; the rest lies underground, pumped to the surface through wells.[2] Of the 88 billion gallons of groundwater used each day in the United States, about two-thirds is used for irrigation; the remainder is used for industrial purposes and in public drinking water systems and private wells *(see graph, p. 125)*.

Groundwater is one of the least understood of the nation's natural resources. For years it was thought to run in underground streams or rivers. The soil above it was once believed to trap or neutralize all harmful wastes dumped there, leaving the subsurface water supply pure and safe for human consumption. Both notions proved wrong. "Only recently has the limited capacity of natural soil processes to change contaminants into harmless substances, before they reach groundwater, become widely recognized," a recent Office of Technology Assessment (OTA) study said.[4]

Groundwater collects in permeable strata of rock, sand or gravel called aquifers that usually lie within half a mile of the surface. The upper level, called the water table, can rise or fall depending on seasonal precipitation cycles and withdrawals by wells. The water in an aquifer flows with the slope of the underground formations at rates that range from a fraction of

---

[1] Persons quoted in this report were interviewed by the author unless otherwise noted.
[2] It is estimated that there are between 12 million and 14 million wells in this country.
[3] Wendy Gordon, *A Citizen's Handbook on Groundwater Protection*, 1984, pp. 10-11.
[4] Office of Technology Assessment, "Protecting the Nation's Groundwater from Contamination," U.S. Government Printing Office, October 1984, p. 5. The OTA is a nonpartisan research arm of the U.S. Congress.

an inch to several feet per day, an important consideration in tracking groundwater pollution. Typical daily flow covers only a few inches. Contaminants most often reach groundwater by percolating down through the soil and spreading out in a plume, like smoke emerging from an upside-down smokestack. The course of the plume is determined by the general groundwater flow *(see chart, p. 127).*

For most of this century, concern among health officials focused on drinking water contaminants, such as viruses and bacteria, that entered public supplies drawn from rivers and lakes. Chlorination was introduced as early as 1908 to rid drinking water of waterborne diseases such as cholera and typhoid. Chlorine works well as a disinfectant, but it has no effect on inorganic contaminants such as heavy metals — chromium, lead, mercury, tin and zinc — or on man-made organic

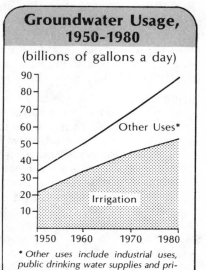

Groundwater Usage, 1950-1980

(billions of gallons a day)

Other uses include industrial uses, public drinking water supplies and private wells.

Source: Wendy Gordon: *A Citizen's Handbook on Groundwater Protection,* Natural Resources Defense Council Inc., 1984.

chemicals, many of which are toxic at levels registering in parts per billion.[5] These are the contaminants that are turning up not only in surface water but also in water pumped from underground.

Groundwater contaminants often reach much higher concentrations than surface water pollutants because there is little mixing and dispersal of toxic substances underground. Once contaminated, groundwater may remain so for hundreds of years. Cleaning a polluted aquifer is extremely difficult, if not impossible, with existing technology. Not surprisingly, the best solution to the problem is prevention.

Gauging the Magnitude of Pollution Problem

Estimates of the extent of groundwater contamination are based on educated guesswork. True levels may never be known because of the cost and technical requirements involved in

---

[5] Organic compounds are derived from carbon. Synthetic organic compounds such as solvents or pesticides are made from carbon-based raw materials.

developing quantitative assessments. Most experts believe that the level of contamination is relatively low. The OTA reported last year that only 1 or 2 percent of the nation's groundwater is believed to be polluted.[6] An Environmental Protection Agency (EPA) survey found that only about 3 percent of public water systems drawn from groundwater are contaminated at levels that exceed standards the agency is considering setting for many contaminants — 5 to 50 parts per billion.[7] But even at 1-3 percent, contamination is significant because it often appears in heavily populated areas where groundwater use is increasing.

And there is evidence that contamination is increasing:
● The Council on Environmental Quality reported in January 1981 that man-made organic chemicals had contaminated groundwater in at least 34 states.
● An EPA report released in June 1982 documented trace levels of one or more man-made organic compounds in 17 percent of the 285 small and 29 percent of the 181 large water systems randomly selected from the nation's 48,000 public drinking water systems drawn from groundwater.
● The following December, an EPA survey of 929 hazardous waste sites nationwide documented groundwater contamination at 128 and suspected contamination at 213 others.
● An OTA study issued in October 1984 found that incidents of groundwater contamination have now been reported in every state. Some 175 organic chemicals, 50 inorganic chemicals, biological organisms and radioactive contaminants have been detected in various groundwater supplies.

Many of these pollutants are known or suspected to cause adverse health effects, including skin and eye damage, damage to the central nervous system, kidney and liver disease, and cancer. Accurate information linking specific contaminants to specific health problems frequently is not available. People often do not know they are drinking bad water because many contaminants are colorless, odorless and tasteless. Even when it is known that people drank polluted water, medical science seldom can establish a definitive link between the bad water and disease.

One exception occurred in Woburn, Mass., where two city water wells were contaminated with chloroform and TCE (trichloroethylene). In February 1984 doctors reported that there was a statistically significant relationship between the

[6] Office of Technology Assessment, *op. cit.,* p. 21.
[7] Environmental Protection Agency, "Ground Water Protection Strategy," U.S. Government Printing Office, August 1984, p. 17.

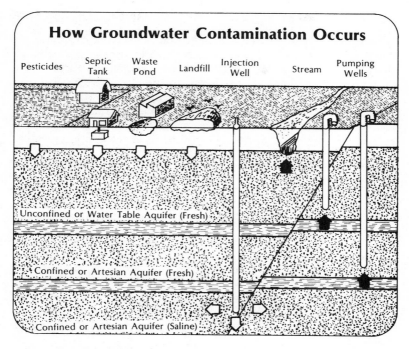

How Groundwater Contamination Occurs

Pesticides | Septic Tank | Waste Pond | Landfill | Injection Well | Stream | Pumping Wells

Unconfined or Water Table Aquifer (Fresh)

Confined or Artesian Aquifer (Fresh)

Confined or Artesian Aquifer (Saline)

Contamination from both "point" sources such as landfills and waste ponds and "non-point" sources such as pesticide runoff can leach into the soil and reach groundwater. Injecting hazardous liquid wastes into deep wells can also cause contamination if the well leaks or the liquid escapes through cracks and faults in the rock layers containing it. Contaminated groundwater reaches the surface through pumps, rivers and streams.

contamination and an increased incidence of childhood leukemia, birth defects and childhood disorders.

Multiple Sources of Water Contamination

A major source of groundwater contamination is improper or unsafe disposal of hazardous waste. More than 19,000 abandoned hazardous-waste dumps have been reported to the EPA; it is not known how many are polluting groundwater. Landfills not licensed to accept hazardous wastes may nonetheless contain substances that contaminate groundwater. EPA has identified 75,000 industrial landfills, about which little is known. In addition, there are 18,500 municipal landfills, but few states require regular monitoring of groundwater quality at these facilities. No one knows how many are leaking contaminants.[8] The number may be high because landfills frequently have been located on terrain regarded to have little commercial value, such as marshland, abandoned sand and gravel pits, old strip mines or limestone sinkholes, all of which act as conduits for contaminants.

---

[8] *Ibid.*, p. 14.

127

Similar problems affect 181,000 ponds and lagoons used to treat, store or dispose of wastes generated by oil and gas production, mining, numerous industrial processes, agricultural activities and urban populations. Most are not lined with a protective shield to prevent wastes from percolating into the soil. EPA has reported that about 40 percent of the industrial and municipal impoundments are located in areas with thin or permeable soils, over aquifers that are or could be used for drinking water.

Leaking storage tanks, primarily those below ground, pose another threat to groundwater. Tanks are used to store everything from gasoline and toxic chemicals to waste products. Some experts say that between 75,000 and 100,000 of the estimated 1.4 million gasoline storage tanks buried at service stations nationwide are leaking.

These "point sources" of pollution are the most thoroughly documented and regulated. "Non-point" sources generally escape regulation but also pose serious hazards. Major non-point pollution sources include highway de-icing salts, pesticide and fertilizer runoff from fields, tailing piles used in mining operations to dispose of rock and dirt, and accidental spills and leaks.

The nation's 20 million household septic tanks and seepage from livestock manure and agricultural fertilizers are major sources of nitrate contamination. The U.S. Geological Survey's 1984 National Water Summary reported that about 8,000 of nearly 124,000 wells surveyed contained nitrate concentrations that exceed federal standards for drinking water. Nitrate by itself is relatively harmless, but it can be converted to nitrite in the human body, causing a life-threatening disease in some infants and cancer risks among adults. The implications of the Geological Survey report may be more significant than the nitrate levels themselves. "The question is, if you have nitrates, what else do you have?" asked David W. Moody, chief of the agency's Water Summary and Long Range Planning Office.

Curbing Contaminants

A COMPREHENSIVE FEDERAL groundwater protection policy does not exist. In 1980, the last year of President Carter's administration, EPA proposed a national protection plan that would have classified groundwater according to use and encouraged states to develop their own protection plans. Many states, especially those in the arid West, objected to what they considered as federal interference in state water issues. The Reagan administration — already committed to reducing federal regulation — withdrew the proposal in 1981 for revision.

In August 1984, EPA issued its new "Ground Water Protection Strategy." The agency affirmed its belief that contamination is a severe problem growing worse, but it proposed no comprehensive federal legislation. Instead it said that EPA should provide support to state and local governments to help them develop groundwater contamination programs. Environmental groups said the agency had ducked the issue. "This is EPA's non-strategy," said Jackie Warren, who heads the Toxic Waste Project at the Natural Resources Defense Council in New York.

The following month the House approved a reauthorization of the 1974 Safe Drinking Water Act that required the EPA to monitor regularly underground drinking water sources and required the states to adopt plans, approved by the EPA, to protect those groundwater sources from contamination. Disagreement with the Senate over those and other provisions killed that bill. The House in June passed another reauthorization bill containing similar language. The differences between it and a Senate-passed version, which does not require the states to adopt groundwater protection plans, must be resolved before a final bill can be sent to the president. The Reagan administration opposes both measures in their present form.

The Safe Drinking Water Act is the only federal law designed to ensure safe water at the tap. In that law, Congress gave the EPA the authority to set quality standards and testing requirements for ground and surface water used by water systems serving more than 25 people and to regulate the disposal of liquid wastes into deep wells *(see p. 132)*. The agency has been criticized for moving too slowly in both areas.

Since 1974, the EPA has set 22 drinking water standards covering coliform bacteria, turbidity (cloudiness), man-made and naturally occurring radioactive materials, six pesticides and trihalomethanes — organic chemicals that contain chloroform, a carcinogen frequently found in drinking water. Environmental groups contend that the EPA has been too cautious in issuing regulations to remove many other contaminants from drinking water. "The legislative history [of the drinking water act] says that if there is uncertainty, err on the side of safety," Warren said. "In 10 years, their list does not contain most of the hazardous chemicals found in groundwater. The EPA says, 'We don't know, we're not sure.' But are we going to continue to use the public as a testing laboratory?"

Arnold Kuzmack, acting deputy director of the EPA's Office of Drinking Water, cast the agency's efforts in a different light. "The regulatory process requires more and more detailed back-up that will stand up to court challenges. That means it takes a lot longer to make certain any piece of regulation is absolutely right." He added that the agency intends to issue standards for a number of additional organic chemicals later this year. Both the House and Senate reauthorization bills would require EPA to set standards for more than 60 contaminants within three years.[9]

Cleaning Up Abandoned Toxic-Waste Dumps

Congress also is working on measures to extend and expand the Superfund program to clean up abandoned hazardous-waste dumps, many of which have polluted or threaten groundwater.[10] Five years after Congress first passed Superfund legislation, it is clear that waste-dump contamination of soil and water is far more pervasive, more expensive to handle and more difficult to remedy than initially thought. The EPA currently estimates that there are from 1,400 to 2,200 waste sites that eventually will require cleanup. The OTA puts the figure as high as 10,000. Depending on the actual number of sites, the cleanup could cost between $10 billion and $100 billion and take up to 50 years to complete, according to the technology office. Funding for the first five years was set at $1.6 billion.

Of the 800 sites on the EPA's priority cleanup list at the end of 1984, only six have been fully restored. The agency has begun to clean up 62 more sites and won commitments from private parties to clean up 72 others. In some cases, the problems have only been transferred elsewhere. "Some restoration efforts have consisted merely of transferring wastes from the contaminated areas to [hazardous waste] landfills, which themselves could be leaking," the Congressional Budget Office (CBO) said in a recent report.[11]

The OTA has urged the EPA to change its cleanup strategy. Rather than trying to clean permanently a limited number of the worst sites, leaving most abandoned dumps untouched, the OTA in an April report advised a limited cleanup of all sites on the priority list. "Initial responses that accomplish the most significant and cost-effective reduction of risks and prevent sites from getting worse might cost about $1 million per site for most sites," the OTA said.[12] To minimize groundwater

[9] For background on the Safe Drinking Water Act renewal, see *Congressional Quarterly Weekly Report*, June 22, 1985, p. 1216.
[10] For background, see *Congressional Quarterly Weekly Report*, June 29, 1985, p. 1281.
[11] Congressional Budget Office, "Hazardous Waste Management: Recent Changes and Policy Alternatives," U.S. Government Printing Office, May 1985, p. 31.
[12] Office of Technology Assessment, "Superfund Strategy," U. S. Government Printing Office, April 1985, p. 3.

Wastes from dumps can leach into the soil, causing groundwater contamination.

contamination, the strategy emphasized covering sites and storing wastes, and excavating wastes only where technically and economically feasible. Phase two of the strategy would focus on permanent cleanup once specific goals were set and technologies available to remedy the problem.

Controlling Disposal of Hazardous Wastes

Congress passed the Resource Conservation and Recovery Act (RCRA) in 1976 to prevent future hazardous-dump problems. The act set minimum requirements for storage, treatment and disposal of corrosive, explosive, ignitible or toxic wastes. Facilities covered under the law included storage tanks; surface impoundments; waste piles; land treatment sites; landfills; incinerators; thermal, physical and biological treatment operations; and injection wells. It required those who generate or handle hazardous wastes to obtain an operating permit from the EPA or from states with RCRA programs approved by the agency. Under the act, the EPA has listed more than 400 specific wastes for regulation. A tracking system requires an EPA manifest to accompany each of these wastes at each stage of shipment, storage, treatment, recycling and final disposal. The agency delegates most enforcement to the states.

The EPA got off to a slow start in implementing RCRA. Final regulations for land disposal of hazardous wastes, for example, were not issued until Jan. 26, 1983. Through 1984, the EPA and states with approved programs had issued only 968 final permits to the estimated 5,000 treatment, storage and disposal facilities that eventually must have permits to stay in operation. Moreover, even facilities that meet RCRA guidelines may not be safe over the long run. According to the Congressional Budget Office, 45 RCRA-regulated facilities have been closed and are now listed for cleanup under the Superfund. "[I]t is unclear whether the EPA can prevent more RCRA-regulated sites from becoming future Superfund candidates," the CBO said.[13]

Congress attempted to strengthen RCRA last year with passage of the Hazardous and Solid Waste Amendments of 1984. The toughest new provision would ban land disposal of all bulk liquid hazardous wastes. It also set a series of deadlines for the EPA to determine whether 400 hazardous wastes adversely affected health or the environment. If the EPA did not act by the deadline for each specified contaminant, land disposal of that contaminant would be banned. Operators of hazardous-waste landfills were required to provide double liners, groundwater monitoring, leak detection and collection of contaminants that leach into the surrounding soil. The amendments also regulated underground storage tanks, primarily gasoline tanks, for the first time.

Under the original act, the EPA did not require generators of less than one metric ton (2,200 pounds) a month of hazardous waste to dispose of their wastes in RCRA-approved facilities. Consequently, these wastes often were dumped into city landfills or sewers connected with city wastewater treatment plants. To protect both surface and underground public water supplies, the amended act lowered the regulatory threshold to 100 kilograms a month.[14]

The cost of compliance with RCRA regulations runs into the billions annually and is expected to climb under the new amendments. The CBO put annual industry expenditures, without considering available tax benefits, between $4.2 billion and $5.8 billion in 1983. The figure is expected to increase to between $8.4 billion and $11.2 billion in 1990.

Concern Over Safety of Deep-Well Disposal

The RCRA amendments imposed relatively few restrictions on deep-well injection operations. Environmental groups consider this a loophole in the law that could result in greater groundwater contamination. Deep-well injection already handles 58 percent of the nation's hazardous wastes, an estimated 10 billion gallons a year. With land disposal limited by the 1984 RCRA amendments, deep-well injection has become more attractive as a cheap alternative to recycling or destroying hazardous wastes. "I've personally witnessed a flood of deep-well injection permit requests [nationwide] since passage of the RCRA amendments," said Suzi Ruhl, a lawyer with the Legal Environmental Assistance Foundation in Tallahassee, Fla. The

[13] Congressional Budget Office, *op. cit.*, p. 62.
[14] For background, see *1984 Congressional Quarterly Almanac*, p. 305.

EPA has estimated that it costs roughly $8 a ton to inject wastes into deep wells, $28 a ton to impound them in ponds and $50 a ton to dump them into landfills.[15] Resource recovery and treatment technologies can run into hundreds of dollars a ton, although many of these techniques are in a competitive range with deep-well and surface disposal *(see p. 137)*.

Injection of hazardous wastes into deep wells began in the 1950s as environmental laws began to protect surface waters from pollution. The wells carry wastes to porous sedimentary formations, typically sandstone, that lie between one-quarter mile and a mile below the surface. The wells are separated from drinking water aquifers by an impermeable layer of rock that theoretically seals the waste in an underground tomb *(see chart)*. In practice, however, liquid waste occasionally has found its way to the surface, raising the specter of major groundwater pollution problems. Leaks also have been found in well casings, allowing pollutants to escape into the soil.

A 1984 EPA survey found 525 active hazardous-waste deep wells at 90 separate sites nationwide. Approximately two-thirds of the wells are in Texas and Louisiana. The next largest grouping, about 20 percent, are in the Great Lakes region. The chemical industry is the biggest user of deep-well injection, followed by the petroleum refining and petrochemical industries. The EPA reports that about 41 percent of the injected wastes are corrosive and 36 percent are organic compounds. It is feared

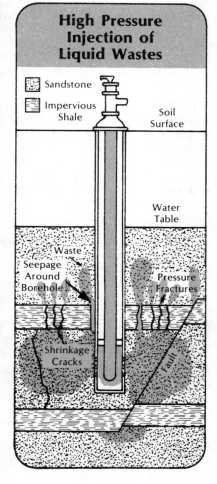

High Pressure Injection of Liquid Wastes

Sandstone

Impervious Shale

Soil Surface

Water Table

Waste Seepage Around Borehole

Pressure Fractures

Shrinkage Cracks

Fault

[15] Wendy Gordon and Jane Bloom, *Deeper Problems: Limits to Underground Injection as a Hazardous Waste Disposal Method,* Natural Resources Defense Council, June 1985, p. 6.

that corrosive waste may eat its way through the impermeable overlying rock and escape into groundwater.

It is the inability to ensure that wastes injected underground will remain where they are placed that most troubles those opposed to the method. "Great gaps in our knowledge of the subsurface and our inability to predict accurately the movement of wastes underground make it difficult, if not impossible, to ensure that, once pumped down the well, hazardous wastes will permanently remain within the zone of confinement," wrote Jane L. Bloom, an attorney for the Natural Resources Defense Council.[16]

In their book, *Deeper Problems: Limits to Underground Injection as a Hazardous Waste Disposal Method*, Bloom and Wendy Gordon cited 13 deep-well failures from "a lengthy list of documented instances" and noted that "several resulted in contamination of drinking water supplies and groundwater resources." One of the most recent occurred in Vickery, Ohio, where in 1983 it was discovered that 20 million gallons of waste had leaked from a commercial deep-well injection facility.[17]

The House version of the Safe Drinking Act reauthorization would bar disposal of hazardous waste by underground injection above or into any geological formation within one quarter mile of a drinking water source. Environmentalists contend that at the least deep-well operators should be subject to the same standards as operators of land disposal facilities. Currently, deep-well operators are not required to demonstrate financial responsibility for cleanup activity or payment of damages to those harmed by leaks. Nor are they required to monitor groundwater near injection sites for contamination. Although monitoring of the well casing is required under the Safe Drinking Water Act, slow leaks often escape detection.

At congressional direction, the EPA studied deep-well injection operations, issuing an interim report in May. "The critical item of information is that we have found only three cases of drinking water contamination [from deep-well injection]," the EPA's Arnold Kuzmack explained later. "And all three would have been prevented under current regulations. We have no cases of contamination that the current regulatory framework wouldn't handle. We find it difficult to conclude that there is a terrible problem. We certainly don't have the problem with deep wells that we have with landfills."

[16] Jane L. Bloom, "The RCRA Amendments and Groundwater," *Environment*, January/February 1985, p. 44.
[17] Chemical Waste Management, owner of the facility, was fined $10 million by the Ohio Environmental Protection Agency and $2.5 million by EPA. Together, the fines represent the largest administrative penalties in EPA history.

"The only way they haven't found problems is they haven't looked," said Ruhl, who has traveled extensively in her work on deep-well problems. Richard C. Fortuna, executive director of the Hazardous Waste Treatment Council, said the EPA surveyed only 20 of the 90 deep-well injection sites nationwide when the agency should have surveyed them all. "The Office of Drinking Water clearly is in love with the technology it is charged to regulate," said Fortuna, who represents 40 firms in the business of hazardous-waste treatment, recycling and disposal.

Turning to Alternatives

BY DISCOURAGING land disposal of hazardous wastes, the 1984 RCRA amendments were intended to promote the use of safer methods, such as chemical treatment to reduce hazards, incineration to destroy wastes, and chemical stabilization to neutralize hazardous wastes so they are no longer harmful. Yet, current incentives for waste reduction and treatment may be inadequate, the CBO warned in its hazardous-waste report. "[W]aste reduction incentives could easily disappear in an atmosphere of regulatory uncertainty," the report said.[18] If industry delays investments in waste reduction measures until the last minute, or commercial treatment facilities cannot be built fast enough to keep up with demand, the landfill ban might have to be eased, the CBO analysts said. If industry makes no effort to reduce its volume of hazardous waste, national production may rise from the 266 million metric tons recorded in 1983 to about 280 million metric tons in 1990, according to the budget office.

Disturbed by this prospect, some have urged Congress to approve a waste disposal tax to prod industry to generate less waste and to force development of treatment technologies.[19] The tax on wastes disposed of in landfills would be higher than the tax on safer disposal methods. Twenty states already have imposed various types of waste-end taxes on hazardous-waste generators.[20] But the EPA says it is unclear if these taxes have had their intended effect. "All personnel responding to the survey were cautious about ascribing [reported] management

---

[18] Congressional Budget Office, *op. cit.*, p. 61.
[19] A tax of $2.13 a dry weight ton is already levied for certain hazardous-waste disposal units to help finance the Superfund.
[20] The states are Alabama, California, Colorado, Connecticut, Illinois, Indiana, Iowa, Kansas, Kentucky, Louisiana, Maine, Minnesota, Mississippi, Missouri, New Hampshire, New York, Ohio, South Carolina, Tennessee, and Wisconsin.

changes directly to the waste-end tax," the EPA reported after surveying eight of the 20 states.[21]

The Reagan administration has proposed a waste-end tax to help finance Superfund. It would tax waste disposal on land at $10.78 a metric ton; waste disposed of by other methods would be taxed at $2.87 a metric ton. To maintain a stable revenue base for Superfund cleanup operations, waste-end tax rates would go up each year as waste production went down.

The Congressional Budget Office, however, questioned whether the proposal would bring about the anticipated shift toward safer waste management practices, saying an $8-a-ton tax difference was "too small to erode the cost advantage currently held by landfills over more advanced technologies." [22] The budget office said at least a $20-a-ton difference was needed to accomplish the goal of recycling and incineration. It suggested a schedule of $25 a metric ton for untreated wastes placed in landfills, $5 a metric ton for treated wastes, $4 a metric ton for wastes injected into wells, and no tax for wastes that are incinerated, recycled or reused.

Environmental groups contend that the administration's proposal would only encourage the continued use of deep wells. "Taxing deep-well injection at one-third or one-fifth of what you tax land disposal isn't the way to encourage recycling or destruction of wastes," said Warren of the Natural Resources Defense Council. "As long as deep-well injection is cheap, we won't see much change."

For similar reasons, environmental groups also oppose the so-called "dry weight" tax of $50 a ton recommended by the Chemical Manufacturers Association. Dry weight is measured by subtracting the free water content of wastes from the total weight, which would exempt from taxation roughly 95 percent of what is pumped into deep wells. The Hazardous Waste Treatment Council also opposes the dry weight tax. "If a waste-based tax is included [in Superfund, it should] ensure that injection is taxed on a wet weight basis and on par with other land disposal methods," the council's Executive Director Fortuna told a House subcommittee in May.

The House Energy and Commerce subcommittee version of the Superfund reauthorization envisions a $1.5 billion waste-end tax but has left the specifics to the tax-writing Ways and Means Committee. The Senate bill, which was awaiting floor action at the beginning of July, contained no waste-end tax.

---

[21] Environmental Protection Agency, "Draft Survey of States' Experience with Waste-End Taxes," EPA Office of Policy Analysis, September 1984, p. 9.
[22] Congressional Budget Office, *op. cit.,* p. 70.

Other Federal Laws Affecting Groundwater

In addition to the Safe Drinking Water Act, the Resource Conservation and Recovery Act and the "Superfund" law, several other federal statutes affect groundwater quality.

Among these are the Clean Water Act of 1977, which is designed to restore and maintain the quality of the nation's ground and surface water supplies; the Coastal Zone Management Act of 1976, which contains provisions to prevent salt water intrusion into freshwater supplies; and the Federal Insecticide, Fungicide, and Rodenticide Act, which regulates pesticide use, storage and disposal.

The Hazardous Liquid Pipeline Safety Act of 1979 and the Hazardous Materials Transportation Act of 1974 seek to control the safe transport of hazardous substances. And the Atomic Energy Act of 1954 regulates storage and disposal of radioactive wastes.

The debate over a waste-end tax raises an important question: Are there available alternatives to the current methods of hazardous-waste disposal? The answer, Fortuna said, is an unequivocal "yes." "There is no doubt that a method or combination of methods exist to manage every waste being deep-welled in an alternative manner that is protective of human health and the environment," he told the House subcommittee.

Technologies for Recycling, Reducing Waste

Gordon and Bloom cited four existing alternatives in their book: [23]

● Acidic wastes can be neutralized by mixing them with alkalines, or vice versa. "[N]eutralization is a straightforward and inexpensive treatment that yields a nonhazardous effluent that can be discharged to a waterway," Gordon and Bloom wrote, adding that the treatment costs between $23 and $101 a ton.

● Highly dilute waste (95 percent or more water) can be treated with the PACT system, which uses activated carbon — an adsorbent — in conjunction with conventional biological waste treatment. Operating costs are estimated at $4-$6 a ton.

● Moderately toxic wastes can be treated with a thermal process called wet air oxidation. The wastes are heated to temperatures between 450 and 600 degrees Fahrenheit at high pressure ranging up to 3,000 pounds a square inch. The process breaks down wastes such as cyanides, sulfides, hydrocarbons, pesticides, herbicides, scrubbing liquors and cleanup residues into simple bio-

---

[23] Gordon and Bloom, *op. cit.*, p. 33-39.

degradable substances. While wet air oxidation facilities are expensive to build, operating costs can be as low as $4-$8 a ton.

● Highly concentrated wastes can be incinerated, which is effective for all but a few highly persistent chemicals. Fuel costs to incinerate highly dilute waste ranges between $150 and $1,000 a ton. But costs can be reduced by mixing wastewater with concentrated solid wastes that become fuel for the process.

Fortuna noted that the Japanese already are using activated carbon treatment and wet oxidation to destroy wastes generated by the production of ethylene, a major organic chemical used as a building block for thousands of products, and acrylonitrile, a common component of plastics.

However efficient these processes may be, they are in short supply and cost millions to install, the CBO observed. For example, it could cost $15 million to build an incinerator to handle roughly 24,000 metric tons of waste a year, considered an average flow for a petrochemical manufacturer. To comply with the RCRA amendments, companies that cannot afford to install treatment facilities will be forced to ship their wastes to commercial facilities. The budget office calculates that demand for off-site treatment will double from 10 million metric tons a year to between 17 million and 25 million metric tons by 1990. "This increase should easily outstrip existing treatment capacity, causing shortfalls if new facilities are not built," the budget office warned.[24] Collecting and transporting hazardous waste to off-site treatment facilities also poses safety problems involving spills or accidents.

Benefits to Business of Waste Prevention

Because getting rid of hazardous waste is becoming increasingly expensive and difficult, some companies are looking for ways to prevent or reduce wastes. "People are just beginning to find that control at the end of the pipe is a pretty expensive proposition," said Robert P. Bringer, executive director of environmental and pollution control at Minnesota Mining & Manufacturing Co.[25] 3M pioneered the notion that "pollution prevention pays" a decade ago. One example: last year the company redesigned its sandpaper-making operation. The modifications are expected to save the company $845,000 a year and cut hazardous-waste production by 400 tons a year.

U.S. Steel has also reported success with waste reduction. The company has cut waste production in half and reduced landfill

[24] Congressional Budget Office, *op. cit.*, p. 61.
[25] Quoted by Alix M. Freedman in "Firms Curb Hazardous Waste to Avoid Expensive Disposal," *The Wall Street Journal*, May 31, 1985, p. 25.

use by 80 percent in five years. For example, sludge residues from coke plants now are mixed with tars and converted into fuel rather than discarded.

These are not isolated examples, says Donald Huisingh, an environmental studies professor at North Carolina State University in Raleigh and an editor of *Making Pollution Prevention Pay*. "There are many technologies already on the shelf that are technically, economically and financially sound," he said. Huisingh documented successful efforts taken by 25 North Carolina companies that cut waste production between 25 and 100 percent. In each case, he added, "the benefits paid for the process modifications in a short period of time."

"We've spent 20 years adding things on the tail end of production to control pollution," Huisingh said. "Now it's time

---

"We've spent 20 years adding things on the tail end of production to control pollution. Now it's time to ... redesign industrial systems to think of pollution prevention."

Donald Huisingh
Editor, *Making Pollution Prevention Pay*

---

to redirect our thinking to redesign industrial systems to think of pollution prevention. 3M has saved $192 million over 10 years with its pollution prevention program. And they still haven't run out of ideas."

A combination of government policies and enlightened industrial self-interest has the potential to reduce the current hazardous-waste threat to the nation's groundwater resources. But there are still questions about how to control groundwater contamination from pesticide and fertilizer runoff, septic tank seepage and other non-point sources. And there remains the question whether solutions to these problems are best left to the individual states or should be addressed by a coordinated program at the federal level.

Selected Bibliography

Books

Gordon, Wendy, *A Citizen's Handbook on Groundwater Protection,* Natural Resources Defense Council, 1984.

Gordon, Wendy, and Jane Bloom, *Deeper Problems: Limits to Underground Injection as a Hazardous Waste Disposal Method,* Natural Resources Defense Council, 1985.

Huisingh, Donald, and Vicki Bailey, eds., *Making Pollution Prevention Pay: Ecology with Economy As Policy,* Pergamon, 1982.

Keough, Carol, *Water Fit to Drink,* Rodale Press, 1980.

Pye, Veronica I., Ruth Patrick and John Quarles, *Groundwater Contamination in the United States,* University of Pennsylvania Press, 1983.

Welsh, Frank, *How to Create a Water Crisis,* Johnson Books, 1985.

Articles

Culver, Alicia and Rose Marie Audette, "Danger's in the Well," *Environmental Action,* March/April 1985.

"How Safe is Deep-Well Disposal of Waste?" *Chemical Week,* Nov. 21, 1984.

Reports and Studies

California Assembly Office of Research, "The Leaching Fields, A Non-Point Threat to Groundwater," March 1985.

Congressional Budget Office, "Hazardous Waste Management: Recent Changes and Policy Alternatives," May 1985.

Council on Environmental Quality, "Contamination of Groundwater by Toxic Organic Chemicals," U.S. Government Printing Office, January 1981.

Editorial Research Reports: "Environmental Conflicts in the 1980s," 1985 Vol. I, p. 121; "America's Disappearing Wetlands," 1983 Vol. II, p. 613; "Drinking Water Safety," 1974 Vol. I, p. 121.

Environmental Protection Agency, "Groundwater Protection Strategy," August 1984.

Feliciano, Donald V., "Underground Injection of Wastes," Congressional Research Service, Report No. 83-195 ENR, Oct. 20, 1983.

General Accounting Office, "Federal and State Efforts to Protect Groundwater," U.S. Government Printing Office, GAO/RCED 84-80, Feb. 21, 1984.

Office of Technology Assessment, "Superfund Strategy," U.S. Government Printing Office, OTA-ITE-252, April 1985.

——, "Protecting the Nation's Groundwater From Contamination," U.S. Government Printing Office, OTA-O-233, October 1984.

U.S. Geological Survey, "National Water Summary 1984," U.S. Government Printing Office, 1985.

Graphics: Cover illustration, p. 133 graphic by Assistant Art Director Robert Redding; p. 127 graphic by Patrick Murphy; p. 125 graphic by Staff Artist Kathleen Ossenfort; photo, p. 131, Louisville *Courier-Journal.*

WHALING:
END OF AN ERA

by

Marc Leepson

**Sept. 27
1 9 8 5**

Editor's Update: Although the International Whaling Commision's (IWC) moratorium on commercial whaling went into full effect with the current season, several nations continued limited whaling operations. Japan made its promise to end all commercial whaling by March 1988 dependent on reversal of U.S. court decisions reducing Japanese fishing rights in American waters. Seeking such a reversal, the Reagan administration appealed to the U.S. Supreme Court, whose decision is expected before the 1986 term ends.

The Soviet Union, its U.S. coastal fishing quota cut in half in retaliation for whaling operations, engaged in no direct fishing in U.S. waters in 1985. The Soviets had indicated their intention to suspend commercial whaling by 1988.

Like Japan and the Soviet Union, Norway had filed with the IWC an objection to the moratorium. Such an objection frees a country from obligation to observe the moratorium, and by March 1986 Norway had not yet indicated whether it will follow Japan and the Soviet Union by setting a date for halting its whaling.

The Marcos government in the Philippines, although it had not filed an objection to the moratorium, had indicated it would continue whaling; the government that replaced Marcos in February 1986 has enunciated no whaling policy. Brazil has indicated it would not engage in whaling, but Iceland and South Korea informed the IWC they would hunt whales for "scientific research."

WHALING: END OF AN ERA

HERMAN MELVILLE shipped out on the whaling vessel *Acushnet* early in 1841 from New Bedford, Mass., bound for Cape Horn and the South Pacific. The 22-year-old was between jobs during a period of hard times. But it was a boom time for the New England whaling industry. More than 700 American ships prowled the seas in search of whales during the 1840s. New Bedford was the busiest whaling port in the world. Crewing on a whaler was difficult and dangerous, and Melville left his ship in mid-voyage after 18 months. But his adventures were the fodder for *Moby Dick*, which many believe is the quintessential American novel.

Commercial whaling changed radically just a few years after the 1851 publication of *Moby Dick*. By the late 1860s the explosive harpoon had replaced the hand-thrown weapon used in Melville's day, and steam-powered catcher boats allowed whalers to hunt faster-swimming whales and to range farther in search of them. By the end of the 1930s whaling fleets from around the world had drastically depleted the numbers of eight of the nine largest species of whales, a group of mammals known as the great whales.

World War II interrupted nearly all commercial whaling, but in the late 1940s a handful of nations resumed operations. At the same time several nations with whaling industries took steps to ensure a continuous supply of whales, an effort that until recently was characterised more by political dissension than success. However, all but a handful of countries — notably the Soviet Union and Japan — have agreed to end commercial whaling in 1986, and those two countries have indicated they will end their operations in 1988.

Some conservationists believe that may be too late for some species. Whalers were prohibited from hunting the slow-swimming right whale in 1936. But it is estimated that fewer than 4,000 right whales live today. "The population is at best stabilized, or at worst continuing to decline...," said Peter Dykstra, a spokesman for Greenpeace, the environmental action group.[1] Bowhead whales, which swim in extreme northern waters, also were decimated in the late 19th century. Although

---

[1] Dykstra and others quoted in this report were interviewed by the author unless otherwise indicated.

bowheads have not been hunted commercially since 1935, there are believed to be fewer than 5,000 alive today. Six other great whales — the gray, blue, fin, sei, humpback and sperm — are considered endangered due to overharvesting.[2]

IWC Imposition of Commercial Moratorium

Concerned by a decline in whale stocks, several whaling nations set up the International Whaling Commission (IWC) in 1946 to try to safeguard the whales and keep the industry alive *(see p. 154)*. The commission was empowered to set limits on the catches of different species. Nearly everyone agrees that the IWC has failed to achieve either goal. "It is widely known that the International Whaling Commission . . . presided during the first 20 years of its existence over the depletion of nearly all the world's whale populations," British biologist Sidney Holt, a longtime international fisheries expert, asserted. "And the whaling industry, instead of enjoying an orderly development, experienced a disorderly, though long drawn-out, collapse." [3]

The discovery in the 1960s that the blue whale, the largest creature that has ever lived on Earth, was in danger of extinction sparked an international "Save the Whales" campaign.[4] Wildlife, environmental, animal-welfare and conservation groups lobbied heavily to get nations to stop commercial whaling. The IWC first discussed a ban in 1972. But 10 years passed before the commission in 1982 voted to phase out all commercial whaling by 1986.

Under the terms of the IWC charter, nations that file formal objections to commission rulings do not have to abide by them. Japan, Norway and the Soviet Union — the nations with the largest commercial whaling operations — promptly filed the requisite formal complaints.[5] Japan and Norway claimed that the ban was not based on scientific evidence and would wipe out profitable domestic whaling industries. The Soviet Union said that "political considerations," not scientific information, motivated the whaling ban. Since that time, however, Japan and the Soviet Union have indicated they would end their commercial ocean whaling operations by 1988. And it is expected that Norway will follow suit. "The handwriting is on the wall for

---

[2] The Bryde's whale, the ninth great whale, is not considered to be in danger of extinction. The great whales are cetaceans, as are smaller whales such as minke, pilot and killer whales, dolphins and porpoises.

[3] Sidney Holt, "Let's All Go Whaling," *The Ecologist*, Vol. 15, No. 3, 1985, p. 114. Holt has served as director of the United Nations Food and Agriculture Organization's division of fisheries resources and operations, as a scientific adviser to the Republic of the Seychelles' IWC delegation and as a consultant to several governments on marine mammal affairs.

[4] Blue whales can be as much as 100 feet long and weigh about 150 tons — about the same as 25 full-grown African elephants.

[5] Japan and the Soviet Union each account for about one-third of the whales killed in recent years. The other whaling nations — Iceland, Spain, Peru, Brazil, South Korea and the Philippines — did not file complaints.

Members of the IWC

Antigua, Argentina, Australia, Belize, Brazil, Chile, China, Costa Rica, Denmark, Egypt, Finland, France, Iceland, India, Ireland, Japan, Kenya, Mauritius, Mexico, Monaco, Netherlands, New Zealand, Norway, Oman, Peru, Philippines, St. Lucia, St. Vincent, Senegal, Seychelles, Solomon Islands, South Africa, South Korea, Soviet Union, Spain, Sweden, Switzerland, United Kingdom, United States, Uruguay, West Germany.

commercial whaling," Patricia Forkan of the Humane Society of the United States commented.[6]

The Soviet Union announced its intention to end commercial whaling on the first day of the 1985 IWC annual meeting. "The Soviet Union plans a temporary stop in the antarctic commercial whaling [after the] 1987-1988 season due to technical reasons," I. V. Nikonorov, Soviet commissioner to the IWC, said in his July 15 opening statement. Western observers said that a "temporary" halt would be tantamount to permanent cessation because nearly all the Soviet Union's whaling takes place in the antarctic. Furthermore, it would be economically unfeasible for the Soviet Union to start up operations after a hiatus because of

[6] Forkan, the Humane Society's vice president for programs and communications, has attended IWC meetings since 1973 to lobby for humane killing by commercial whalers.

.the deteriorating condition of its whaling fleet. "They're having terrible problems," said Craig Van Note, executive vice president of a consortium of animal-welfare groups. "Their fleet this last whaling season had major breakdowns. They were laid up for three weeks in the Falkland Islands for major repairs. It's very difficult for them to keep their whaling fleet going." [7]

The Soviet statement also was prompted by a recent step taken by the United States. On April 4, 1985, the Reagan administration announced it would halve the number of fish the Soviets could take in U.S. waters. The reason: The Soviet Union exceeded its IWC-allocated quota of minke whales by about 500 in 1984. The U.S. action was taken under the terms of a 1979 law *(see p. 147)* that imposes mandatory penalties on nations that violate directives of groups such as the IWC. Another law that has not yet been applied allows the president, at his discretion, to prohibit the importation of Soviet fishery products — which are worth some $17 million a year — into the United States. "Those sanctions are hurting [the Soviet Union]," Van Note said. "They've lost half their fish and they'll lose the rest next April if they don't stop."

Emotional, Political Uproar Caused in Japan

The IWC decision in 1982 caused an emotional and political uproar in Japan, the world's leading whaling nation. Japanese government and whaling industry officials lashed out at the IWC, vowing that Japan would continue its commercial whaling operations. In 1981 Japanese whalers caught some 14,000 whales, about 40 percent of the annual world catch. Japan complained that non-whaling nations unfairly dominated the IWC, and that the fight against Japanese whaling was being led by the United States and Britain, the two countries that 150 years earlier had taken large numbers of whales from Japanese waters. Japanese leaders also complained about the economic loss, saying that the ban would shut down the nation's $44-million-a-year whaling industry, which directly employs some 1,300 persons and is responsible for some 50,000 jobs in related industries.

Japan's emotional reaction to the ban is explained in part by the role whales and whaling have played in the country's cultural heritage. The Japanese have been taking whales from their coastal waters and eating whale meat since the 8th century. "The New World wasn't founded when the Japanese were whaling," marine mammal specialist Charles Potter of the Smithsonian Institution's Natural History Museum said. Japan's repre-

---

[7] Van Note, who attended this year's IWC meeting, represents Monitor: The Conservation, Environmental and Animal Welfare Consortium. The Washington-based group is supported by the American Society for the Prevention of Cruelty to Animals, Friends of the Earth, the Fund for Animals, Greenpeace and the Humane Society of the United States, among other groups.

sentative to the IWC meeting this summer said that whaling "is deeply rooted in our culture and socio-economy, particularly in the life of certain local communities." The desire for whale meat, according to the Japanese Whaling Association, "has traditional roots embedded in the Japanese psyche." [8]

It is one of the ironies of history that the United States after World War II virtually ordered the Japanese to begin pelagic (oceangoing) whaling and to consume whale meat. Gen. Douglas MacArthur's occupation forces, "in trying to feed this starving nation said, 'You will go whaling.'" Potter commented. "That was one of the ways that the allied forces felt they could bring red meat to the Japanese populace." Whale meat consumption peaked in Japan during the late 1940s and then began dropping steadily. By the early 1970s whale meat accounted for less than 10 percent of the meat consumed in Japan. Still, whale steak, raw whale slices and whale sausages could be found at restaurants that specialized in whale meat.

Today, however, Japanese are much more likely to eat at one of that nation's ubiquitous fast-food hamburger restaurants than at the increasingly rare whale meat eateries. "Whale meat is not a staple of the diet in Japan today," Dykstra said. "Some of the most prime cuts are considered a delicacy and bring an extremely high price in restaurants and gourmet shops. Other inexpensive cuts are used as fillers in things such as school lunch programs. All in all, whale meat accounts for less than 1 percent of the protein intake in Japan."

United States-Japan Tensions Over the Issue

Dietary questions notwithstanding, Japan formally objected to the IWC's ban on commercial whaling, as well as to a separate ruling in 1981 that phased out Japan's sperm whale hunting. The formal objections permitted the Japanese to hunt whales without fear of disciplinary action by the IWC. However, Japan faced American sanctions under the terms of two laws enacted by Congress in the 1970s. The Pelly Amendment, named after its sponsor Rep. Thomas M. Pelly, R-Wash. (1953-73), was added in 1971 to the 1967 Fishermen's Protective Act. It authorized the president to ban the importation of fish products from countries whose activities "diminished the effectiveness" of any international fishery conventions. [9]

Eight years later Congress amended the 1976 Fishery Conservation and Management Act to impose immediate, mandatory sanctions on nations that failed to observe international

---

[8] Quoted in *The New York Times*, July 28, 1982.
[9] For background, see Congressional Quarterly's 1971 *Almanac*, p. 798.

whaling agreements. The 1979 law, the Packwood-Magnuson Amendment, required the secretary of state to cut in half the number of fish a nation violating IWC agreements could catch in U.S. waters. If compliance seemed unlikely within a year, the offending nation could lose all of its U.S. fishing privileges.[10]

Although the Reagan administration invoked the amendment against the Soviet Union last April, it did not use it against Japan after that nation began catching sperm whales in 1984 in violation of the IWC ban. Instead, Commerce Secretary Malcolm Baldrige negotiated a bilateral agreement in November 1984 in which Japan agreed to end sperm whale hunting at the end of the 1987 season and to end all commercial whaling by April 1, 1988. Japan would be permitted to take up to 400 sperm whales each in 1984 and 1985 and 200 each in 1986 and 1987 without risking a reduction in the amount of fish it could take from U.S. waters.[11] The agreement, Baldrige said in a statement released Nov. 13, "is a positive step toward ending whaling throughout the world."

Conservationists had a very different view. "For 13 years the United States has led the international battle to save the great whales from extinction," Van Note told the House Subcommittee on Human Rights and International Organizations May 8. "Now we are witnessing an attempt by high-level U.S. officials to reverse this noble policy and accommodate the demands of a defiant bureaucracy and whaling industry in Japan." Twelve conservation and animal-welfare organizations subsequently filed suit to overturn the agreement and force the U.S. government to impose the terms of the Packwood-Magnuson Amendment. On March 5, Judge Charles Richey of the U.S. District Court for the District of Columbia decided in favor of the environmentalists, ruling that the administration had a legal obligation to enforce economic sanctions against Japan. The government, claiming that Japan's willingness to end whaling in 1988 precluded implementation of U.S. sanctions, appealed the decision to the U.S. Court of Appeals for the District of Columbia.

Then, on April 5, 1985, Japan announced formally that it would end all commercial whaling by March 1988, provided that Judge Richey's decision was overturned. However, the appeals court on Aug. 6 upheld the lower court decision. In a 2-1 decision the court ruled that the Commerce Department is obligated to enforce the fishing sanctions. The court, though, delayed implementation of the ruling for 90 days, and on Sept.

---

[10] The measure was sponsored by Sens. Bob Packwood, R-Ore., and Warren G. Magnuson, D-Wash. See Congressional Quarterly's 1979 *Almanac,* pp. 679-680.
[11] It is estimated that there are about one million sperm whales in the world's oceans. They are nonetheless considered endangered.

18 the administration appealed the case to the full court of appeals.

Japanese government and fishing industry spokesmen expressed anger and disappointment over the appeals court ruling. Some U.S. observers predicted that the decision would exacerbate the current tensions between the United States and Japan over the huge trade imbalance between the two countries. But others say that the latest court ruling virtually assures that Japan will abide by IWC regulations and end commercial whaling. "Japan will be forced to choose between its $500-million-a-year fishing industry [in U.S. waters] and its $50-million-a-year whaling industry," Greenpeace Chairman David McTaggart said the day the appeals court ruling came out. "This signals the final demise of the whaling bloc." [12]

Whaling's Long History

PEOPLE have been eating whale meat and using whale bones since the earliest days of civilization. Anthropological evidence indicates that humans who lived near sea coasts during the Stone and Bronze ages took full advantage of beached whales. In the Orkney Islands of northern Scotland, for example, about 5,000 years ago the Pict inhabitants stripped stranded whale carcasses for the meat and "used the ribs and jaw-bones of whales as rafters in the roofs of their stone-built huts, and the smaller bones for making bowls and other domestic utensils," L. Harrison Matthews wrote in *The Natural History of the Whale*.[13]

Historians believe that the first humans to hunt whales were the Alaskan Eskimos and Indian tribes on the East and West coasts of North America. About 2,000 years ago, these primitive whalers went after small whales with harpoon-like weapons made of bone, horn, flint and slate. The earliest recorded whaling in Europe came in the 9th century in Norway and Flanders. About 200 years later, the French and Spanish Basques began the first systematic whaling operations, hunting the Biscayan, or North Atlantic, right whale. Right whales, the third-largest species, contain vast amounts of oil and blubber, as well as large, long baleen (whalebone) plates in their upper jaws. The right whale earned its name because it is a slow-swimming animal that lives near land and floats when it is killed, thus making it the "right" whale to hunt.

---

[12] Quoted in *The New York Times*, Aug. 7, 1985.
[13] L. Harrison Matthews, *The Natural History of the Whale* (1978), pp. 1-2.

The Basques made the first oceangoing whaling voyages in the 15th century, sailing as far as the Grand Banks off Newfoundland and the Gulf of St. Lawrence. They later turned to northern waters off Iceland and Greenland in search of the Greenland or Arctic right whale, a larger variety than the Biscayan right. Basque sailors, much prized for their harpooning and flensing (blubber stripping) abilities, worked on whaling ships owned by British, German, French and Dutch companies. The Dutch set up the first large-scale whale-processing operation in the early 1600s on what is now the Norwegian island of Svalbard, then known as Spitsbergen, just below the Arctic Circle.

North American whalers first began going after right whales in the western North Atlantic along the seaboard near Massachusetts and Long Island in the mid-1600s. Then, in 1712, Nantucket whalers, blown off course in a storm, killed a sperm whale. That accidental catch launched what became known as the "Yankee" whaling industry, which Melville described so vividly in *Moby Dick*. The enormous sperm whales "contained a vast amount — sometimes as much as fifteen barrels — of the valuable spermaceti oil, used in the manufacture of expensive smokeless candles," author and illustrator Richard Ellis noted. "[T]his whale was responsible for the rise of a major New England industry and for the ascendancy of such whaling ports as New Bedford, Nantucket, Mystic and Sag Harbor." [14]

The search for the prized sperm and right whales took American whalers to the Azores in 1765 and to the coast of Brazil in 1774. From there, Americans circled Cape Horn and began whaling in the Pacific, first along the coasts of Chile and Peru and later throughout the Pacific. By the early 1820s dozens of American vessels were taking sperm whales off the Japanese coast. The Yankee whaling industry peaked in 1846 when 729 American whalers sailed the seas. U.S. vessels killed more than 6,100 right whales and nearly 4,200 sperm whales that year. [15]

Yankee whaling went into decline in the 1850s for several reasons. First, it began to take increasingly longer to find and catch the rapidly decreasing numbers of right and sperm whales. Second, finding crews became a problem. "In the middle of the 19th century, labor and capital were shifted away from whaling and shipping and into agricultural and mineral development, where greater profits existed," the authors of a

---

[14] Richard Ellis, *The Book of Whales* (1980), p. 13. Spermaceti, sometimes called "sperm oil," is a waxlike substance used in ointments, cosmetics and candles. Whale oil, rendered from the blubber of sperm and other types of whales, contains genuine fats and is edible. Whale oil was used for lighting, lubrication, in the tanning and textile industries and in the manufacture of softer types of soap.

[15] Statistics from *Marine Fisheries Review,* special section on the status of endangered whales, No. 4, 1984.

Whalers on the Sunbeam in 1904 gathering spermaceti from the whale head.

recent article on sperm whales noted. "A skilled worker could earn two or three times as much onshore as he could in whaling." [16] Perhaps the most telling reason was the discovery of petroleum in Pennsylvania in 1859, which greatly decreased the demand for whale oil, as did the development of mineral, cottonseed and linseed oils. The U.S. whaling industry never again reached the levels it had in Melville's sailing days. Most whaling was confined to gray whales off the coast of California, which were rapidly depleted.

The Yankee whalers, like their European counterparts, worked from open rowboats launched from sailing ships when

[16] Merrill E. Gosho, Dale W. Rice and Jeffrey M. Breiwick, "The Sperm Whale, *Physeter macrocephalus,*" *Marine Fisheries Review, op. cit.,* p. 61. Gosho, Rice and Breiwick are with the National Marine Fisheries Service's Marine Mammal Laboratory in Seattle.

the whales were spotted. The whalers struck their prey with hand-thrown harpoons, held on when the wounded animal dove under water and waited for it to surface. "Once the whale had tired of dragging behind it the boat, its occupants and a great weight of rope it rose to the surface and the men were able to row alongside to commence the kill," one historian explained. "Long lances were repeatedly thrust into the body until the vital organs were destroyed and the sea around was colored red with gallons of blood pouring from the severed arteries and veins." [17]

1867: Advent of the 'Modern' Whaling Era

The nature of commercial whaling changed markedly in 1867 when Sven Foyn, a Norwegian seal trapper, devised new techniques that greatly increased whalers' effectiveness: the steam-driven whaling boat and the grenade harpoon launched by a cannon. The powered whale catchers meant whalers could hunt the fast-swimming and powerful blue and fin whales. Foyn's harpoon not only killed the whale, but also injected it with compressed air, which made the carcass float and thus easier to retrieve.

"With the introduction of the modern method the Industrial Revolution had made its entry into whaling," Norwegians J. N. Tonnessen and A. O. Johnsen wrote in their history of modern whaling.[18] Another boost for whalers was the invention of hydrogenation, which, Tonnessen and Johnsen said, "meant that whale oil was now a highly important raw material in the production of margarine."

Foyn and other Norwegians first used his inventions in the fjords along Norway's northern Finnmark region in the early 1880s. Their ships sailed from about a dozen shore stations to which they later towed their prey to be rendered into margarine and soap. For two decades Norwegian whalers hunted blue, fin, humpback and sei whales from the Finnmark bases. Then, when the number of whales began declining drastically around the turn of the 20th century, they began hunting other populations of those same species at the other end of the globe — in the antarctic.[19]

Period of Great Antarctic Pelagic Whaling

The abundance of whales in the antarctic oceans and the development of gigantic floating factories to process whales at sea brought about what was to become the last great whaling era. Antarctic whalers developed the floating factory ships early

[17] Arthur G. Credlund, *Whales & Whaling* (1982), p. 6. Credlund, a zoologist, is a whaling curator at Britain's Hull Museum.
[18] Tonnessen and Johnsen, *The History of Modern Whaling* (1982), p. 7.
[19] See "Future of Antarctica," *E.R.R.* 1981 Vol. I, pp. 469-488.

in the 20th century, but these first ships were not suited to the rough waters of Antarctica because choppy seas made it extremely difficult to flense the whales alongside the ship. With the invention in the 1920s of the slipway — a mechanism at the rear of the ship that permitted whalers to haul entire carcasses on deck — factory ships and their whale catchers could venture into every section of the vast antarctic waters in search of their quarry.

Antarctic whaling was immensely profitable because the waters were not under the jurisdiction of any country. Whaling there "was free from any regulations imposed by governments on the work of shore stations, as also from taxation on their production and license fees payable to the owners of the land," Matthews wrote.[20] Dominated by the Norwegians and British, whaling in the Antarctic Ocean flourished in the late 1920s and early 1930s. According to Tonnessen and Johnsen, the number of whales taken in the region went from 13,775 in the 1927-28 season to 20,341 the following year, and to 40,201 in the 1930-31 season. At its peak in 1930, the antarctic whaling industry consisted of six shore stations, 41 floating factories and 232 whale catchers.

Not long after reaching its zenith, antarctic whaling began a steady decline. A resurgence of whaling followed World War II, but by the early 1960s only the Soviet Union and Japan maintained extensive whaling operations. Those two nations, along with Norway, Iceland, Brazil, South Korea, Denmark, Peru, Spain and the Philippines, are the only countries with commercial whaling industries today. A drop in whale oil prices during the worldwide Depression of the 1930s accounted for some of the decline. But the more important factor by far was the decimation of virtually every species of antarctic whale. The relatively slow-swimming humpback was the first to be hunted — and the first to be overharvested. Antarctic whalers killed so many humpbacks beginning in 1904 that they all but disappeared by 1916. Then the blue whale was hunted practically to extinction. "When there were too few blue whales to hunt, the whalers turned to the next largest species, the fin whale, then to the sei [in the mid-1960s], and finally to the little minke [in the mid-1970s]," Richard Ellis noted.[21]

Efforts to Regulate the Taking of Whales

During the 1930s the antarctic whaling nations entered into several voluntary agreements designed to protect whales. Some of them — including the Geneva Convention of 1931, the eight-nation London Agreement of 1937 and a British-German-

---

[20] Matthews, *op. cit.,* p. 194.
[21] Ellis, *op cit.,* p. 13.

Questions of Killing

One of the more emotional aspects of the whaling debate is whether whales should be killed at all and if they are, what methods should be used to ensure that they do not suffer unnecessarily.

Some conservationists and all animal-rights groups believe that it is ethically indefensible to kill whales. "It's not the sort of thing where it's a necessity; nothing is needed. It's a frivolous practice . . . ," said Patricia Forkan of the Humane Society of the United States.

Those opposed to killing them point out that whales, like humans, are warm-blooded mammals that live in extended family units and have large, highly developed brains. "The sperm whale, for example, has by far the largest and the most convoluted brain that ever evolved on the planet," said Thomas Garrett of Greenpeace. "In some ways they must have a far more developed intelligence than ours . . . ."

Ethical arguments against whale killing brought popular support to the "Save the Whales" campaigns that began in the early 1970s. But whaling nations dismissed them. They contend there is little difference between killing whales and slaughtering hogs and cattle. "The whole idea of the whales as a superior group of animals . . . has very, very little scientific background to it," said Tom McIntyre of the National Marine Fisheries Service.

As far as killing whales humanely, the IWC rejected all such pleas until the early 1970s. After years of lobbying, primarily from conservationists in the United States, Great Britain, and Australia, the IWC passed a resolution in 1983 outlawing the use of the cold harpoon, a type of harpoon containing a delayed reaction explosive head.

Norwegian agreement signed the following year — succeeded in reducing the number of whale catchers and limiting the time periods for hunting some species. But none of those agreements stopped the whales' decline. The International Whaling Commission, which came into being in 1946 following a conference of whaling nations in Washington, was the first international body given the power to grant complete protection to endangered species and set up yearly hunting quotas for the other species.[22] In addition, the IWC could limit whaling to specific seasons and ban the taking of nursing whales, whale calves, and adults under certain sizes. The commission also carries on regular inspections of whaling operations.

---

[22] Fourteen nations signed the International Convention for the Regulation of Whaling, establishing the IWC in 1946: Argentina, Australia, Brazil, Canada, Chile, Denmark, France, the Netherlands, New Zealand, Norway, Peru, the Soviet Union, the United Kingdom, the United States. Japan, which did not become a major whaling nation until after World War II, joined in 1951.

154

It is generally conceded that, despite its unprecedented powers, the IWC did little to safeguard diminishing whale species until the 1970s. Still, unlike its predecessors, the commission continued to operate. The IWC "is really a remarkable organization in that it's managed to hold together through all these years and still has a certain amount of legitimacy. It actually seems to function," biologist Scott Krauss of the New England Aquarium in Boston said. "It may not function to the likings of Greenpeace, and it may not even function to my likings, but it does still function." Under increasing pressure from conservationists, the IWC in the late 1970s began cutting quotas and working toward implementing a total moratorium on commercial whaling. This led to the total ban that the commission adopted at its 1982 meeting.

The first unilateral U.S. restrictions on commercial whaling came with passage of the Endangered Species Act in 1969, which placed eight of the nine great whales on the U.S. endangered list *(see p. 157)* and barred the granting of whaling licenses for those species. At the time there were only two small commercial whaling operations in this country, the Del Monte and Golden Gate Fishing companies in Richmond, Calif. The Marine Mammal Protection Act of 1972, which put a permanent moratorium on most killing of ocean mammals within the U.S. fishing zone and on importation of their products, "was the nail in the coffin for any commercial whaling in the United States," said Tom McIntyre, marine resource management specialist with the National Marine Fisheries Service.[23]

Chances for Survival

COMMERCIAL WHALING almost certainly will end within the next few years. But that does not mean that all other types of whaling also will cease. Article VII of the 1946 International Convention for the Regulation of Whaling gives countries the right to kill whales "for the purposes of scientific research." Thus far Iceland and South Korea have officially notified the IWC that they intend to carry out comparatively widescale whaling for scientific purposes in the late 1980s. Whalers in Japan and Brazil reportedly are pushing for those nations to undertake scientific whaling as well. Iceland plans to kill 80 fin whales, 80 minke whales and 40 sei whales annually from 1986-89. South Korea has said it will take 200 minkes a year from 1986-89.

[23] For background see Congressional Quarterly's 1972 *Almanac,* pp. 961-969.

Icelandic and South Korean officials maintain that the whales will be taken solely for research studies. But conservationists say those nations are actually trying to circumvent the IWC ban on commercial whaling. Conservationists point out that Iceland plans to export the meat from its whales to Japan. "Iceland has made no bones about the fact that they intend to sell [the whale meat] to Japan," Forkan said. "What we are looking at is the potential to make over the four years $30 million or so for a million and a half dollars' worth of research. We think that's commercial whaling."

The IWC allows another exception to its whaling bans, including those on catching totally protected species. IWC regulations permit the taking of whales so long as "the meat and products are to be used exclusively for local consumption by the aborigines." Aboriginal whaling has been permitted in recent years in Greenland where the Eskimos kill fin and humpback whales, in the Soviet Union where Siberian Eskimos take gray whales and in the United States where Alaskan Eskimos kill bowheads. Conservationists have strenuously objected to these aboriginal whaling activities, alleging that the meat of the gray whales killed in Siberia is used illegally to feed animals on fur farms and that the Eskimos in Greenland and Alaska are killing too many of the rare humpbacks and bowheads.

"U.S. Eskimos are wreaking havoc on the bowhead stocks," Potter said. The problem is not so much the number of whales killed, but the much larger number of those struck and not killed, nearly 90 percent of which die. "The number of whales struck and not landed skyrocketed in the late '70s, early '80s," Potter said. "Given the very low population estimates of these bowhead whales, there is great concern that [the Eskimos] are clearly taking more animals than are being reproduced each year. If you've only got a couple of thousand, it doesn't take long to extinct the species." Some IWC scientists have pushed to end Alaskan bowhead aboriginal whaling. The U.S. government, under pressure from the Alaska Eskimo Whaling Commission, requested that the IWC allocate 35 bowhead strikes for 1985. The commission eventually allocated the Eskimos 26 strikes a year for 1985, 1986 and 1987.

Then there is the issue of coastal whaling. At the 1985 IWC meeting Japan asked the commission to give "special consideration" to whaling that takes place solely within 200 miles of a nation's coastline. It would be "totally improper," the Japanese said, for the IWC to have jurisdiction over "any additional species whose utilization is confined exclusively to the 200-mile zone." This was the start, conservationists say, of a Japanese lobbying campaign to reclassify coastal whaling as subsistence

How Many Whales:
Estimated Populations of Whales
On U.S. Endangered Species List

Species/Reporting Area	Current Estimate
Gray Whale	
Eastern North Pacific	13,450-19,210
Western North Pacific	nearly extinct
Blue Whale	
North Atlantic	100
North Pacific	1,400-1,900
N. Indian Ocean	*
Antarctic	1,000-8,000
Subantarctic Indian Ocean	5,000
Fin Whale	
North Norway	*
West Norway/Faeroe Island	low hundreds
Spain/Portugal/British Isles	*
Denmark Strait	1,791-11,584
W. North Atlantic	3,590-6,300
North Pacific	14,620-18,630
Antarctic	85,200
Sei Whale	
North Atlantic	4,957
North Pacific	22,000-37,000
Southern Hemisphere	9,800-11,760
Humpback Whale	
E. North Atlantic	*
W. North Atlantic	5,257-6,289
Northern Indian Ocean	*
North Pacific	1,200
Southern Hemisphere	2,500-3,000
Bowhead Whale	
E. Greenland-Spitsbergen	nearly extinct
Davis Strait	low hundreds
Hudson Bay	low hundreds
Western Arctic	3,617-4,125
Sea of Okhotsk	low hundreds
Right Whale	
North Atlantic	low hundreds
North Pacific	low hundreds
Southern Hemisphere	3,000
Sperm Whale	
North Atlantic	99,500
Eastern North Pacific	274,000
Western North Pacific	198,100
Southern Hemisphere	410,700

* No published estimate
Source: *Marine Fisheries Review*, Vol. 46, No. 4, 1984, p. 4.

whaling, which would be exempt from IWC jurisdiction. Norway and other nations are expected to join Japan in seeking unrestricted coastal subsistence whaling.

The Controversy Over Counting Populations

What continued hunting means for the various whale populations is unclear. The International Whaling Commission has been setting quotas based on whale populations for decades. Yet the process of counting whales is an inexact science at best. This has led to charges by conservation groups that the IWC, bowing to pressure from whaling nations, continually overestimates whale populations. Whaling nations and IWC officials, for their part, claim that conservation groups deliberately understate their figures. "We tend on a worldwide basis to set quotas for the numbers of whales that can be killed without any firm idea of how many there are and whether or not those numbers may be harmful," said Dykstra of Greenpeace. "If you were to talk to a scientist who works for the Japanese government . . . [and] a scientist who works for a country that may tend towards conservation, you might find as much as a 5,000 percent difference in the estimate of a certain stock."

Biologists use several methods to estimate whale populations. One of the oldest involves shooting harmless stainless steel darts (called discovery tags) into schools of whales. Scientists recover the tags after the whales are killed, and estimate the population based on "the percentage of returns versus the number of animals tagged," Krauss said. The main problem with this method, he explained, is that it is difficult to tag a representative sampling of a population because whales tend to swim in groups segregated by sex and age.

Keeping track of the time it takes to catch whales is a more commonly used method. "If the whale boats go out for 10 hours and catch 10 whales and they do that year after year, they say there's no evidence that the population is declining," Krauss said. "On the other hand, if you go out and each year for 10 years you get nine whales and then six whales and then two whales, or if you have to increase your effort to get the same amount of animals, you see the catch per unit effort declining and therefore the population is declining." This method, however, "does not give you absolute estimates; it just gives you an index of abundance," Krauss said.

Biologists also use aerial and shipboard visual surveys to estimate whale populations. Those estimates, though, are not totally reliable because whales spend a good deal of their time underwater. A fourth method is to take photographs of selected populations and rephotograph them at later dates for comparison. But this method can only be used on slow-swimming, low-population whales such as the rights and humpbacks. The failings of the various methods of counting whales, Krauss said, mean that "you tend to get estimates that have plus or minus figures that are equal to the estimate." He gave an example: "One recent estimate for right whales in the North Atlantic was 380, plus or minus 644. There aren't 'negative' whales, but this is the way the statistics work out."

Debate Over Whether Species are Endangered

Political considerations also have spilled over to the U.S. endangered species list. Conservationists do not even consider it a debatable point that eight of the largest great whales are endangered. "The major whale stocks were destroyed, there are just no ifs, ands or buts about it," Garrett of Greenpeace said. But some biologists and government officials say that political pressures have caused some populous species of whales to be listed as endangered. "The endangered species lists are highly political," Potter said.

Potter and other scientists believe that the California gray whale and certain populations of the sperm and fin whales are not at all endangered. "There are probably more California gray whales today than there were back when they were being heavily exploited . . .," Potter said. "In the last 50-60 years they seem to have completely recovered." The National Marine Fisheries Service, in fact, intends to propose by the end of October that the California gray whale be downgraded from endangered. The service is currently debating whether the whale should be listed as "threatened," which would foreclose commercial hunting, or to "de-list" the animal altogether.

Krauss said that most of the whales being hunted today are "not endangered in the biological sense of the word." The fin and sei whales, Krauss said, "may be listed in the United States Endangered Species Act because everybody's concerned about whales going extinct. But the fact of the matter is that where the Russians, the Japanese and the Icelanders take whales the take . . . does not endanger the populations."

There is no disagreement, however, over the endangered status of the bowhead, humpback, right and blue whales. In some areas of the world those species are close to extinction. Nor is there any argument that the number of all whales swimming in the world's oceans is a fraction of what it once was. Most scientists, conservationists and government whaling officials agree that the ban on commercial whaling — politically motivated or not — is a prudent step that may ward off the extinction of some of the largest animals ever to have lived on Earth.

Recommended Reading List

Books

Credlund, Arthur G., *Whales and Whaling*, Seven Hills Books, 1983.
Ellis, Richard, *The Book of Whales*, Knopf, 1980.
Frost, Sidney, *The Whaling Question*, Brick House, 1979.
Lockley, Ronald M., *Whales, Dolphins and Porpoises*, Norton, 1979.
Matthews, L. Harrison, *The Natural History of the Whale*, Columbia University Press, 1978.
——, *The Whale*, Simon & Schuster, 1968.
Melville, Herman, *Moby Dick: Or, the Whale*, Random House, 1950.
Phillips, Marion, *The Whale*, Exposition Press, 1978.
Schevill, William, ed., *The Whale Problem: A Status Report*, Harvard University Press, 1974.
Small, George L., *The Blue Whale*, Columbia University Press, 1971.
Tonnessen, J. N. and Arno Johnsen, *The History of Modern Whaling*, University of California Press, 1982.
Whipple, A. B., *The Whalers*, Time-Life Books, 1979.

Articles

CEE Report (published by the Center for Environmental Education), selected issues.
Forkan, Patricia, "Japan Declares War on Whaling Moratorium," *The Humane Society News*, winter 1985.
Greenpeace Examiner, selected issues.
Holt, Sidney, "Same Old Swan Song: One More Verse," *BBC Wildlife*, July 1985.
——, "Let's All Go Whaling," *The Ecologist*, No. 3, 1985.
Marine Fisheries Review (published by the National Marine Fisheries Service), selected issues.
Norman, Colin, "U.S. Sanctions Required to Enforce Whaling Ban," *Science*, March 22, 1985.
Stoler, Peter, "Stirring Up a Whale of a Storm," *Time*, Dec. 3, 1984.

Reports and Studies

Editorial Research Reports, "Troubled Ocean Fisheries," 1984 Vol. I, p. 429.
Center for Environmental Education, "Position Paper on Bowhead Whales," 1985.
Greenpeace, "Greenpeace Information on Whales," April 1985; "Scientific Whalers? The History of Whaling Under Special Permits," 1985.
U.S. Department of the Interior, Fish and Wildlife Service, "Endangered and Threatened Wildlife and Plants," July 20, 1984.

Graphics: Cover from Dick Sutphen Studios; p. 145 photo of humpback whale by Mason Weinrich, Cetacean Research Unit, Gloucester Fisherman's Museum, Gloucester, Mass.; p. 151 photo, The Whaling Museum, New Bedford, Mass.

REQUIEM FOR RAIN FORESTS?

by

Roger Thompson

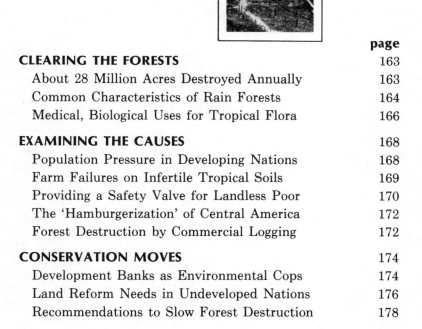

**Dec. 20
1 9 8 5**

REQUIEM FOR RAIN FORESTS?

IN THE HEART of the Amazon rain forest, the Brazilian government bulldozes a new road, No. 429. Thousands of landless peasants follow its progress, swarming over the land that flanks the unpaved strip. Pioneers in quest of a dream, they hack and burn the forest to make way for crops. Lured by government land agency promises of a better life, Renato and his wife, Maria, claim a 15-acre homestead. They clear the trees in six months and plant 2,200 coffee seedlings, corn, pumpkin and melons. "I won't leave here," says Renato, a former sharecropper, as he anticipates his first harvest. "Here one works for one's self. Plant today, eat tomorrow." But after only a year, they give up and move on. "This land is not good. Nothing grows," Renato says. "It's impossible to stay." [1]

Renato and Maria are small players in a worldwide game of ecological roulette. Each year 28 million acres (an area roughly the size of Pennsylvania) of the Earth's remaining tropical forests are cleared, primarily to grow crops but also for logging and cattle ranching. Nearly half of the rain forests already have been cleared, mostly in this century. The rural poor — whether in tropical Latin America, Africa or Asia — are the main agents of destruction, although poverty and skewed land distribution are the real causes. Sometimes the soil is good enough to support long-term farming. Most often it is poor and the land is abandoned after only two or three years of diminishing harvests. Regeneration of the forest, if it happens at all, can take hundreds of years.

Landless peasants, often with government encouragement, repeat this cycle year after year. They have no other means of meeting their daily survival needs. The governments have no land or jobs to offer elsewhere. The cumulative effect of this routine destruction adds up to an ecological disaster of major proportions. "The deforestation occurring in the tropics today is one of the great tragedies of our time," said T. N. Khoshoo, former Secretary of the Environment of India. "It is a classic example of a Third World problem the industrial nations cannot afford to ignore." [2]

---

[1] Quoted in the House Science and Technology Subcommittee on Natural Resources, Agriculture and Environment, "Tropical Forest Development Projects: Status of Environmental and Agricultural Research," 1985, pp. 6-9.
[2] Quoted in an Oct. 22, 1985, press release by the World Resources Institute.

At the current pace the world's rain forests will disappear in 72 years, 2057.[3] Gone too will be the capacity of the natural environment to support more than a billion people projected to inhabit tropical forest areas by then. The loss of forest resources could bring on population collapse from mass starvation, internal political turmoil in Third World nations and chaos in international financial markets as affected nations lose valuable trade commodities and default on their foreign debts.

Ecologists have a different but no less urgent reason to prevent tropical deforestation. Rain forests are the most biologically diverse regions on Earth, containing roughly half of the world's five million plant, animal and insect species, all on just 2 percent of its land surface.[4] Biologists now warn of a mass extinction of species on a par with the large scale losses of life that mark the boundaries of at least six geologic ages over the past 500 million years. Thomas Lovejoy, a biologist with the World Wildlife Fund, has estimated that tropical forest destruction could push 15-20 percent of living species to extinction by the year 2000. Scientists also predict disastrous changes in the world's climate *(see box, p. 177)*.

The biological richness of tropical forests provides a bounty of uses worthy of protection. Wild plant varieties are particularly important to agriculture because they provide a gene pool for the development of new crops resistant to pests and diseases. Tropical plants also are pharmaceutical factories, providing raw materials for analgesics, antibiotics, heart drugs, hormones, laxatives and many other medical products. At least 1,400 plant species are believed to offer some potential in fighting cancer.[5] Viewed as a renewable resource, rain forests produce billions of dollars annually in lumber, fruits, oils, gum, resins, waxes, edible oils, rattans, bamboo, spices, pesticides and dyes.

Slowing rain forest destruction won't be easy. "You can't just tell Third World people to stop cutting the rain forests for aesthetic beauty, or for their biological diversity," said Michael H. Robinson, director of the National Zoo in Washington, D.C. "You have to provide them with an alternative to cutting. You have to change the hard facts of survival in the Third World." [6]

Common Characteristics of Rain Forests

Most of the world's tropical forests are sandwiched between the Tropic of Cancer and the Tropic of Capricorn *(see map,*

---

[3] Nicholas Guppy, "Tropical Deforestation: A Global View," *Foreign Affairs*, Spring 1984, p. 929.
[4] Catherine Caufield, *In the Rainforest*, Alfred A. Knopf, 1985, p. 60.
[5] Norman Myers, *The Primary Source*, W. W. Norton and Co., 1984, p. 212.
[6] Persons quoted in this report were interviewed by the author unless otherwise indicated.

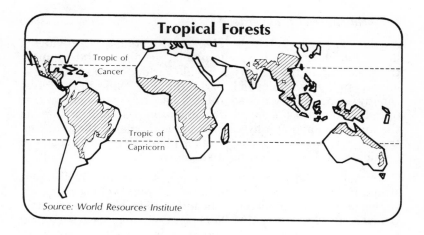

Tropical Forests

Tropic of Cancer

Tropic of Capricorn

Source: World Resources Institute

above). These global bands mark the farthest points of the Sun's seasonal migration into the northern and southern latitudes. Within this zone the Sun's rays strike more directly than in the temperate zones, providing one determinant element for the luxuriant growth of tropical forests: warmth. The annual average temperature registers at least 75 degrees Fahrenheit.

The second element is rainfall. The amount that falls on a tropical forest determines whether it will be "open" or "closed." Open forests occur in semi-arid areas where the tree cover is so thin that the forest floor receives enough sunlight to support a dense, continuous cover of grass. Most of the trees are deciduous. Annual rainfall generally measures 35 to 47 inches. African nations have roughly two-thirds of the world's open tropical forests.[7]

Closed tropical forests occur in areas that receive at least 79 inches of rain a year, producing a broad-leaved evergreen canopy so dense that grass cannot get enough sunlight to grow underneath. True rain forests exist in areas receiving over 13 feet of rain a year. Equatorial Brazil, Zaire and Indonesia account for about half of the world's closed tropical forests *(see box, p. 167).* Favorable climatic conditions also produce some rain forests outside the tropical latitudes, notably in northern India and Burma and south China.

The diversity of life is so great that scientists have divided the forest into vertical strata. The main canopy is formed by the interlocking crowns of the middle strata of trees, generally 100 to 130 feet high. Above them stand a few taller trees, called emergents. Below is a canopy of shorter trees,

---

[7] U.S. Congress, Office of Technology Assessment, "Technologies to Sustain Tropical Forest Resources," U.S. Government Printing Office, March 1984, p. 68. Tropical scrublands grow in areas receiving less than 35 inches of annual rainfall. Seventy-one percent of the scrubland also is in Africa.

roughly 50 to 80 feet high. The sparse understory provides a home for shrubs, non-woody plants, seedlings and younger trees. Adding to the density is a wide variety of woody vines — lianas, epiphytes, bromeliads and ferns. The lianas in the forest canopy sometimes grow so thick that they can hold a tree upright after it has been cut by a chainsaw.[8] Orchids are among the most common epiphytes, non-parasitic plants that grow on trunks, branches and leaves of other plants. Up to 50 species of orchids have been found on a single tree.

Animals of the rain forest have adapted to life in different strata. Each layer is a different habitat. Tree-dwelling monkeys, sloths, marsupials, squirrels, rats and mice rarely come to earth. Ornithologists estimate that 95 percent of the birds accustomed to forest shade will not fly across a clearing during daylight. Animals on the ground, such as tapirs, wild pigs and anteaters, have long snouts for rooting out insects from the earth and rotting logs. Insects on the forest floor provide a crucial service in breaking down leaf litter and other debris, freeing nutrients for living plants.

Medical, Biological Uses for Tropical Flora

The biological richness of the forest is its main asset. A typical four-square-mile patch of rain forest is a cornucopia: 1,500 species of flowering plants, 750 of trees, 125 of mammals, 400 of birds, 100 of reptiles, 60 of amphibians and 150 of butterflies.[9] Tiny Panama has as many plant species as all of Europe. The forest of Madagascar, an island in the Indian Ocean, has 2,000 species of trees, compared with 400 in all of North America.

The benefits of this diversity are not limited to those who live in tropical regions. Developed nations import billions of dollars annually in tropical timber, fruits and nuts. Medical and biological benefits are less well known, but perhaps more essential. Forest-dwelling Indians of the Amazon reportedly use at least 1,300 plant species for medical purposes. Traditional healers in Southeast Asia use an estimated 6,500 plants in treatments for malaria, stomach ulcers, syphilis, and various other disorders. Scientists have learned how to use many of these plants in modern medicine. Roughly one in four drugs purchased in a pharmacy today owes its origin in some way to a tropical plant or animal. Yet scientists have screened only one tropical plant in 10 for medical applications. Only one in 100 has received intensive scrutiny.[10]

The claims of folk medicine led researchers to test the anti-

---

[8] Myers, *op. cit.,* p. 27.
[9] Caufield, *op. cit.,* p. 60.
[10] Myers, *op. cit.,* pp. 209-210.

Major Tropical Forests*
(in square kilometers)

Country	Total Forest Area	Undis-turbed Forest†	% of Nation's Total	Unpro-ductive Forest‡	% of Nation's Total
Brazil	3,562,800	2,886,300	81.0%	556,500	15.6%
Indonesia	1,135,750	389,150	34.3	400,000	35.2
Zaire	1,056,500	797,400	75.5	255,300	24.2
Peru	693,100	373,200	53.8	259,900	37.5
Colombia	464,000	386,000	83.2	69,000	14.9
India	460,440	48,850	10.6	76,860	16.7
Bolivia	440,100	177,600	40.4	141,600	32.2
Papua-New Guinea	337,100	138,150	41.0	196,750	58.4
Venezula	318,700	76,000	23.8	126,600	39.7
Burma	311,930	141,070	45.2	80,700	25.9
Total	8,780,420	5,413,720	61.7%	2,163,280	24.6%
Other Countries	2,829,930	1,270,430	45.0	838,550	29.6
World Total	11,610,350	6,684,150	57.6	3,001,830	25.9

* Broad-leaved humid and dry forests with closed canopy.
† Productive forest that has never been disturbed or has not been logged in the last 60 years.
‡ Unproductive forest is not suitable for wood production.

Sources: Nicholas Guppy, "Tropical Deforestation," Foreign Affairs, Spring, 1984.

cancer effects of the Madagascar periwinkle plant. Now children with lymphocytic leukemia have an 80 percent or better chance of remission. Fifty-eight percent of adults with Hodgkin's disease survive 10 years with treatment. For four thousand years Hindu healers treated nervous disorders with a compound derived from the so-called snakeroot plant. Today a chemical from the plant supplies the base for tranquilizer products and materials for the treatments of hypertension, anxiety and schizophrenia. Chemicals extracted from plants also serve as the building blocks for semi-synthetic drugs. A leading example is diosgenin, derived from a lowly yam found in tropical Mexican. The compound is used in the manufacture of oral contraceptives. Of all steroidal drugs on the market, 95 percent depend on diosgenin as a raw material.

The untapped potential of tropical plants is the driving force behind the work of ethnobiologists like Mark Plotkin of Harvard University. "We're working with people to find out what plants they know how to use," said Plotkin. "Well over 90 percent of the Brazilian flora has not been investigated for its chemical value," he added. "This type of work is really snowballing, because if we don't get the information now, we're never going to get it." As development pushes deeper into untouched areas, the native population gradually is assimilated and abandons its traditional ways. "The knowledge is going fast," Plotkin said. "With the advent of religion and modern medicine, the shamen have no one to pass the knowledge on to."

Tropical regions also provide irreplaceable gene pools for the improvement of many of the world's leading crops. Only three species of grass — corn, wheat and rice — provide half of the protein and calories for the world's four billion inhabitants. Another 10 crops — soybeans, barley, oats, peanuts, potatoes, millet, sorghum, rye, sweet potatoes and coconuts — provide all but 10 percent of the rest. Of these, five have ancestors in tropical rain forests.[11] The world's food supply depends upon maintaining the pest and disease resistance of these crops. Resistance often is restored by cross-breeding hybrid plants with those found in the wild. But as forests are cleared, wild species and ancient varieties are being lost even before they are discovered.[12]

Examining the Causes

RISING POPULATION pressure is a major force behind the current rate of deforestation. Seventy-six nations with a population of two billion people, half the world's total, lie totally or largely within the tropical latitudes. In just 30 years the population of tropical nations is projected to double. Already, 40 percent of the closed forests have been cleared or logged, leaving roughly 2 billion acres worldwide.[13] Latin America has 57 percent of the remaining rain forests, Southeast Asia and the Pacific islands 25 percent and Africa 18 percent. But each year, 18.5 million acres of closed forest (more than 30 acres for every minute of every day) and 9.5 million of open forest are cleared for other uses *(see box, p. 173)*.

Mainland India, Bangladesh, Haiti and Sri Lanka have no primary rain forests left. At current rates of destruction, the lowland rain forests of peninsular Malaysia, Thailand, the Philippines, Guatemala, Panama, Sierra Leone and the Ivory Coast will be reduced to patches as early as 1990, according to the Food and Agriculture Organization (FAO) of the United Na-

---

[11] Caufield, *op. cit.*, p. 227.
[12] See "Advances in Agricultural Research," *E.R.R.*, 1981 Vol. I, pp. 169-88.
[13] World Resources Institute, "Tropical Forests: A Call for Action," October 1985, p. 3.

tions. Nigeria and the Ivory Coast will lose all remaining rain forests by 2000. In Latin America, Ecuador, Honduras and Nicaragua will lose more than half of their remaining forests by the end of the century; Mexico and Colombia one-third.[14] Indonesia will lose 10 percent and Brazil 8 percent over the same period. Brazil's loss actually is larger than it appears, representing 63 million acres, an area two and one-half times the size of Portugal.

People who depend on wood for heating and cooking are the greatest threat to the open forest areas of Africa and India *(see box, p. 959)*. Closed forests are most threatened by the spread of agriculture, whether for crops or cattle. The FAO estimates that 88 million people live in rain forests — about 28 million in Asia, 20 million in Africa and 40 million in Latin America. Most of these are itinerant farmers whose slash-and-burn methods were not a threat to rain forests until recently because of the relatively small number of people involved over vast areas.

The population explosion experienced by tropical nations since World War II, however, has sent more inexperienced farmers into the forests, stretching their limits to recover from slash-and-burn activity. The agricultural population grows by about 1 percent a year in tropical Latin America, 2 percent in tropical Africa, and 1.5 percent in tropical Asia.[16]

Farm Failures on Infertile Tropical Soils

It seems ironic that crops do not flourish where massive trees once stood. But the luxuriant growth of rain forests belies the poor quality of the soils. An estimated two-thirds of the soils in humid tropical areas are low in nutrients and high in acid.[17]

In a temperate-zone forest, the soils build rich organic layers from leaf litter and vegetative decay that supply most of the forest's nutrients. But in a rain forest, most of them are found in the trees and other plants. Constant high temperatures and abundant rainfall over eons have broken down the soil; nutrients that fall on it are quickly leached out. Evolutionary processes have developed a highly efficient system for quickly delivering natural fertilizers to plants. Nutrients from rain, a major source, are caught and absorbed by epiphytes, lichens and algae. At ground level, a thick mass of tree roots, as much as a foot thick, soaks up nutrients washed into the soil.

"Some studies have shown that as little as one-tenth of 1

---

[14] Caufield, *op. cit.*, p. 38.
[15] Office of Technology Assessment, *op. cit.*, p. 45.
[16] Jean-Paul Lanly, "Tropical Forest Resources," Food and Agricultural Organization of the United Nations, 1982, p. 35.
[17] Caufield, *op. cit.*, p. 66..

percent of forest nutrients ever penetrate below the first 5 centimeters [2 inches] of soil in tropical rain forest," Adrian Forsyth and Ken Miyata wrote in *Tropical Nature.* Specialized fungi called mycorrhizae make this high level of efficiency possible. Where mycorrhizae are destroyed by burning or other soil disruptions, the rain forest may never be able to return.

The poor quality of tropical soils sets the stage for slash-and-burn farming. Ashes from burned vegetation act like fertilizer, bestowing temporary fertility to the soil. After two or three years nutrients from the ashes are used up, and the farmer is forced to move on. But continuous crop production is possible even on poor soils, says Pedro A. Sanchez, a soil scientist at North Carolina State University.

His research in the Peruvian Amazon has shown that three grain crops can be produced annually on acid, infertile soils with "appropriate fertilizer inputs." [18] Sanchez contends that the crop rotation and fertilization methods he developed in Peru could slow deforestation elsewhere in the Amazon basin because every acre placed in permanent cultivation spares several acres of forest from the itinerant farmer's ax.

Critics have pointed out, however, that most forest farmers do not have access to fertilizer or to a farm credit system that would allow them to purchase it on loan. University of Georgia ecologist Carl F. Jordan questioned the economic justification of hauling fertilizer into remote areas. "You can pasture on the moon," said Jordan. "All you have to do is send up enough nutrients and water." [19]

Providing a Safety Valve for Landless Poor

Despite well-known soil deficiencies, development of tropical rain forest regions continues, often with government assistance. Brazil has conducted large relocation projects in its attempt to open the Amazon to colonization. In the late 1960s the nation launched a patriotic "New Frontier" program to build highways to encourage settlement in its northern areas. Between 1966 and 1975, 28 million acres of forests were cleared for roads and farms. Waves of immigrants arrived, spurred by hopes of a new life, but most small farms failed within two to three years because of poor soil.

Disenchantment with resettlement projects led the Brazilian government in the late 1970s to concentrate on grand development projects backed by Brazilian and foreign entrepreneurs.

---

[18] Pedro Sanchez, et. al., "Amazon Basin Soils: Management for Continuous Crop Production," *Science,* May 21, 1982, p. 821
[19] Roger Stone, *Dreams of Amazonia,* Viking, 1985, p. 126.

One such project was undertaken by Daniel Ludwig, reputed to be the world's richest man. He poured hundreds of millions of dollars into a 250,000-acre tree plantation and paper mill before abandoning it in 1982.

A major hydroelectric project was more successful. The Tucurui Dam constructed by Eletronorte, northern Brazil's state electric company, cost $4 billion and spans 12 miles on the Tocantins River, a southern tributary of the Amazon. When the gates closed last year, the dam flooded 800 square miles of virgin rain forest. The project is expected to produce 8,000 megawatts of electricity, equal to six Three Mile Island nuclear power plants, and supply development needs in the Amazon basin for years to come.

While the government aided massive projects, thousands of landless farmers from the south of Brazil began migrating into the forests of Rondonia, a largely uninhabited region in the southwestern Amazon basin, bordered by Bolivia *(see inset)*. The government in 1981 decided to assist the chaotic "occupation" of Rondonia and created a colonization project called Polonoroeste. It involves paving 930 miles of highway through Rondonia, building numerous unpaved feeder roads and developing 39 rural settlement centers. The area covers territory the size of Great Britain.

The government has promoted the area as "Good land, appropriate land ... these lands offer excellent possibilities for the expansion of agricultural productivity." Yet Jose Lutzenberger, a Brazilian agronomist, contends that much of the land is so poor that, "It is quite common to see settlers give up their clearings after the first meager harvest." He contends that the government is promoting the project as a "safety valve for the political and social pressures" caused by the nation's 2.5 million landless poor.[20]

A similar forest colonization program is now underway in

[20] House Science and Technology Subcommittee on Natural Resources, Agriculture and Environment, *op. cit.,* p. 18.

Indonesia. Millions of landless Javanese have been "transmigrated" to four of the nation's sparsely inhabited islands, Sumatra, Kalimantan (Indonesian Borneo), Sulawesi and West Irian. Kalimantan alone has received four million people, despite the fact that less than 2 percent of the island's soils are thought to be permanently cultivable.[21] Critics of the plan say the government is attempting to "Javanize" the indigenous people of the outlying islands, who have their own cultures, languages and religions.

The 'Hamburgerization' of Central America

Cattle ranching, rather than farming, is the largest threat to rain forests in Central America, Panama and the southern area of Mexico. Two-thirds of Central America's rain forests already have been cut. What remains is disappearing at a rate of 1,544 square miles a year. Ranching also has spread rapidly in Brazil, where 38,600 square miles of forest have been converted to pasture over the past 20 years.

The effects of expanding cattle ranching are dramatic. About two-thirds of Central America's farm land now is devoted to cattle. Pastures commonly are abandoned after 10 or 15 years primarily because of declining soil fertility.[22] Overgrazed pasture on the Peninsula of Azuero in Panama is causing the Sarigua Desert to advance an estimated 100 yards annually. In Brazil nearly all the ranches established before 1978 have been abandoned.

The American appetite for beef is a primary cause of this upward trend in cattle ranching. The United States buys about three-quarters of all exported Central American beef, which costs about half as much as U.S. beef. But the grass-fed beef of the tropics is too lean for steaks, so it is sold to food processors for pet food and processed meat and to fast-food restaurants for hamburger meat. Critics refer to this link as the "hamburgerization" of Central American rain forests. Burger King and Roy Rogers have acknowledged using imported beef,[23] although a spokesperson for Roy Rogers said the restaurant now only used a small amount of Costa Rican beef. But McDonald's, the giant of the fast-food restaurants, uses "only USDA inspected, American beef," said spokesman Bob Keyser. "It is just patently false" that the chain uses any imported beef, he added. Burger King did not respond to several phone calls.

Forest Destruction by Commercial Logging

Commercial logging and itinerant farming are the largest threats to rain forests in the Pacific islands, West and

[21] Guppy, *op. cit.*, p. 943.
[22] Office of Technology Assessment, *op. cit.*, p. 96.
[23] Caufield, *op. cit.*, p. 110.

Tropical Closed Forest Losses
(Projected Change, 1980 to 2000)
(in square kilometers)

Kind of Forest	Tropical Africa	Tropical America	Tropical Asia
Undisturbed	− 15%	− 14%	− 48%
Logged or managed	− 18	+ 4	+ 3
Fallow	+ 33	+ 28	+ 26
Unproductive or protected	− 3	− 15	+ 9

Source: U.S. Congress, Office of Technology Assessment; U.N. Food and Agriculture Organization

Central Africa and parts of Latin America. Logging often is a forerunner to farming and ranching. Logging companies bull-doze roads through the forest that later are used by landless peasants in search of homesteads.

The world's consumption of all kinds of commercial timber has grown enormously this century and now totals roughly 1.5 billion cubic yards annually. That figure is likely to double by 2000 and double again by 2025, conservationist Norman Myers predicts.[24] Commercial logging in tropical forests is proceeding at an official rate of 16,984 square miles a year: 8,106 for Southeast Asia; 2,895 for tropical Africa and 5,983 for Latin America.

These figures, however, do not include what is widely re-garded as a significant amount of illegal harvesting. Timber poaching is a major problem in several countries. Substantial quantities of Thailand's prized teak are smuggled over the border into Cambodia and Laos by guerrillas to raise capital for their activities. In the Philippines official figures showed 365,441 cubic meters of wood exported to Japan in 1981. But Japanese import figures show more than three times as much delivered from the Philippines, suggesting a huge illegal trade.[25]

Indonesia, Malaysia and the Philippines account for half of all tropical hardwood exports. Other major suppliers are the Ivory Coast, Gabon and Brazil. The world's largest single im-porter of tropical hardwoods is Japan, which accounts for over half of the developed world's imports. The second largest im-porter is the United States.[26]

Timber provides a steady flow of cash for developing nations.

[24] Myers, *op. cit.*, p. 95.
[25] *Ibid.*, p. 109.
[26] *Ibid.*, p. 100.

But only 15 to 20 kinds of tropical trees are marketable among the thousands of known species. This highly selective cutting means that upwards of 90 percent of the trees are left unused, but as many as two-thirds of them may be damaged beyond recovery by cut trees crashing to the forest floor and by bulldozers and other heavy equipment used in logging. This destruction is compounded by land-hungry peasants who follow logging trails into the forests. "In virtually all areas of Southeast Asia and West Africa," Myers wrote in *The Primary Source,* "areas where the cropland squeeze hits hardest at land-hungry peasants — logging sites are subject to a slash-and-burn agriculture of such intensive form that the forest gets little chance, if any, to regenerate." [27]

Conservation Moves

D EVELOPED NATIONS must share the blame for the destruction of rain forests. Their demand for timber and beef have created huge economic incentives for Third World nations to exploit forest resources for quick profit, showing little regard for long-term environmental repercussions. Many forest development projects, particularly logging and ranching, receive substantial financial support from multilateral development banks such as the World Bank and the Inter-American Development Bank.

An estimated one-half of the World Bank's lending for agriculture in Latin America over the past 20 years has gone directly or indirectly into livestock, according to Bruce Rich, a senior attorney for the Environmental Defense Fund. The development banks also finance roads, pulp mills and hydroelectric projects, all of which destroy forests.

Environmental groups in the United States and the borrowing nations are stepping up their criticism of the lending agencies for failing to consider the environmental impacts of development projects. A prime example is the World Bank's funding of the Polonoroeste project in Brazil. The bank has approved six loans totalling $443 million for the colonization project. The loans stipulate a number of environmental safeguards, including setting aside park land and biological preserves, protection of lands for 15 Indian tribes and a ban on settlement in areas with unsuitable soils or soils of unknown quality. The bank, however, was criticized for failing to enforce

---

[27] *Ibid.,* p. 109.

Wood Gatherers Threaten Forests

Almost 70 percent of the people in developing nations use wood for heating and cooking. Cutting trees and woody vegetation to meet this demand is the leading threat to tropical forests in large parts of Africa, principally in the arid and semi-arid regions south of the Sahara, and Asia, in the Himalayas and the hills of South Asia.

In rural areas, women and children are the wood collectors, often walking miles a day in search of fuel. Competition for fuel wood around populated areas can lead to the destruction of all trees and shrubs. In some countries, malnutrition develops when people have little or no wood for cooking; quick-cooked or uncooked meals often are less nutritious than hot meals.

Intensive fuel wood collection has adverse consequences for the land. Where wood is not available, people substitute crop residue and animal dung, which deprives the soil of important nutrients and hastens the infertility of agricultural land. The rural poor burn an estimated 400 million tons of dung a year to cook meals and keep warm.

Stripping land of trees and depleting agricultural soils leads to soil erosion and can, in extreme cases, turn once-forested land into desert. An estimated 300 million people on three continents — Africa, Asia, and Latin America — already live on land showing signs of turning to desert.

the terms of the loan. "What is now occurring in the Polonoroeste region is an ecological, human and economic disaster of tremendous dimensions," Rich told the House Natural Resources Subcommittee in September 1984.[28] Most environmental safeguards had been ignored and Indian lands had been overrun by settlers, he added.

The following month, an international coalition of environmental groups wrote World Bank Chairman A.W. Clausen, raising a number of questions about the project. When they received an unsatisfactory reply from a lower official, they turned in frustration to Sen. Bob Kasten, R-Wis., who chairs the appropriations subcommittee overseeing the U.S. contribution to development banks. Kasten fired off a sharp letter to Clausen demanding a full response. Clausen answered with a conciliatory letter on March 1 of this year. Later that month the bank quietly halted disbursements on its Polonoroeste loans. It was the first time the bank had ever stopped loans for environmental reasons, Rich said. Disbursements resumed in late summer after the bank won a number of concessions from the Brazilian government. Meanwhile, Kasten has continued to

---

[28] House Subcommittee on Natural Resources, Agriculture and Environment, *op. cit.*, p. 99. When he testified, Rich was with the Natural Resources Defense Council.

push for tighter multilateral development bank controls over the environmental impact of their projects.

The United States wields considerable influence in this area because it provides roughly one-fifth of the funds used by development banks, three times as much as the next largest contributor. On Nov. 1, the Senate Appropriations Committee approved Kasten's proposal directing development banks to crack down on environmental problems or face loss of funding.[29] The language directs the banks to hire additional environmental staff and requires the U.S. Treasury to set up board meetings of the major development banks to discuss environmental problems. "The bottom line is that handouts from taxpayers to finance development projects which ravage the environments of host nations are going to stop," Kasten said.

Development banks are being thrust into the role of environmental cop of the Third World largely by default. Most nations are short on trained foresters, biologists and technicians needed to conduct research and shape policy. Economics is a more important factor. The staggering international debts owed by many Third World nations put a premium on development activity that will yield immediate cash for foreign exchange.

Attention is being focused on the World Bank "because we are the biggest target. If they [environmentalists] can lean on us, we'll bring the others along with us," said an official who asked to remain anonymous. "Sure there have been projects with unforeseen and regrettable consequences," the official continued. "But the bank's position is that we are doing these projects at the request of the governments. And sometimes they have other concerns that transcend the concerns of environmentalists. They are trying to feed hungry people. And they don't feel they can be as sensitive to these issues as environmentalists in developed nations. It is very hard to put our standards on a society that can't afford to make the same decisions we can. It is really hard for us to force our borrowers to accept something they don't necessarily think is in their best interest."

Land Reform Needs in Undeveloped Nations

Development banks and Third World nations also are criticized for financing agricultural projects that promote land consolidation at the expense of the small farmer and landless poor. In Latin America an estimated 7 percent of the land owners possess over 90 percent of the arable land. In the Philippines 4 percent of the farms cover one-third of the cropland.

---

[29] The language was subsequently attached to a continuing appropriations resolution the Congress cleared Dec. 19.

Effects of Deforestation on Climate

Many scientists contend that what happens to the world's rain forests concerns everybody because of potential impacts on climate. While no one knows for sure what might happen if the rain forests are destroyed, Jim Lovelock, a British ecologist who works with world climate models, has come up with an unsettling hypothesis: He concludes that temperate areas, such as North America, Europe and the Soviet Union, would become dryer, turning much productive farm land into desert.

Scientists also are concerned that slash-and-burn activities are contributing to the so-called greenhouse effect, the trapping of solar heat that warms the atmosphere. The effect is caused by the ability of carbon dioxide to absorb radiant energy. The amount of carbon dioxide in the atmosphere began rising with the advent of the Industrial Revolution during the 19th century, and has accelerated in this century.

Tropical forests contain an estimated 340 billion tons of carbon, equal to about half of all carbon in the atmosphere. Continued cutting and burning of vast forest areas would speed up the anticipated climate effects of fossil fuel burning. Some scientists now predict a significant warming of global temperatures next century, possibly by as much as 5 degrees Fahrenheit. Such an increase would be accompanied by shifts in global rainfall patterns and melting of polar icecaps. Sea levels could rise by 15 to 20 feet by the end of the next century.

In Kenya, 3,000 large farms contain more land than 750,000 small holdings.[30]

Most agricultural projects follow the "green revolution" model, which is capital rather than labor intensive. It relies on mechanization, chemical fertilizers and monoculture (single crop) plantings of crops for export, such as wheat, soybeans, sugar cane, cotton, oranges and coffee. "The social and ecological consequences of this green revolution in Brazil have really been shockingly apparent," said Brent H. Millikan, an advisor for the Foundation for Economic Investigation and Research at the University of Sao Paulo.[31] The winners, he said, have been the big farmers and multinational corporations that supply machinery and plant chemicals. "At the same time, it has drastically increased concentration of land and rural incomes, pushing more and more of Brazil's small farmers off the land" and into settlement areas such as Polonoroeste. Nicholas Guppy, former Conservator of Forests in British Guyana, contends that Brazil has enough cultivable land outside the Amazon basin to

---

[30] Myers, *op. cit.*, p. 150.
[31] House Subcommittee on Natural Resources, Agriculture Research and Environment, *op. cit.*, p. 165.

give every individual 2.3 acres. "Yet as a result of government policies disadvantageous to small farmers, smallholders are selling up and moving elsewhere," Guppy said.[32]

Latin American land law, grafted from Spanish law, also is a major contributor to deforestation. Under the law, peasants have a right to work unoccupied land, but gaining title is extremely difficult. The quickest way to stake a claim is to improve the land. "The fastest way to improve it for legal purposes is to cut all the trees down regardless of whether you have a use for the wood or not," said William McLarney, who is conducting a land tenure project in Costa Rica.[33] "If you are in an area where you know your neighbors, there isn't much pressure to do this. But when a highway comes through, or population pressures start to rise, the campesino is afraid of waking up one day and finding some stranger has moved onto his [forest] land."

Recommendations to Slow Forest Destruction

International concern over deforestation is on the rise. "A large number of groups are now coalescing on the issue," said Robinson of the National Zoo. "At least we may be moving in the right direction." His own bid for saving the remaining tropical rain forests is admittedly idealistic. "We need to have a moratorium on destruction, like a nuclear test ban treaty, until we have time to figure out how to use the forest constructively. . . ."

Ira Rubinoff, director of the Smithsonian's Tropical Research Center in Panama, has proposed a worldwide system of tropical preserves to protect 10 percent of the remaining rain forests. Currently about 4 percent of the forests in Africa, 2 percent in Latin America and 6 percent in tropical Asia are protected by parks or preserves. Not all of these are rain forests.[34] Rubinoff contends 10 percent is the minimum amount necessary to protect biological diversity.

Rubinoff suggests that funds to finance his plan could come from a progressive tax assumed by 43 developed nations with a per capita gross national product of over $1,500. The United States, for example, would contribute one-third of the $3 billion needed annually to fund the project. Much of the money would go to establish preserves, but a substantial amount would be used to compensate developing countries for the loss of revenue for shielding forests from development. "Unless there is some sort of large scale program to deal with the harsh economics of deforestation, I don't foresee much change," Rubinoff said.

---

[32] Guppy, *op. cit.*, p. 939.
[33] McLarney is a founder of the New Alchemy Institute, an environmental group that conducts research in ways to live on small tracts of land and conserve resources.
[34] Lester R. Brown, et. al., *State of the World 1985*, W.W. Norton and Co., 1985, p. 145.

Payments from the project would be incentive for nations to abide by its provisions. "Fundamentally, you get what you pay for," he added.

Guppy contends that underpricing of tropical timber has caused much deforestation. He has proposed creation of an Organization of Timber Exporting Countries (OTEC) made up of the 17 nations that hold 90 percent of the world's tropical forests. Like the Organization of Petroleum Exporting Countries, OTEC would raise prices and, through a taxation system, channel billions of dollars each year into resettlement projects, reforestation and improved management of forest resources. "We have only a few years in which to set in motion such an organization. It should be urgently considered by all the countries concerned," Guppy wrote in *Foreign Affairs* magazine.[35]

The idea that has received the most attention is also the most recent. The World Resources Institute, a private policy research group based in Washington, proposed in late October a five-year, $8 billion plan involving forest management, reforestation, improvement of agricultural practices, land-use planning and conservation research in 56 tropical countries.[36] Developed with the backing of The World Bank and the U.N. Development Programme, half the funds would come from development agencies and international lending institutions and the remainder from the private sector and governments of tropical nations.

At a news conference, World Bank President Clausen and Peter McPherson, administrator of the U.S. Agency for International Development (AID), praised the plan and said they were committed to its goals. But neither was prepared to commit his organization to a specific contribution. They emphasized that the governments and peoples of tropical nations would have to cooperate to make the plan work.

Clausen said that development agencies historically "have focused heavily on the problem of alleviating rural poverty through increased food production. However, we are increasingly coming to realize that that is only part of the story." It is now clear, he added, that "development policies cannot succeed unless we include provisions for protection of the ecological environment on which sustainable agriculture is built."

Bill Burley, who is directing the project for the institute, said he was optimistic that the plan would succeed. "We see some very encouraging responses within the World Bank and U.S.

[35] Guppy, *op. cit.*, p. 965.
[36] The institute was founded in 1982 and is aimed at providing "accurate information about global resources and populations, identifying emerging issues and developing politically and economically workable proposals. It is funded by private foundations, the United Nations, governmental agencies and corporations.

AID. That does not mean lots of new money right away, but very likely it will in the long run." As for support from developing nations, he said, "To the extent they realize this is in their best interest, they will commit the money to it." But, he continued, "What this will translate to in the future is hard to tell."

Recommended Reading List

Books

Brown, Lester, et al., *State of the World 1985,* W. W. Norton and Co., 1985.
Caufield, Catherine, *In the Rainforest,* Alfred A. Knopf, 1985.
Goodland, R. J. A., and H. S. Irwin, *Amazon Jungle: Green Hell or Red Desert?,* Elsevier Scientific Publishing Co., 1975.
Forsyth, Adrian, and Kenneth Miyata, *Tropical Nature,* Charles Scribner's Sons, 1984.
Myers, Norman, *The Primary Source, Tropical Forests and Our Future,* W. W. Norton & Co., 1984.
Stone, Roger D., *Dreams of Amazonia,* Viking, 1985.

Articles

Guppy, Nicholas, "Tropical Deforestation," *Foreign Affairs,* Spring 1984.
Maybury-Lewis, David, "Societies on the Brink," *Harvard Magazine,* January/February 1977.
Rubinoff, Ira, "If We Lose the Tropical Forests, No Birds Will Sing," *The Washington Post,* Aug. 5, 1984.
Sanchez, Pedro, et. al., "Amazon Basin Soils: Management for Continuous Crop Production," *Science,* May 1982.
"Wound in the World," *Asiaweek,* July 13, 1984.

Reports and Studies

House Science and Technology Subcommittee on Natural Resources, Agriculture Research and Environment, "Tropical Forest Development Projects: Status of Environmental and Agricultural Research," No. 143, U.S. Government Printing Office, 1985
Lanly, Jean-Paul, "Tropical Forest Resources," Food and Agriculture Organization of the United Nations, 1982.
Office of Technology Assessment, "Technologies to Sustain Tropical Forest Resources," U.S. Government Printing Office, OTA-F-214, March 1984.
World Resources Institute, "Tropical Forests: A Call for Action," October 1985.

Graphics: Cover photos courtesy World Wildlife Fund-U.S., right by Andrew Young, left by Douglas R. Shane; map p. 165 by Assistant Art Director Robert Redding; map p. 171 by Patrick Murphy.

SOIL EROSION: THREAT TO FOOD SUPPLY

by

Marc Leepson

Mar. 23
1 9 8 4

Editor's Update: Although House-Senate differences blocked 1984 action on "sodbuster" legislation *(see p. 194)*, the omnibus farm bill enacted in December 1985 included popular new programs for soil conservation. The sodbuster provision will deny any federal farm benefits to farmers who till highly erodible soil, and a "swampbuster" program will give similar protection to much of the nation's wetlands.

To further encourage farmers to take fragile land out of crop production, the bill also established a "conservation reserve" of at least 40 million acres. Over the next five years, the secretary of agriculture will be required to take steps to help farmers place farm land in the reserve for 10 to 15 years, and to help pay the cost of planting grass, trees or other ground covering.

SOIL EROSION:
THREAT TO FOOD SUPPLY

A LIST of the most pressing problems confronting modern civilization certainly would include the threat of nuclear war, worsening air and water pollution, overpopulation in Africa, Asia and Latin America and the depletion of worldwide supplies of fossil fuels. Agriculture experts add another candidate to that list: the potentially catastrophic consequences of soil erosion. "[T]he loss of soil is in some ways the most serious of the threats civilization faces...," writes Lester R. Brown, president of Worldwatch Institute. "[T]here are no widely usable substitutes for soil in food production. Civilization can survive the exhaustion of oil reserves, but not the continuing wholesale loss of topsoil." [1]

"Soil erosion is absolutely a tragedy of mounting proportions in some of the developing world," said R. Neil Sampson, executive vice president of the National Association of Conservation Districts. In the United States, he added, "the soil erosion rates are pretty alarming. There's no amount of rationalization to make them go away. They are pretty serious." [2]

Erosion — the wearing away of earth — occurs whenever rain and wind come into contact with soil *(see box, p. 187)*. Some erosion therefore occurs naturally on all types of land. But agricultural practices that take little account of erosion control add greatly to the natural loss of soil. Agricultural scientists say that land with deep topsoil can lose as much as five tons an acre each year and land with thin layers of topsoil as much as three tons an acre annually without adversely affecting crop production potential. But on some 141 million acres of U.S. cropland — about 34 percent of the total — annual erosion averages more than five tons an acre, according to data compiled by the U.S. Department of Agriculture.[3] In the "Corn Belt" states of Iowa, Missouri, Illinois, Indiana and Ohio, soil erosion averages twice

---

[1] Lester R. Brown, *Building a Sustainable Society* (1981), p. 14. Brown is a former administrator of the International Agricultural Development Service in the U.S. Department of Agriculture. Worldwatch Institute is a Washington, D.C., non-profit research organization that focuses on natural resources, human needs and environmental threats to food production.

[2] Sampson is author of *Farmland or Wasteland* (1981). Remarks by Sampson and others in this report, unless otherwise indicated, are taken from interviews with the author in January.

[3] U.S. Department of Agriculture, Soil Conservation Service, "1977 National Resources Inventories," p. 5.

that of any other region. Cropland erosion also is particularly serious in Hawaii, western Texas and eastern New Mexico, the Palouse Basin of eastern Washington and the western border of the Idaho panhandle, east-central Texas' Blackland Prairie and the southern Mississippi Valley Delta.

Altogether, some two billion tons of soil wash away from U.S. croplands each year. Three billion tons of soil vanish from range land, forests and pastures. The yearly erosion from all lands adds up to more than the amount washed away during the "Dust Bowl" years of the 1930s *(see p. 190)*. What is lost cannot easily be regained. "It takes nature more than 100 years to produce a single inch of topsoil," Sen. William L. Armstrong, R-Colo., told the Senate recently, "but that inch of soil can blow away in less than an hour if not protected against erosion." [4]

As bleak as the erosion problem is in the United States, the situation in many other parts of the world — especially in developing nations — is exceedingly more serious. The problems of soil conservation in the Third World "are much worse and the difficulties of applying the solutions are much greater" than in the United States, said Norman W. Hudson, vice president of the World Association of Soil and Water Conservation. [5]

Although there are no reliable statistics measuring the extent of soil erosion around the world, extremely serious problems exist in Australia, China, Ethiopia, Haiti, India, Indonesia, Nepal, Pakistan, South Africa, the Soviet Union and Zimbabwe. Most soil scientists agree with Lester Brown's assessment that erosion "has now reached epidemic proportions." [6] A 1977 survey undertaken by the U.N. Conference on Desertification estimated that excessive erosion exists on about one-fifth of the world's cropland. Other experts, including Brown, say that the problem is much worse. "Close to half the world's cropland is losing topsoil at a debilitating rate," Brown said. A 1980 report commissioned by President Carter to assess international environmental problems categorized erosion and other soil deterioration as "perhaps the most serious environmental development" facing the world. [7] The report predicted that soil losses from erosion "can be expected to accelerate, especially in North and Central Africa, the humid and high-altitude portions of Latin America and much of South Asia."

---

[4] Speaking Nov. 18, 1983, on the Senate floor.

[5] Writing in the *Journal of Soil and Water Conservation*, November-December 1983, p. 446. Hudson is professor of field engineering at the National College of Agricultural Engineering in Silsoe, Bedford, England.

[6] Writing in *State of the World, 1984: A Worldwatch Institute Report on Progress Toward a Sustainable Society* (1984), p. 5.

[7] Council on Environmental Quality and U.S. Department of State, "The Global 2000 Report to the President: Entering the Twenty-First Century," Vol. I, 1980, pp. 32, 33.

Soil Erosion: Threat to Food Supply

This large-scale loss of soil through erosion causes two basic environmental problems. First, the washing away of the most fertile topsoil makes eroded cropland much less productive. The soil is unable to supply plants with nutrients; its capacity to retain water is diminished. In short, as a government report put it, "crop production suffers as erosion progresses." [8] Second, billions of tons of soil — along with residues from chemical fertilizers and pesticides — wash into the world's waterways, lakes and reservoirs, restricting water flow, increasing flood damage, reducing water quality and damaging fish and wildlife habitats.

Experts say that over-population and the resultant increased demand for food greatly exacerbate the soil erosion problems around the world. "It's the basic demand pressures pushing farmers into doing things they would not otherwise do," Brown said. In the United States the pressure to produce more grain to meet demand and mortgage payments has prompted farmers to plow up marginal grass and pasture lands. In developing countries, Brown said, the demand for food output has forced farmers "to farm more intensively in some situations where the land doesn't hold up very well under more

USDA - Soil Conservation Service

Runoff from spring rains

intensive cultivation." [9] In addition, Brown said, more and more farmers have been "pushed up the hillsides, particularly in much of the Third World. And so a lot of the steeply sloping land is being farmed, and when you see it plowed, you know 15 years from now there won't be any agriculture there."

It is thought that the Soviet Union, which has the most cropland of any country, may also be losing the most topsoil. Again, the cause is the push to expand production — in the

---

[8] Office of Technology Assessment, "Impacts of Technology on U.S. Cropland and Rangeland Productivity," August 1982, p. 35.

[9] Brown estimates that the world demand for grain doubled between 1950 and 1973 and could double again by the end of the century. See Brown, et. al, *State of the World 1984, op. cit.*, p. 53.

Soviet Union's case to grow enough grain for self-sufficiency. Brown blamed the Soviet erosion problem on the government's high grain production quotas. "In trying to meet a production quota you don't want to worry about spending your time and energy building terraces and developing [crop] rotations and whatever else is needed" to fight erosion, he said.

Damage to Ecology From Deforestation

Adding significantly to erosion problems around the world are two closely related environmental phenomena: deforestation and desertification. Trees and forests are among nature's most powerful anchors, holding the soil in place. When they are absent there is little to prevent wind and rain from playing freely with the soil and, in the world's arid places, turning the land into desert.

Growing demand for food, fuel and housing — especially in Third World countries — is leading to widespread deforestation. "In a tremendous number of poor countries you have this problem of tree cutting for houses or firewood," said Nicholas Raymond, external relations director for the U.N. Food and Agriculture Organization (FAO). "Since forests are the main block against soil erosion — especially water, but also wind — if you cut down the woods, you're in a mess."

Although accurate statistics are impossible to pin down, the FAO estimates that some 18.5 million acres of closed forest and 9.4 million acres of open tree formations are cleared annually, mainly to extend croplands and supply firewood. Because newly plowed former forest lands generally are marginal and unsuitable for cultivation, however, serious soil erosion often occurs, as it has throughout Central America and large portions of Africa, northern India, Thailand, the Philippines, Nepal, Haiti, Brazil, Chile, Venezuela, the Peruvian and Colombian Andes and West Java in Indonesia.

"The situation in West Java is bad," said Emil Alim, Indonesia's minister of state for development supervision and the environment. "It has no plantation history and as long ago as 1918 it was called the 'Dying Land.' To a visitor [today] it looks like the surface of the moon. Nothing can grow." [10] In Haiti, Nicholas Raymond said, "where you have steep slopes and heavy rains, the people have gone up and cut the trees and tried to plow. When the rains came, the soil went away. And when the soil goes away, it doesn't come back.... You can look at any local painting made of Haiti and see those grey, barren hills all over the place. Those used to be covered with forests. It's a disaster down there."

---

[10] Quoted in *People,* (a quarterly publication of the London-based International Planned Parenthood Federation) Vol. 10, No. 1, 1983, p. 18.

Types of Erosion

Soil erosion is caused by wind and water. Wind erosion occurs when the wind is strong enough to lift particles of unprotected, dry soil into the air. The Great Plains and Western states are most susceptible to wind erosion.

There are four basic types of water erosion; the first two are the most damaging:

● **Sheet erosion** — the removal of a fairly uniform layer of soil from the land surface by the action of rainfall and surface runoff.

● **Rill erosion** — the formation of numerous small channels that occurs primarily on recently cultivated soil.

● **Gully erosion** — an advanced state of rill erosion in which water accumulates in channels and washes away soil to depths ranging from one to two feet to as much as 75 to 100 feet.

● **Streambed erosion** — the widening of streams.

In Ethiopia erosion caused by deforestation and overgrazing — in combination with a lengthy drought — has led to greatly diminished food production and food shortages. Moreover, a guerrilla war has disrupted food supply lines and forced thousands of persons to leave their homelands. Experts believe that as many as 4.5 million Ethiopians — about 14 percent of the population — are now facing malnutrition and starvation.

At one time forests covered nearly all of Ethiopia's mountainous highlands, where more than 70 percent of the nation's population lives. But by the 1960s, according to a recent report by the U.N. Environmental Program, forest cover had been reduced to some 20 percent. Today only 3.1 percent of the mountainous land is covered by trees. This drastic depletion of forest cover, along with overgrazing, has led to severe soil erosion in about half of the country.[11] "Enough topsoil has been lost that Ethiopia may never get the food situation straightened out during our lifetimes," said Lester Brown.

Fast-Growing Desertification Situation

Desertification — the spread of deserts and desertlike ecological conditions onto formerly arable land — destroys both vegetation and fertile soil. Once desertification occurs, crops cannot grow on the land until it is somehow reclaimed. Restoration of such land can take years to accomplish and is extremely costly. Some 11.58 million square miles — about 20 percent of the Earth's land surface — "are under direct threat of desertification," according to Jon Tinker, director of the environmental group Earthscan.[12] Desertification, evident

---

[11] See "Land Degradation in Ethiopia," *Newsletter* of the World Association of Soil and Water Conservation, September 1983, p. 4.
[12] Writing in *People, op. cit.,* 9.

throughout the world, is a serious problem in Africa, the Middle East, Iran, Afghanistan and northwestern India. In the United States, overgrazing of sheep is contributing to desertification on the Navajo Indian reservation in northern Arizona and New Mexico.

Overgrazing, overcultivation and deforestation — all of which stem from overpopulation — are the primary causes of desertification. "With population growth, agricultural people — people who don't know how to do anything else — are going to start moving farther and farther from good, traditional agricultural land onto marginal land," said Nicholas Raymond of the FAO. "Then two things happen. They cause erosion, and when the whole thing breaks down, that adds to the number of people who go hungry."

By far the world's worst case of desertification is in the eight African countries of the Sahel: Chad, Niger, Mali, Upper Volta, Mauritania, Senegal, Gambia and Cape Verde. Desertification in this belt of land, which is situated directly below the Sahara Desert, was one of the causes of a devastating famine that killed hundreds of thousands of Africans in the region in the early 1970s. Only a monumental international relief effort and the return of rains in 1974 eased the suffering.

The same conditions that caused the famine a decade ago — a drought, the destruction of vegetative cover, wind erosion on cultivated fields and high population growth — once again are causing severe food shortages in most of the Sahel. Sen. John C. Danforth, R-Mo., who recently returned from a fact-finding tour of the region, described what he saw in Senegal: "One drives for miles through a land with no ground cover and scattered scrub trees to the dust-shrouded village of Mafré. No rain has fallen for more than a year. No crop has been produced. Once the villagers owned 300 head of cattle. Now they own six. Of 40 families that lived in Mafré several years ago, only five remain." [13]

Erosion in America

IN THE UNITED STATES erosion has been a problem since colonial times. But only a few perceptive soil conservationists and scientific farmers recognized its potential seriousness and sought to control it. Among them were George Washington and

---

[13] Writing in *The Washington Post*, Jan. 25, 1984.

Dust storm, 1936, Cimarron County, Okla. Photo by
Arthur Rothstein for the Farm Security Administration

Thomas Jefferson. Washington "fought erosion with . . . zeal,"
agricultural historian Edward Jerome Dies wrote. "Each year
the rains would wash topsoil down into his 'Muddy Hole' farm,
and each year he would haul it back to its proper place. . . ."
Jefferson, Dies said, "noted that rainstorms washed both crops
and soils down the hillsides of many farms. He attacked the
problem and at length introduced horizontal or terraced
plowing. Marked benefits resulted."

But few farmers adopted these erosion control methods. One
reason was the availability of vast new areas of land. As Dies put
it: "Planters simply opened new acreage when the soil of old
fields was exhausted, for as Thomas Jefferson observed, it was
cheaper to buy a new acre than to fertilize an old one." [14]

One area that appeared to be closed to farming was the Great
Plains, a stretch of land that lies between the 100th Meridian
and the Rocky Mountains. Atlases published between 1820 and
1850 showed this region as "The Great American Desert," and it
was thought at the time that no farm economy could be sustained on these seemingly desolate lands. Attitudes toward the
"Great Desert" changed drastically in the following decades.
The new transcontinental railroad companies, land speculators
and civic boosters who advertised the region as heaven on earth
and the prospect of free land provided by the Homestead Act of
1862 lured thousands of pioneers to the plains.

Settlement of the plains coincided with development of agricultural equipment — particularly the steel plow in 1839 —
which allowed the homesteaders to farm the hard prairie sod.
But the plains had comparatively little water even in the best of
times, and the periods of drought that beset the region roughly

[14] Edward Jerome Dies, *Titans of the Soil* (1976 reprint), pp. 15, 25-26.

every 20 years from the time the homesteaders arrived drove many of them away. But by then the damage to the soil had been done. Winds blew the loosened particles away and the rains, when they finally came, washed away more soil.

The farmers persisted, however, slowly turning the land into what would become the world's breadbasket. In the second decade of the 20th century, drought-induced scarcities, together with the food demands of World War I, drove farm prices up, prompting farmers to plow up pasture land to grow more grain. When farm prices fell after the war, farmers returned many of their wheat fields to grazing land. Then, in the early 1930s, the nation experienced a sustained drought. The damage done by cultivating the former grasslands in the prairie states was compounded by the lack of rain. Beginning in 1934 a series of devastating dust storms smothered crops, buried buildings, destroyed pasture land and forced many farmers to leave their land.

May 1934 brought some of the worst storms to the Great Plains, particularly in western Kansas, Texas, Oklahoma and eastern Colorado. Hugh H. Bennett, the pioneering soil scientist and the first head of the USDA's Soil Conservation Service, described the May 12, 1934, storm as "a disturbance that was completely without precedent in American history." The dust lifted from the prairies, Bennett said, "darkened the sun over the nation's capital, sifted through the screens of tall office buildings in New York City and moved on for hundreds of miles over the Atlantic Ocean." [15] A presidential commission, directed in 1934 to assess the erosion problem, reported that some 35 million acres of former farm land had been destroyed by gullying and that nearly 140 million acres had been stripped of much of its topsoil. Severe damage occurred not only in the Great Plains but in many parts of the South and Far West as well.[16] The storms and the farmers they forced onto the relief rolls focused national attention on soil conservation for the first time and influenced Congress to institute the first federal erosion control programs.

Federal Commitment to Soil Conservation

In 1933 Congress took two steps to curb erosion. The first was the creation of the Civilian Conservation Corps (CCC) intended to put jobless men — some of them farmers forced off the land by the dust storms they helped to create — back to work on conservation projects throughout the United States. In its first

---

[15] Hugh Hammond Bennett, *Soil Conservation* (1939), p. 56. For further information on the Dust Bowl, see R. Douglas Hurt, *The Dust Bowl: An Agricultural and Social History* (1981).
[16] See Frederick Merk, *History of the Westward Movement*, Alfred A. Knopf, 1978, p. 551.

PIK and Erosion

Under the 1983 Payment-in-Kind (PIK) program, the U.S. Department of Agriculture allowed wheat, corn, sorghum and rice farmers to take up to 50 percent of their cropland out of production and receive surplus government crops in return. The idea was to cut back on federal farm program outlays and help stabilize farm prices. Although it was not designed as a conservation measure, the PIK program required farmers to plant clover or alfalfa on the idle acreage to cut down on erosion.

Peter Myers, head of the USDA's Soil Conservation Service, and Everett Rank, head of the agency's Agricultural Stabilization and Conservation Service, in March 1983 estimated "soil savings at around three tons per acre, for a total in excess of 240 million tons of soil which may be kept on farms as a result of the PIK program in 1983."

However, a preliminary USDA report issued in February estimated that only about 1.6 tons of soil were saved on each of the approximately 82 million acres set aside under PIK and a related program. Environmental and wildlife groups have charged that many farmers disregarded the requirement to plant cover crops on the fallow soil. Instead, millions of PIK acres were left bare and unprotected or covered with the previous year's crop residue and weeds, providing little protection against erosion.

USDA officials say they are generally satisified with the conservation aspects of the PIK program. "I would have been satisfied if we had just held our own," said Wayne Chapman, an SCS soil conservationist. The soil saved, Chapman added, is "a positive showing that [PIK] was really worthwhile from a conservation standpoint."

year, the CCC built 420,000 erosion control dams, planted 100,000 acres of trees and put up 4,000 miles of fence.[17] The second was creation of the Soil Erosion Service within the Department of the Interior. Using CCC workers, the Soil Erosion Service set up dozens of erosion-control demonstration projects.

After the dust storms of 1934 the federal government undertook a greater commitment to soil conservation and erosion control. On March 25, 1935, the Soil Conservation Service (SCS) was established as a permanent agency within the Department of Agriculture. Its first director was Hugh Bennett, who had run the Soil Erosion Service and worked to bring the problems of erosion to the attention of the government and the American people. Since 1937 the SCS has worked directly with farmers through soil conservation agencies set up by individual states and local conservation districts. The first local district was set

---

[17] "Soil and Water Resources Conservation Act, 1980 Appraisal, Part I" Department of Agriculture, March 1981, p. 11.

up in August 1937 in Anson County, N.C., Bennett's home. Today, according to the National Association of Conservation Districts, there are 2,950 districts covering virtually the entire country.

Most observers agree that this new federal-state-local cooperation made significant progress in controlling soil erosion. "[T]he national goal of soil and water conservation was translated into local action programs designed to fit local conditions and guided by locally elected leaders," Neil Sampson wrote. "Through conservation districts, the SCS could bring a national research and testing effort and the knowledge of skilled technicians to the farmers of America. . . . The federal agent did not have any authority over the landowner; the district provided a local agency to establish a cooperative, voluntary arrangement." [18]

With SCS advice and the help of federal loans and subsidies, many farmers began using conservation and erosion-control methods. Marginal lands were left unplowed and used for pasture. Farmers practiced crop rotation, planting corn or wheat one year followed by cover crops such as hay, grass or soybeans. Fields were plowed in contours rather than straight rows to cut down on rain-induced erosion. Artificial terraces were bulldozed into place on erosive slopes. Fences were built and tree rows planted to ward off wind-borne erosion.

Consequences of Stepped-Up Production

Progress in the fight against erosion continued until the early 1970s when a new surge in demand led many farmers to sacrifice control measures in their quest to increase production. Three factors contributed to the heightened production. First, crop failures in many parts of the world increased demand for U.S. grains. Second, the dollar was weak compared with other currencies and so American grain was cheaper to import. Third, the Nixon administration in 1972 signed an agreement that sent $1.1 billion worth of U.S.-grown grain to the Soviet Union.

The federal government encouraged the increased production; Agriculture Secretary Earl Butz called on the nation's farmers to plant "fencerow to fencerow." And in 1973 Congress passed a farm bill designed to spur farmers on to higher productivity.[19] Blessed with good weather and ample rain, farmers produced bumper crops. They also abandoned many long-standing soil conservation practices.

"In the all-out push for production we began to lose some of the old soil conservation practices," said Norman Berg, the

---

[18] Neil Sampson, *Farmland or Wasteland* (1981), p. 260.
[19] For background see "World Grain Trade," *E.R.R.*, 1973 Vol. II, pp. 709-732.

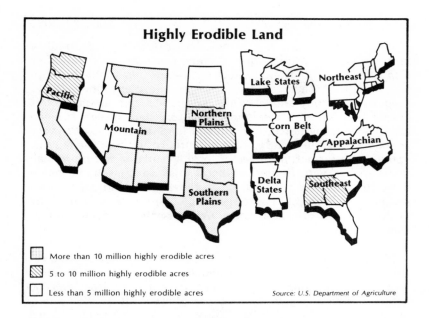

Highly Erodible Land

Pacific
Mountain
Northern Plains
Lake States
Northeast
Corn Belt
Appalachian
Southern Plains
Delta States
Southeast

☐ More than 10 million highly erodible acres

☒ 5 to 10 million highly erodible acres

☐ Less than 5 million highly erodible acres

Source: U.S. Department of Agriculture

former Soil Conservation Service head who now represents the Soil Conservation Society of America in Washington, D.C. By the late 1970s, Neil Sampson said, "We found ourselves . . . with a very specialized, very intensive agriculture that had abandoned the age-old techniques for controlling soil damage, such as crop rotations. . . . Suddenly we were out there with huge new tractors farming land that was a great deal steeper or sandier or rougher just because we had the power and the mobility and the ability and technology to do it."

Even falling farm prices do not necessarily mean that farmers will take some land out of production. They are just as likely to till even more land in an effort to pay their often staggering production bills and keep their income levels stable. That is what happened after 1976 when bumper crops in the Soviet Union and elsewhere cut demand for American grain and left farmers with huge surpluses and depressed prices.

The amount of U.S. farm land under cultivation in this country hit a post-World War II low of 333 million acres in 1969. But the number of acres under cultivation began rising steadily in 1972 and stands today at some 413 million acres. Some of that newly plowed land, which had been used for grazing, is highly susceptible to erosion. Soil scientists estimate that about 10 percent of the land now under cultivation in this country — about 40 million acres — is subject to average annual erosion rates of from 10-30 tons per acre. Moreover, experts say, about 250 million acres of fragile lands may be plowed in the near future *(see map, above)*.

The federal system of economic incentives designed to allow farmers to make profits while keeping consumer food costs low also had an unintentional effect on the erosion problem. Price supports and other federal farm programs encourage "land speculators to buy and plow up rangelands that should be left alone," Sen. Armstrong said in a Nov. 18 Senate speech. In some cases, Armstrong noted, the value of land doubles "by the very act of plowing," no matter how potentially erodible the land is. "So when a farmer, an investor, or a speculator can plow such lands with a very limited economic risk to himself, he has a powerful incentive to plow. . . . If the crop should grow, price supports will roughly cover the cost of production. If not, the farmer can get crop insurance, even disaster payments under some circumstances. . . ."

In Montana, for example, the Soil Conservation Service estimates that between 750,000 and two million acres of rangeland have been plowed in the last 10 years. At least 250,000 acres of Montana grazing land was plowed out in 1983 alone, according to SCS estimates. "Most of that land is considered highly erodible," said Bill Laycock, a range management specialist with the USDA's Agricultural Research Service in Fort Collins, Colo. "It's grazing land that had never been plowed before."

Financial pressures compound the problem. Many farmers' "options are reduced on the way they use their land" because of pressing financial problems, said SCS soil scientist Don McCormack. "They have to use it pretty intensively and therefore risk soil erosion in order to make their commitments for the annual production costs, plus any investments they have in land." The array of federal farm programs can become the deciding factor when such farmers opt to put marginal lands under the plow. "Under such circumstances," Sen. Armstrong said, "a farmer or rancher trying desperately to eke out a living under what are already difficult conditions may be led to conclude he should plow fragile lands even when his best instincts warn against such a move."

On Nov. 18, 1983, the Senate passed a bill sponsored by Armstrong that would prohibit the payment of some government incentives to farmers who plowed up highly erodible land. The measure, informally referred to as the "sodbuster" bill, was endorsed by a long list of farm organizations and conservationist groups — two sectors that do not usually agree on farm policies. A companion measure, introduced in the House on June 30, 1983, by Rep. Ed Jones, D-Tenn., combines the sodbuster plan with much broader financial incentives to get erosion-prone land out of crop production on a long-term basis.[20] Observers say some form of this legislation likely will be passed by Congress in 1984.

Search for Solution

S OLVING the world's erosion problems is going to be, at best, an extremely difficult task. Some fear it may be impossible, especially in some of the Third World countries. But there are some encouraging signs. In the United States new techniques of tilling that reduce erosion are gaining popularity. The mold-board plow that made it possible to bust the sod is giving way, if slowly, to conservation tillage systems that in some cases barely disturb the soil.

There are many types of conservation tillage systems — also known as plowless farming, reduced-tillage, no-till, and eco-till, among other terms. These methods have three things in common: They do not use the moldboard plow; they leave some residue on the soil surface to fight erosion and help retain mosture; and they depend primarily on herbicides for weed control.

The traditional moldboard plow has a series of curved plates that dig into the soil, lift it and turn it over. Disks and harrows are then dragged over the plowed soil to break up clumps of sod. Once seed is planted, a farmer may repeatedly run a cultivator between the rows to destroy weeds. Even on fields that are contour-plowed or otherwise treated to reduce erosion, the exposure of land to wind and rain can still result in high levels of erosion.

The invention of the chisel plow, described by an Office of Technology Assessment (OTA) report as "the primary tool of conservation," has reduced reliance on the traditional tilling methods.[21] Chisel plows typically expose only enough soil to plant each row, leaving crop residue on the surface. This helps the soil retain moisture and thus reduces soil runoff and wind erosion. Chisel plowing and other types of conservation tillage

---

[20] See *Congressional Quarterly Weekly Report*, Sept. 17, 1983, p. 1942. An expanded version of Rep. Jones' bill was approved by the House Agriculture Conservation Subcommittee March 6. The bill would deny federal assistance for crops grown on highly erodible land and offer farmers cost-sharing payments for conservation practices on fragile lands taken out of crop rotation.

[21] Office of Technology Assessment, "Impacts of Technology on U.S. Cropland and Rangeland Productivity," August 1982, p. 95.

systems disturb the soil less than conventional tillage methods do, but the amount of disturbance varies widely. Some tillage techniques churn up as much as 95 percent of the ground, while no-till planters seed new crops directly into existing crop residues with minimal disruption of the soil.

One of the newest types of conservation tillage, called slit planting, has been developed by soil scientist Charles Elkins of the USDA's Soil and Water Research unit. This method uses blades that cut slits 15 inches deep and only one-sixteenth of an inch wide at the base, into which the seeds are dropped. Slit planting leaves topsoil and crop residues in place and at the same time penetrates the hardpan beneath the topsoil allowing better root development. Successful tests of this method on soybeans, sunflowers, okra and peanuts have encouraged USDA soil scientists to try to develop a farm implement that could make large-scale slit planting practical.

Soil scientists continue to develop and refine tilling technologies that cut back on erosion and still give farmers high crop yields. "Too often tillage systems are combinations of operations applied in a broad manner without regard for all the needs of the plant or for conservation," said agricultural engineer Robert L. Schafer, director of the USDA's National Tillage Machinery Laboratory in Auburn, Ala. "Future tillage systems must be much more specific than present systems. Specific crops, soil types, and environments must receive their own special treatment." [22]

Prospects for Future of Reduced Tillage

Conservation tillage practices are "taking off faster than any agricultural technology we've ever seen, but it'll take a while to make a full contribution to the problem," Neil Sampson said. In some areas of the country significant numbers of farmers have put erosion-control systems into place. In Ohio, for example, a 1980 survey of 808 farmers indicated that 43 percent used some type of conservation tillage practice.[23] According to the Maryland conservation service, nearly 85 percent of the corn crop in Howard County (located between Baltimore and Washington, D.C.) is farmed with no-till technology.[24] On a nationwide basis, however, the percentage of farmers using conservation tillage is much lower than in Ohio or Howard County. A survey released Feb. 8 by the National Association of Conservation Districts found that nearly 87 million acres of cropland were planted in

---

[22] Quoted in the USDA publication, *Agricultural Research*, April 1983, p. 8.

[23] See Howard Ladewig and Ray Garibay, "Reasons Why Ohio Farmers Decide For or Against Conservation Tillage, *Journal of Soil and Water Conservation*, November-December 1983, pp. 487-488.

[24] See Kenneth Cook, "Slip, Sliding Away," *Environmental Action*, November 1981, pp. 18-21.

Traditional plow, left, turns over soil, exposing it to wind, water erosion. Conservation tillage, right, disturbs less earth, leaves crop residue to retain moisture, slow erosion.

some form of conservation tillage in 1983, more than 31 percent of the total cropland planted.[25] "That is up from very, very negligible amounts five or six years ago," Sampson said.

Many farmers have turned to conservation tillage primarily because it saves expensive fuel and precious time. In those cases erosion control is a secondary benefit. And some experts believe that conservation tillage must be used with other conservation methods to be most effective. Norman Berg of the Soil Conservation Society of America, for example, said that conservation tillage systems "are very promising providing they are combined with other erosion-control methods such as contour or terraced planting. They may eventually apply to most of the agricultural soil in America." Conservation tillage systems also present a major unknown — namely, how their heavy reliance on chemical herbicides affects the environment. "While current evidence suggests that herbicides have relatively minor effects on the environment, the evidence is incomplete," noted Pierre R. Crosson, a senior fellow at Resources for the Future. "As more information becomes available, controls on the use of herbicides may greatly restrict the spread of conservation tillage." [26]

[25] "1983 National Survey: Conservation Tillage Practices," prepared by the National Association of Conservation Districts' Conservation Tillage Information Center.
[26] Pierre R. Crosson, ed., *The Cropland Crisis* (1982), p. 15. Resources for the Future is a Washington, D.C., food and agricultural research organization.

One stubborn problem in the fight against soil erosion is that most of those who employ conservation practices are successful farmers who work rich land that is not subject to severe erosion. Unfortunately, the converse also is true: Very few farmers working land that suffers from severe erosion use conservation tillage practices. Conservation tillage is generally used by farmers with better soils, Sampson said, "because the payoffs are better and also because those farmers are using their financial condition to take the risk, for example, of buying a new piece of machinery or trying an untested technology. The last place these technologies go is on the marginal farms where the risks are already so marginal in terms of both economics and production that taking new risks is hard to do." The OTA report observed that the suitability of particular soil conservation technologies are "site specific, as are the soil and water savings they will achieve." Nevertheless, the report concluded, if conservation tillage and no-till systems are applied to the worst areas of erosion in this country, and if they are "well designed and adequately funded," they could "significantly reduce the nation's overall erosion problem and protect some of its most fragile lands."

Erosion Control in Developing Countries

If the United States has not been able to solve its erosion problems "with all the advantages of research, extension, and conservation services, plus wealthy, educated farmers on good land with a gentle climate ... then what hope is there for struggling countries that have few, or none, of these advantages?" asks Norman Hudson of the World Association of Soil and Water Conservation.[27] The answer to that question, most agricultural experts say, is that soil conservation problems, particularly erosion, are so intractable in many developing countries there may not be any near-term solutions.

Nonetheless, several nations have made strong commitments to fight soil erosion and put soil conservation plans into practice. A presidential commission for soil conservation has been set up in Kenya, for example. And Indonesia instituted a "Greening Program" of soil conservation and reforestation in 1983. Peru's National Agrarian University soon will offer its first postgraduate program in forestry science in a cooperative project with the University of Toronto in Canada. Soil scientists in South Africa have been experimenting with conservation tillage methods of corn in the country's Highveld region.

Several international organizations also are involved in the fight against soil erosion. The World Bank, for example, is backing reforestation programs in the Sahel, including an am-

---

[27] Hudson, *op. cit.*, p. 446.

Soybeans planted in "no-till" wheat straw

bitious irrigated plantation of eucalyptus trees in Niger. The FAO's Soil and Water Division has helped design erosion-control programs for specific countries. A new international organization, the World Association of Soil and Water Conservation, was set up in January 1983 to promote cooperation on soil and water conservation issues among governments, international agencies and private and public groups. The association, which is still in its formative stages, will monitor, assess and support soil and water conservation practices around the world.

Despite these steps, soil erosion, desertification and deforestation remain extremely serious worldwide problems. The only positive factor Lester Brown named when asked to assess the future of the fight against soil erosion was "that awareness of the issue is gradually rising. . . . When you see the news reports now on famine in Africa they often talk about population growth and soil erosion and recognize it's not just a climatic phenomenon. The drought is clearly bringing a deteriorating situation into focus and there is now a wide awareness that there are some very basic problems that have to be dealt with."

Selected Bibliography

Books

Bennett, Hugh Hammond, *Soil Conservation*, McGraw-Hill, 1939.

Brown, Lester R., *Building a Sustainable Society*, Norton, 1981.

Brown, Lester R., et al., *State of the World, 1984*, Norton, 1984.

Crosson, Pierre R., ed., *The Cropland Crisis: Myth or Reality?* Johns Hopkins University Press, 1982.

Dies, Edward Jerome, *Titans of the Soil: Great Builders of Agriculture*, Greenwood Press, 1976.

Hurt, R. Douglas, *The Dust Bowl: An Agricultural and Social History*, Nelson-Hall, 1981.

Merk, Frederick, *History of the Westward Movement*, Alfred A. Knopf, 1978.

Sampson, R. Neil, *Farmland or Wasteland: A Time to Choose*, Rodale, 1981.

Articles

Agricultural Research (published by the U.S. Department of Agriculture), selected issues.

Cook, Kenneth, "Slip, Sliding Away," *Environmental Action*, November 1981.

Journal of Soil and Water Conservation (published by the Soil Conservation Society of America), selected issues.

Larson, W. E. et al., "The Threat of Soil Erosion to Long-Term Crop Production," *Science*, Feb. 4, 1983.

Steinhart, Peter, "The Edge Gets Thinner," *Audubon*, November 1983.

Wehr, Elizabeth, "Conservation Policy Faces Far-reaching Shift," *Congressional Quarterly Weekly Report*, Sept. 17, 1983.

Reports and Studies

Council on Environmental Quality and the Department of State, "The Global 2000 Report to the President: Entering the Twenty-First Century," Vol. I, 1980.

Editorial Research Reports, "Farm Policy's New Course," 1983 Vol. I, p. 233; "Farm Policy and Food Needs," 1977 Vol. II, p. 807.

General Accounting Office, "Agriculture's Soil Conservation Programs Miss Full Potential in the Fight Against Soil Erosion," Nov. 28, 1983.

National Association of Conservation Districts, "1983 National Survey: Conservation Tillage Practices," February 1984.

Office of Technology Assessment, "Impacts of Technology on U.S. Cropland and Rangeland Productivity," August 1982.

U.S. Department of Agriculture, "A National Program for Soil and Water Conservation: 1982 Final Program Report and Environmental Impact Statement," September 1982.

Graphics: Cover photo courtesy of USDA - Soil Conservation Service; p. 193 map by staff artist Belle Burkhart; p. 199 photo, left, courtesy of USDA; photo, right, courtesy of the USDA - Agricultural Research Service.

INDEX